RACE AND THE OBAMA
ADMINISTRATION

Welcome to Emory!

Andra Gillespie

MANCHESTER
1824
Manchester University Press

RACE AND THE OBAMA ADMINISTRATION

Substance, symbols, and hope

ANDRA GILLESPIE

Manchester University Press

Published by Manchester University Press
Altrincham Street, Manchester M1 7JA
www.manchesteruniversitypress.co.uk

British Library Cataloguing-in-Publication Data
A catalogue record for this book is available from the British Library

ISBN 978 1 5261 0501 1 hardback
ISBN 978 1 5261 0502 8 paperback

First published 2019

Typeset by Out of House Publishing
Printed in Great Britain
by TJ International Ltd, Padstow

For God,
And for Brianna, Brielle, and every kid
who saw the Obama presidency
and felt confident to dream bigger

Contents

Figures

Tables

Acknowledgments

I Corinthians 2:9 says that "Eye hath not seen, nor ear heard, neither have entered into the heart of man, the things which God hath prepared for them for them that love him" (KJV). I could not have imagined the journey that I would take as I wrote this book. I am grateful to God for its completion, and I hope that the finished product is useful and informative to others.

This book was difficult to write. The complexity of the subject was heightened by the fact that I was doing some analysis in real time. Moreover, the unexpected results of the 2016 US presidential election required additional reflection and a rethinking of parts of the manuscript. I do not expect that this is my last word on the Obama Administration by any stretch of the imagination, and I hope that the hard work of this volume "tilled the soil" to help advance future projects on the Obama legacy.

In addition to the substantive challenges, my professional life changed over the course of writing this project. In 2015, my former dean, Robin Forman, asked me to direct Emory's James Weldon Johnson Institute for the Study of Race and Difference. This role is intellectually rewarding. I have been able to use some research sponsored through the Institute to enhance the argument in this book. And I have found that our weekly speakers have challenged me to think about my own work, including this project, in new and creative ways. Administrative work takes time, though. Fortunately, I have a wonderful staff, and I am grateful to them for managing business during those times when I was out of the office writing or just plain distracted. Thank you, Kali-Ahset Amen, Anita Spencer Stevens, and Latrice Carter! I could not have finished without your support.

I am also grateful for the students who assisted me in collecting data for this project: Jennifer Goodman, Rebecca Hartsough, Abigail Heller, Ashton Hughes, Chelsea Jackson, Courtney Miller, Maalik Nickerson, Elvin Ong,

James Szewcyck, Steven Webster, Kirsten Widner, Elizabeth Wiener, and Erin Wrenn. I am grateful to you for all you have done.

I would also like to thank the librarians who make my work possible. Christopher Palazzolo of Emory Libraries helped my students compile the appointments dataset. Unnamed librarians at the Clinton Presidential Library sent transcripts of commencement speeches that were not readily available online. I am grateful for their support. I am especially grateful to Rosemary Magee and her staff at the Rose Manuscript, Archives and Rare Book Library at Emory University. Rosemary had no idea when she showed me letters from a young Barack Obama that they would have any relevance to this project. I was grateful to have been introduced to them, and it is an honor to be able to cite them in this project.

I also want to thank my writing partners on a different project—Niambi Carter, Shayla Nunnally, and Tyson King-Meadows—for letting me preview some of our data in this book. I can't wait for that project to be done, too; but I am most grateful for your friendship and collegiality.

I am extremely thankful for my forbearing editors. This project started at Bloomsbury Press in New York, where Matthew Kopel was an early believer in the project. After it was sold to Manchester University Press, Tony Mason, assisted by Alun Richards, David Appleyard, and Sarah Rendell, have been very patient stewards. My schedule made it very difficult to finish the project, but they have been supportive. I am truly thankful for this, and I hope that they find that this project was worth the wait.

Most of all, I would like to thank my family for their support. I am always grateful to my parents, Celestine Gillespie and James Gillespie, for believing in me (and for pestering me to get this project done). I am also grateful to other relatives who helped me in the home stretch of this project. When I lost power because of Tropical Storm Irma, my cousin Tamika Henderson let me use her electricity. Another cousin, Karen Michelle Knight, ably assisted me with copy-editing at the last minute. This project reminds me of how important family is, and I am grateful for the small sacrifices they make for me on a regular basis and how they pour into my life.

Finally, I would like to thank the anonymous respondents who contributed to the public opinion chapter, especially the qualitative component. We researchers cannot do our work without your willingness to participate. I am grateful to you and to the contacts who helped facilitate those introductions.

Introduction: My president was black. So what?

My president is black, my Lambo's blue
And I'll be goddamned if my rims ain't too
My mama ain't at home, and daddy's still in jail
Trying to make a plate, anybody seen the scale?

-"My President," Young Jeezy

The end of any presidential administration usually brings a slew of retrospectives and reflections on the outgoing president's accomplishments and prospective legacy. Those assessments took on an especially important role as Barack Obama ended his historic term as President of the United States. One could not go past an American newsstand in late 2016 and early 2017 without seeing a newspaper or magazine featuring some article discussing the significance of the Obama presidency. The foci of these articles varied. *Rolling Stone*, for instance, published a special collector's edition compiling all of the feature articles its staff had written about him. The back cover included three of the nine previous covers which featured President Obama's photograph (see Dickinson 2017, 7; *Rolling Stone* 2017). *Time*'s special edition commissioned articles covering President Obama's successes and failures on issues such as foreign policy, LGBT rights, and racial issues (*Time* 2017). *People* magazine featured a breezy interview with Barack and Michelle Obama recounting their fondest memories of their eight years in the White House (Westfall 2016).

Many articles examined the significance of President Obama as the first African American[1] president. The Obamas sat for an interview with *Essence* magazine in which they assessed the racial significance of their tenures as

---

1 Please note I will use the terms "black" and "African American" interchangeably throughout this book.

president and first lady (De Luca 2016). In *Time* magazine, Maya Rhodan wrote that, "For a generation of [black] Americans, the president's race mattered in the most meaningful way" (Rhodan 2017, 53).

In part because of his prominence as a National Book Award winner and MacArthur genius, Ta-Nehisi Coates' cover article for *The Atlantic* was one of the more prominent retrospectives. The title of his article sums it up: "My President Was Black" (Coates 2017, 47). In the article, Coates cited Jay-Z, who recorded a song titled "My President Is Black" in 2010, as the implicit inspiration for his title (Coates 2017, 62). As an Atlantan, though, when I first saw the magazine cover, I thought of Young Jeezy's 2008 song, also called "My President Is Black" (Jenkins and Jones 2008). The song expresses pride at the thought of having a black president—one line even calls for Obama to be memorialized on a $5,000 bill. However, the lyrics still situate Jeezy in his own neighborhood experience: his mother still has to work; his father is incarcerated; and according to those who annotate hip hop lyrics, the protagonist in the song sells drugs to provide for his family (see Jenkins and Jones 2008; *Genius.com* n.d.).

In many ways, Young Jeezy's lyrics, which juxtapose the pride in the prospect of having a black president with the gritty reality of a black life that might not change outwardly because of that presidency, beautifully capture the irony Coates expresses in his tribute to Obama. Coates, who had the benefit of interviewing and interacting with President Obama on numerous occasions, recounts those encounters and his musings about those meetings and the 2016 election in his piece. He makes it clear that he often disagreed tactically with President Obama and found him to be naive on racial issues. He lamented the possibility that a Trump Administration would not stem the tide of police violence against blacks. At the same time, Coates wanted desperately to believe in the post-racial America that Obama imagined possible. Perhaps more important, Coates found himself able to embrace Obama's symbolic importance even as he disagreed with him and even as he realized that Obama's presidency would be followed by the Trump Administration. Coates talks about a feeling—a feeling that transcended his disagreements with the president. A feeling that Obama:

> had been responsible for the only time in my life when I felt, as the first lady had once said, proud of my country ... The feeling was that little black boy touching the president's hair. It was watching Obama on the campaign trail, always expecting the worse and amazed the worst never happened. It was how I felt seeing Barack and Michelle during the inauguration ... rising up out of the limo, rising up from fear, smiling, waving, defying despair, defying history, defying gravity. (Coates 2017, 66)

Clearly, there is no denying the symbolic importance of the Obama presidency. Still, many have struggled with how to critique him. Some, like Tavis Smiley and Cornel West, were marginalized for their critiques and panned for being too personal in their attacks (Malveaux 2016, xxxvii). Others, like Coates, struggled to balance their pride with their ethical and professional obligation to provide necessary critique. Julianne Malveaux, the economist and former president of Bennett College, introduced the anthology of her Obama-era op-ed pieces by using the term "ambivalence" to describe her assessment of the Obama presidency (Malveaux 2016, xxv, xxvi). She confessed that while she campaigned for Barack Obama's 2004 Senate campaign, she thought that as president, Obama "missed too many opportunities to be of special help to the African American community" (Malveaux 2016, xliii).

This echoed academic critiques leveled by political scientists after Obama's first term in office. Michael Dawson, for instance, noted that persistent black–white inequality in areas such as unemployment, income, housing, and health should temper blacks' enthusiasm for the Obama presidency, especially if those problems did not abate (Dawson 2011, 17–18). Similarly, Frederick Harris contended that the election of Barack Obama was symbolically important but substantively lacking. He argued, "If recognition is achieved for black Americans but structural barriers remain intact and unchallenged, then recognition without a commitment to eradicating racial inequality may actually end up further perpetuating inequality, despite the gains made by some" (Harris 2012, 186).

One of the challenges of balancing praise and critique was the reaction in black America. Michael Eric Dyson perhaps said it best when he noted that:

> gales of black pride have swept aside awareness of his flaws, and when those flaws are conceded, gusts of black defiance play down their meaning and significance. Mr. Obama's most ardent black fans ignore how he often failed to speak about race or use his powers to convene commissions or issue executive orders to lessen black suffering; his nastiest black critics lambast him as an ineffectual leader who has done little to protect blacks from racial assault or lift them from economic misery. Neither the haters nor the hagiographers do the Obama legacy justice. (Dyson 2016a, 7)

When Dyson talks about "gales of black pride," he is no doubt referring to President Obama's stratospheric approval ratings among blacks. Figure I.1 shows Gallup's weekly tracking of presidential job approval over the course of the Obama presidency, broken down by race and ethnicity. While President Obama began his presidency with job approval ratings above 60 percent

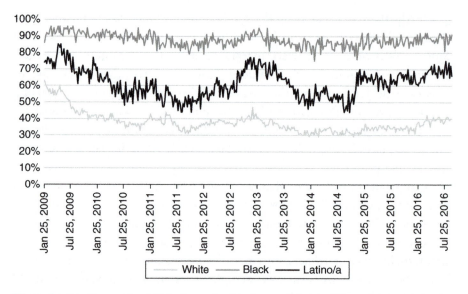

Figure 1.1 Weekly presidential job approval ratings by race/ethnicity, Obama Administration
Source: Gallup (n.d.b).

among blacks, whites, and Latinos/as, his approval ratings quickly plummeted among whites. Though President Obama's ratings started to rebound in the final days of his presidency, he did not receive a job approval score of greater than 50 percent among whites after July 2009. Overall, he averaged a 38 percent approval rating among whites over the course of his presidency. President Obama's approval ratings also quickly fell among Latinos/as, though not as dramatically as they did among whites. His approval ratings rose and fell through the years among Latinos/as but mostly stayed above 50 percent despite the ebbs and flows. While Obama's approval rating among Latinos/as was lower than 50 percent for about 30 weeks during his presidency, it did rebound and generally stayed above 70 percent in the final three months of his term. On average, he enjoyed a 63 percent approval rating among Latinos/as.

Blacks, though, were a completely different story. President Obama enjoyed consistently high approval ratings among African American voters. Over the course of his term as president, Gallup found that Barack Obama's approval rating averaged nearly 88 percent among black voters. In only seven weeks of his presidency did Obama's approval rating fall below 80 percent among blacks—and even then, his approval rating was never lower than 75 percent (Gallup n.d.b).

When Malveaux reflected on her own assessment of the Obama presidency, she spoke of the need for dispassion (Malveaux 2016, xxvii). Now that

Obama is no longer president, I hope to contribute to that dispassionate conversation. In this book, I try to position my analysis somewhere between the haters and the hagiographers, to borrow from Dyson. My hope is to leverage the conclusion of the Obama Administration to start an open-minded examination of the attempts President Obama made to improve the lives of African Americans, which will allow me to make a preliminary assessment of whether or not those efforts worked.

As I write this, I recognize that the quandary of whether to commend or critique that Dyson, Malveaux, Coates, and others discuss is real. For many blacks, this ambivalence will likely not go away. The fact that it is real is worth examining empirically. How do blacks reconcile their pride in Obama's service to their frustration with the things that did not improve in black communities? How do we know for sure what Obama did and did not accomplish? Were our expectations reasonable?

I believe that the best approach to questions like these—especially in an era where evidence is contingent—is to be systematic in data collection and to allow the data to drive the analysis. I would be remiss to ignore the emotionalism—both positive and negative—that engulfs our discourse about the importance of the Obama presidency. However, as a scholar, my greatest contribution to this debate is to collect important new data that can shed empirical insights on Obama's successes and failures.

With this is mind, I submit this book as one the many empirical contributions to the study of the Obama presidency. Some have already entered this space with normative assessments of politics in the Obama era (see Glaude 2016), while others have undertaken quantitative and qualitative analyses of his rhetoric (see Dyson 2016b; Gillion 2016; Price 2016). Additional work has focused on public opinion (see Tesler 2016). These are all fine works, and it is a privilege to engage these scholars in this text. What I intend to contribute, however, is a more comparative tally of what Obama did in office for black Americans. I take seriously Julianne Malveaux's call to get past the emotion of the Obama era to actually count his accomplishments with respect to black uplift—both substantive and symbolic—and to place them in context with other presidents. This will help us see more clearly what he actually did for black people.

Chapter overview

With this in mind, I approach this question of what Obama accomplished for blacks in four steps, using a variety of methodological techniques. First, in Chapter 1, I introduce a normative theory of race and presidential representation. Here, I synthesize the presidential power and deracialization literatures to make the claim that presidents are structurally constrained in their ability to address a host of issues of concern to blacks. As a result, they tend to address issues of race symbolically. Barack Obama, as the first black president and a black politician who rose to power by using deracialization, or a more race-neutral campaign strategy, will be particularly susceptible to resorting to more symbolic means of racial representation.

I then test this theory by examining both the racially substantive policies that have been implemented by the Obama Administration and by charting key indicators of black well-being relative to other racial and ethnic groups in the United States. I organize this examination in parts. First, I examine substantive politics. In Chapter 2, I present a general overview of Obama's performance with respect to race and the state of racial inequality in America on a number of key indicators. Others, such as Michael Dawson, have undertaken similar projects. The benefit of my analysis is that while Dawson charts black–white inequalities to the dawn of the Obama era, I track key indicators throughout Obama's tenure in office. This allows me to gain a sense of how blacks fared socioeconomically, often across his entire term (Dawson 2011, ch. 4).

One of the other benefits of having a longer range of longitudinal data is that it allows the reader to get a sense of the temporal scope of black–nonblack inequality in the United States. Throughout the text, I will be making comparisons between key indicators and how blacks fared in the United States in different presidential administrations. Understanding how well blacks did from 2009 to 2016 is important, but having the contextual knowledge of how well they fared under the administrations of Bill Clinton and George W. Bush is particularly helpful. Comparative analyses were not always possible, but I incorporate them where I can.

I continue the comparative analysis by looking at presidential actions in Chapter 3. In Chapter 1, I suggest that presidents may be structurally constrained from initiating certain types of actions on behalf of blacks. However, they do have certain tools, such as executive orders, at their disposal through which they can set binding policy. To explore this further, I use a comparative content analysis of Presidents Clinton, Bush, and Obama's executive orders to gain a sense of whether these presidents differed in the type and frequency of proactive steps they took to represent the interests of African Americans. I then explore these issues further by doing an analysis of racial actions taken at the Cabinet department level. Here, I use press release data from Departments of Labor, Justice, Health and Human Services, and Education.

In Chapter 4, I start to incorporate an analysis of more symbolic politics. I start with the more substantive aspects of symbolic politics, looking at descriptive representation in presidential Cabinet, sub-Cabinet, and independent agency nominations. Presidential rhetoric can also serve substantive and symbolic purposes. In this chapter, I use a comparative analysis of Presidents Clinton, Bush, and Obama's State of the Union Addresses to gain greater insight into the ways presidents make symbolic gestures toward African Americans and the extent to which they propose policies that are targeted toward black communities. I also examine the ways that presidents respond to questions about race in news conferences.

I shift to an analysis of pure symbolic politics in Chapter 5. Here, I look at arts, culture, and inspirational rhetoric. Who are the president and first lady inviting to the White House to entertain the nation and the world? What does this signal about their racial and cultural commitments? Later in the chapter, I look at the rhetoric of commencement addresses. In addition to examining the content of presidents' commencement speeches, I also incorporate a comparative analysis of first ladies' speeches to determine the ways that Michelle Obama contributed to the symbolic racial politics of her husband's presidency.

I end the empirical study with a look at black attitudes toward Barack Obama and aspirations regarding his presidency. In Chapter 6, I ask black citizens themselves to answer the question of whether symbolism is enough. Using qualitative and quantitative public opinion data, I ask blacks how satisfied they were with President Obama's performance on racial issues. I also examine the relationship between satisfaction with the president's racial performance and general job approval ratings and enthusiastic electoral support for President Obama in 2012.

By the end of the book, I hope to provide readers with important context with which to judge the Obama Administration. By explicitly comparing the performance of the Obama Administration to the Clinton and second Bush Administrations at critical junctures in this analysis, we can gain perspective on the limitations and possibilities of presidential power in being able to unilaterally address issues of racial inequality. Similarly, the comparative analysis of the presidents' symbolic behavior also provides some insight into the extent of President Obama's importance as a racial figurehead. Finally, by exploring public opinion data on reactions to the Obama Administration, we have the ability to understand black voters on their terms and to ascertain what their political desires and expectations were and to make distinctions—if necessary and appropriate—between black mass and elite opinion.

A brief note about what will not be covered

I should note at the outset of this book that there are a few worthy topics related to the Obama presidency that time and space will not allow me to cover. For instance, I will not cover foreign policy or civil liberties debates in this book. I look forward to future volumes which engage these and other important topics. Also, while I do not ignore the concerns of other minority groups, like Latinos/as and Asian Americans, this book focuses primarily on African Americans. Again, I expect that other colleagues will produce important scholarship on these questions. I also hope to contribute to those debates in future projects.

I

The triple bind

If human history is heard as well as seen, an audio-visual record of events and processes, then Obama's election is, at this level, a revolutionary event, not merely in the quantity but the quality of what we can call his "visibility." It is certainly a less than revolutionary event at the level of actual policies, and one of the central issues with Obama's presidency will be measuring the distance between his audio-visual image – what he says and stages – and what he is able to *do*.

-W.J.T. Mitchell (2009, 125)

In a reflection piece for *The Journal of Visual Culture,* University of Chicago Professor (and Obama neighbor) W.J.T. Mitchell pondered the aesthetics of electing the first black president. He came to the conclusion that Barack Obama represented the hopes and dreams of those who voted for him, which put the new president in an interesting position. He writes, "When we analyze the effect of Obama as a 'cultural icon,' then, enumerating the innumerable commodifications of his image, it is important to recognize the extent to which his image is, before any positive content of, say, visible racial marking, a highly ambiguous blank slate on which popular fantasy could be projected" (Mitchell 2009, 126). Obama's election, then, represented not only the shattering of one of the hardest, highest racial glass ceilings in the United States, then (to coopt Hillary Clinton's phrasing); his electoral coalition was comprised of people who projected all of their hopes, fears, anxieties, and expectations onto him.

Because of Barack Obama's status as the first African American president, he was likely an acute victim of voters projecting unrealistic expectations onto him. However, like all other presidents, he had to confront the constraints of his office and make tough decisions about which issues to address or not address (and how to frame those decisions for his many publics) over the course of his term in office. In this chapter, I advance a theory about three considerations that President Obama had to take into account as he crafted his agenda. Those insights will help to frame the discussion of the rest of the book and help to put the Obama record—and black voter reaction to that record—into context.

Simply put, while the election of Barack Obama symbolized the full incorporation of African Americans into American political life, the election of one black person cannot and should not connote the eradication of all forms of structural, social, political, and economic inequality along racial lines in this country. Moreover, it is unrealistic to assume that being president of the United States afforded Barack Obama the ability to end all inequality with the stroke of a pen, though it is not unreasonable for people to have expected him to make progress on these issues. Aside from the fact that it will take more than eight years to reverse nearly 400 years of racial inequality, Barack Obama had to confront the institutional constraints of his office as he pondered the nature of the racial advocacy he would choose to take while in office.

The office confines: presidents cannot do everything

It is easy for Americans to be lulled into thinking of their president as a singularly powerful figure. Anyone who has grown up since the Cold War has likely grown accustomed to hearing the president referred to as the "leader of the free (or Western) world," and such phrasing connotes a certain type of singular power. That impression is not exactly accurate, though. Yes, the American president occupies a prominent leadership role on the global stage, but the Electoral College does not confer omnipotence on one winner every four years.

Instead, the Framers of the American Constitution, who feared despots and monarchies, placed real limits on what presidents can do. And as the country has evolved and put the ideas of the Constitution into practice, political actors have developed their own institutions—complete with their own constraints—to try to carry out their duties. Over time, these factors limit the leverage of even the most well-meaning presidents (even those who serve in times of unprecedented executive power) to address issues of racial inequality without cooperation from other political actors.

The first real constraint on the president is separation of powers. The president shares power with two other branches of federal government, whose different roles are intended to check and balance the power of the other branches. Take voting rights for example. By the 1960s, it was clear that

Southern states were circumventing the 15th Amendment and denying blacks the right to vote through racially neutral, ingenious measures like literacy tests and more informal but explicit measures like intimidation. President Lyndon Johnson could not unilaterally instruct Southern states to let blacks vote. Instead, he had to work with Congress to pass legislation to empower the Executive Branch to oversee voting rights in the states. Despite the fact that presidents do have some capacity to govern via executive order (which we will discuss in Chapter 3), they still rely on Congress to make laws. If there is no law, then the president (and by extension, the rest of the Executive Branch) has nothing to enforce.

Executive Branch constraints came into full view when the Supreme Court overturned parts of the Voting Rights Act in 2013. In the ruling *Shelby County, AL* v. *Holder* (570 U.S. 2 (2013)), the high court declared the preclearance sections of the Voting Rights Act to be unconstitutional. Under preclearance, states and counties which had historically engaged in denying blacks and language minorities the right to vote in the 1960s and 1970s were required to submit any changes to their electoral processes to the Department of Justice (an arm of the Executive Branch) before those adjustments could be implemented. In 2013, the Supreme Court declared that the formula that the Voting Rights Act used to determine which areas of the country required preclearance was antiquated and therefore unconstitutional. According to the majority opinion, it was unfair to penalize states for egregious practices that happened two generations ago when those states may have stopped discriminating against minorities entirely. The Court's opinion allowed Congress to rewrite the preclearance section of the Voting Rights Act and to redefine which jurisdictions were in need of oversight based on current patterns of discrimination. However, it would not allow the Department of Justice to force states and counties to clear election plans with them just because Congress had identified racial disparities in voter turnout in those areas in 1975.

The *Shelby* ruling had immediate consequences for electoral politics. Until that point, the Justice Department had used the power of preclearance to limit the ability of some Southern states to enact laws requiring photo identification in order to vote. Once the Court invalidated preclearance, states like North Carolina and Texas implemented voter identification laws that some critics charge were intended to make it difficult for poor, elderly, and black voters to participate in elections. The Justice Department can still sue states for voter discrimination if necessary, using Section 2 of the Voting Rights Act, but invalidating preclearance removed an important tool from the kit of remedies that the Justice Department uses to defend voting rights (see Fuller 2014; Lopez 2014).

Congress does have the right to revisit preclearance. In their ruling, the majority of the Supreme Court took issue with the idea of using 40-year-old criteria to define which states were more likely to discriminate. If Congress chooses, they can rewrite the Voting Rights Act and develop a more contemporary rubric to determine which states and counties are in need of supervision. As of this writing, though, they have not revised the Voting Rights Act (see Fuller 2014). As such, the Executive Branch has fewer tools at their disposal to help ensure equal access to the ballot than they had before June 2013.

In addition to the constitutional constraints of the office, the scope and magnitude of the Executive Branch (and bureaucracy) present its own challenges for governance and innovation. The federal government employs nearly three million civilian employees in over 500 departments, commissions, and independent agencies (Morone and Kersh 2013, 533). To put this into context, Wal-Mart, the world's largest corporation, only has 1.3 million US employees (2.2 million internationally) (Wal-Mart 2014). The sheer size of the operation is going to make progress slow. When you compound the size of the federal government with accountability measures like public comment periods (where the federal government cannot issue new regulations without soliciting public input), then it becomes clear that the Executive Branch may not always be the most nimble in being able to develop new policies or to swiftly address issues of inequality.

Finally, presidents, like all institutional actors, have to factor the opportunity costs of their decisions. George Edwards argues that presidents are strategic players who wait for opportune times to push certain initiatives. Presidents may have all the good intentions in the world to tackle many issues, but if the structural and political opportunities are not ripe for action, they will not move. Edwards uses Franklin Roosevelt to make his point. Roosevelt took advantage of a supportive Congress, the gravity of the Great Depression, and the public's desire to see some reassuring action in Washington to enact key provisions of the New Deal. Roosevelt appeared most successful when he led from behind—when the Democrat-controlled Congress was most ideologically predisposed to support his initiatives. When he fell out of step with Congress, his initiatives failed and pundits questioned his leadership skills (Edwards 2009, ch. 4).

The idea of leading Congress from behind helps to explain Roosevelt's reticence to address civil rights. Roosevelt needed the votes of Southern segregationists in order to pass his New Deal initiatives. If he pushed for civil rights, he would lose the strong Southern voting bloc which supported his economic initiatives. So, Roosevelt demurred to push for anti-lynching legislation and he allowed for stereotypically black occupations to be written out of the initial Social Security legislation in order to ensure support for the larger economic program. It was only under duress from civil rights groups that Roosevelt introduced anti-discrimination oversight of federal employment (i.e., the Fair Employment Practices Committee (FEPC)), and even then, the FEPC's oversight capacity was weak (see Klinkner and Smith 1999, 126–130, 155–159).

Edwards' observations reflect a larger school of thought among presidential scholars about executive entrepreneurship. Researchers like Stephen Skowronek contend that presidents "make politics" by seizing the opportunities that previous presidents and current events present them. Depending on the context of their ascension, some presidents are in the position of being able to be really innovative and "transformative" (see Skowronek 1997; 2008). Usually, we think of transformative presidents as the ones who governed successfully during times of tremendous crisis or upheaval and/or presidents who followed incompetent or corrupt administrations. Thus, transformative presidents stand out, appear proactive, and are judged positively because (1) they had the fortune (or misfortune) to demonstrate strength in a crisis; and (2) because the previous administrati on was horrible in comparison. Unfortunately, if a president governs during times of peace and prosperity or if their term is not bookended by disastrous administrations, we probably will not count them among the greatest presidents.

The people constrain: the limitations of public sentiment

Presidents factor more than congressional recalcitrance and crises into their decisions about when and on what to act. Public opinion is also a key consideration. Just as presidents do not want to get ahead of Congress, they also do not want to risk getting ahead of public opinion. A classic example of the perils of getting ahead of public opinion would be Bill Clinton's attempt to create universal health care. In post-mortem discussions of the failure of the initiative, political analysts cited general public satisfaction with the existing health care system (or aversion to the uncertainties of the details of the new proposal) as being an important factor in the demise of the effort. This relative satisfaction was captured in the mobilization against the Clinton health initiative. In the infamous "Harry and Louise" ads, a couple express their concerns about losing the insurance plan they liked under the president's proposal. Because the majority of the public preferred their current level of service to a complex new plan they did not understand, they were not supportive of health care reform. They worried change might deliver less familiar, lower quality service (see Clymer *et al.* 1994; Singer 2009).

Pollsters routinely ask Americans to identify the issue that they believe is the biggest concern facing the country. These responses are clues about citizen preferences regarding which issues are most salient and which require immediate attention. The Gallup Organization has intermittently asked voters to identify the most important problem facing America since the mid-1930s. As part of a feature article on issue salience, the *New York Times* created a series of infographics to help visualize changes in American perceptions of the most important issue (Aisch and Parlapiano 2017). I used this infographic to code the number of survey-months[1] in which race was listed as one of the many issues Americans found important. If race was listed in the infographic as one of the most important issues named for that month, I coded it as 1. When race does not appear among the top issues, I code it as 0. I repeat the same coding procedure to identify months where respondents are most likely to name race as the most important domestic and overall issue that month (I code ties as 1). Because I am working with graphics which use size to depict the percentage of respondents who named a particular issue most important, there are a few instances where roughly equal proportions of respondents identified two or more issues as being important. To confirm the proportions, I actually measured the graphics to try to be as accurate as possible. Of course, there is always the possibility of small measurement error.

Overall, race and civil rights were of enough concern to Americans that it often found its place among the top issues of concern to Americans. In 262 of the 371 months for which I have data, enough people mentioned race for it to be listed as a concern (as opposed to its being lumped into the "other issues" category). Most of the time, though, race was not the most important issue to a plurality of respondents, as measured by the percentage of respondents naming it as their most important issue. Race was the most important domestic issue (as opposed to international or economic issues) in only 61 of the months studied. Those months are shown on the second tier of Figure 1.1. As the figure shows, race is the most important domestic issue at the height of the second phase of the civil rights movement in the mid-1950s to 1960s.

The third tier of Figure 1.1 indicates the months where pluralities of respondents mentioned race as the most important issue overall, inclusive of international and economic issues. Gallup respondents only named race and civil rights as the most important issue overall in 14 of the months studied. Again, respondents were most likely to list race as most important between

---

1 There are 15 months where the *New York Times* reports multiple infographics. I assume that there were multiple surveys conducted in these months. If at least one survey that month lists race as one of the oft-mentioned most important issues, I code the month as 1. Most of the time, issue salience is consistent across a month. The one exception was September 1984.

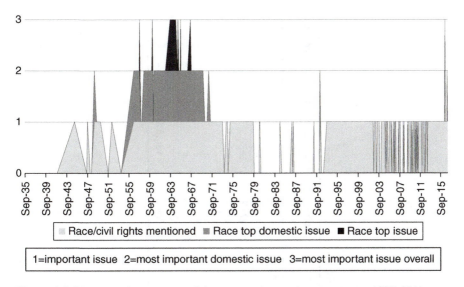

Figure 1.1 Mentions of race as one of the most important American issues, 1935–2016
Source: Author's compilation from Aisch and Parlapiano (2017).

1963 and 1965. Gallup does register an increase in the salience of racial issues toward the end of President Obama's term in office.

Figure 1.1 shows that while race has never entirely receded as an issue of concern for some Americans, it has rarely been the most important issue. To delve further into how salient racial issues were over the course of the Obama Administration, Table 1.1 ranks the top issues (by annual averages) that Gallup respondents indicated were the most important issues facing America over the course of the Obama presidency. With a few exceptions, four issues consistently ranked among the top concerns of Americans: the economy, jobs, health care, and government dysfunction. While only one-third of respondents ranked the economy or unemployment as most important in the latter part of Barack Obama's presidency, more than half ranked these issues most important throughout his first term (2009–2012). This suggests that during President Obama's initial years in office, Americans had an implied expectation that he should focus on rebuilding the American economy from the Great Recession.

Economic issues continued to dominate the public imagination into the second term. General economic issues ranked as the first or second most mentioned issue from 2013 to 2016. However, during this time period Americans increasingly began to cite government dysfunction and poor leadership as a concern. When a plurality of Americans were not citing the economy as the most important issue, they were mentioning government dysfunction as their most important issue (and vice versa).

Table 1.1 Annual ranking of respondent perceptions of most important issue facing America, 2008–2016

	Budget deficit/debt	Economy	Gas prices	Government dysfunction	Health care	Iraq	Jobs	Race relations	Immigration
2008	–	1st (39%)	3rd (10%)	–	4th (8%)	2nd (18%)	–	–	–
2009	–	1st (40%)	–	4th (7%)	3rd (15%)	–	2nd (16%)	–	–
2010	–	1st (29%)	–	4th (12%)	3rd (13%)	–	2nd (27%)	–	–
2011	4th (12%)	1st (30%)	–	3rd (12%)	–	–	2nd (29%)	–	–
2012	4th (10%)	1st (31%)	–	3rd (13%)	–	–	2nd (25%)	–	–
2013	–	1st (22%)	–	2nd (20%)	4th (10%)	–	3rd (16%)	–	–
2014	–	2nd (17%)	–	1st (18%)	4th (10%)	–	3rd (15%)	–	–
2015	–	2nd (13%)	–	1st (16%)	–	–	3rd (8%)	4th (8%)	3rd (8%)
2016	–	1st (16%)	–	2nd (13%)	–	–	3rd (9%)	–	–

Source: Gallup (Smith and Saad 2016).

It should be noted that the annual rankings of public perceptions of the most important problem facing America are based on an annual average of monthly polls. At two points throughout 2014, issues of concern to blacks and Latinos/as ranked highly for one month. In July 2014, 17 percent of respondents ranked immigration as the most important issue, most likely because of reports of unaccompanied minors from Central America fleeing into the United States. In December 2014, 13 percent of respondents ranked race relations as the most important issue, most likely as a result of media attention around officer-involved killings of black men and boys in Ferguson, Missouri, Staten Island, New York, and Cleveland, Ohio and the subsequent decisions to not indict the police officers involved in these cases (see Riffkin 2015). And in the last two years of Obama's second term, racialized issues did rank among the top four most important issues facing America. In 2015, immigration tied as the third most mentioned issue; and in 2016, race relations was mentioned as the fourth most cited issue.

Racial inequality and economic inequality are closely linked. Unfortunately, differences about the best approach for addressing inequality persist along racial lines. In his analysis of 2008 American National Election Study data on racial policy preferences, Vincent Hutchings (2009) found racial gaps in policy preferences, even after controlling for ideology and 2008 vote preference. Blacks were more likely than whites to support aid to blacks and fair jobs initiatives. Whites who harbored anti-black stereotypes were less likely to support such initiatives. Even liberal and pro-Obama whites were less supportive of these initiatives if they harbored anti-black stereotypes. Hutchings' findings reveal, then, that there was a cadre of liberal Obama supporters who would likely be resistant to targeted policies to help African Americans.

Race still matters

The Hutchings findings underscore the continued importance of race in American politics. When we think about race relations, the election of Barack Obama sent mixed messages about the status of blacks in this country. Considering that in 1958, only 37 percent of respondents told Gallup that they would vote for a black president, Obama's election represents serious progress (Keeter and Samaranayake 2007). However, just because Americans overcame long-standing prejudices to put a black man in the White House does not mean that they conquered all bigotry.

Over the course of the Obama Administration, the Associated Press (in conjunction with the University of Michigan) conducted surveys on race relations (see Ross and Agiesta 2012). They found instances of increased, not decreased,

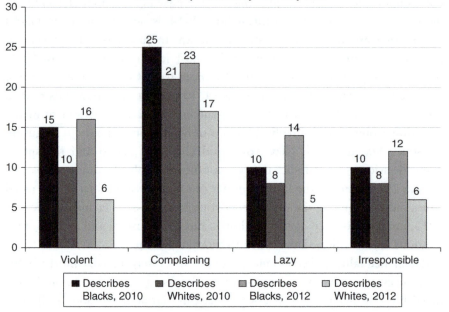

Figure 1.2 Stereotyping of blacks and whites, AP/Knowledge Networks Surveys, 2010 and 2012 Source: Associated Press Racial Attitudes Surveys, 2010 and 2012. The 2010 survey had a sample size of 1,037 and the 2012 survey had a sample size of 1,071. Toplines for both surveys are available at Associated Press (2012).

racial resentment over the course of Obama's first term. Respondents were asked if certain stereotypes described blacks and whites well. Figure 1.2 shows the percentage of respondents who said that "violent," "complaining," "lazy," and "irresponsible" described blacks and whites extremely or very well in 2010 and 2012. For some of these stereotypes, respondents were equally likely to attribute these negative stereotypes to blacks and whites. For instance, in 2010, the two percentage point difference in perceptions that blacks and whites are lazy is not statistically significant. By 2012, though, the gap in perception about laziness increases to nine percentage points, with blacks being perceived as more lazy. Similarly, the five-point gap between perceptions that blacks and whites are violent grew in 2012 to a ten-point gap.

What is a black president to do, then?

Given the continued racial insensitivities in the American population, it is no surprise that Barack Obama and his campaign team opted to use a deracialized, or race-neutral, campaign strategy to get elected. Scholars and political analysts widely accept the notion of Barack Obama as a deracialized black politician (see Gillespie 2009; Ifill 2009; Frasure 2010). Deracialization is a political strategy that emerged in the 1970s as an attempt to help Democrats attract white citizens to the voting booth. It was intended to counter a Republican recruitment strategy that targeted whites who were uncomfortable with the civil rights gains of the 1960s. As Charles Hamilton originally conceived the concept, deracialized politicians (who could be of any race) would refrain from framing policy positions as being solely beneficial to blacks because that would alienate white voters. By presenting racially just policy positions as beneficial for all Americans, Hamilton hoped that Democrats would be able to attract a wide, multiracial coalition to their party (Hamilton 1977).

Deracialization has since evolved into a strategy in which black politicians carefully guard their racial self-presentation in an attempt to appeal to as many nonblack voters as possible. McCormick and Jones identify three primary components of a deracialized campaign strategy: counter-stereotypic self-performance, limited appearances in all-black settings, and a de-emphasis of campaign issues that are strongly associated with blacks. They concede that deracialization is an efficacious strategy, especially for black candidates running in majority-white jurisdictions. (They write soon after Douglas Wilder becomes the first elected black governor in US history. He was elected on the same day that many black mayors won election for the first time in majority-white cities like New York, Seattle, Durham, and New Haven in 1989.) However, they and others express normative concerns with the idea that blacks have to de-emphasize racial issues (in effect, abandon a primary motivation for blacks pursuing political power) in order to get elected. They fear that eschewing difficult discussions about race as candidates will evince a reluctance to address pressing racial issues as elected officials. Thus, blacks will gain little substantively from the increased descriptive representation of blacks among the nation's officeholders (McCormick and Jones 1993; see also Smith 1990).

Many things could have influenced Barack Obama's decision to deracialize, including his biracial background, philosophical commitments to multiculturalism, and his general disposition. However, the status of race relations in 2008 would have also privileged his decision to use a racially risk-averse strategy like deracialization. Obama may not have been the first black person to run for president, but being the first black nominee of a major party was uncharted territory; and while public opinion polls showed that a majority of whites were theoretically willing to vote for a black presidential candidate (see Keeter and Samaranayake 2007), his candidacy had no racial template. Thus, it is not surprising that his campaign took a conservative approach to addressing racial issues.

Once Obama won, though, questions arose about whether he would pivot and become more vocal about racial issues from the Oval Office. Long ago, though, scholars warned that such a move is potentially problematic. Some voters are likely drawn to deracialized candidates out of a sense of "racism fatigue" (McIlwain and Caliendo 2011, 218). For them, deracialized candidates represent the best of both worlds. Voters can use their support of a black candidate as evidence of their lack of racism, and in turn, the candidate implicitly promises not to advocate for blacks as an elected official. Candidates seeking the support of these tired voters, then—especially if they intend to pursue reelection or higher office—have a strategic incentive to try to limit their vigorous advocacy of racial issues (Smith 1990; McCormick and Jones 1993).

Black politicians face other obstacles once they get elected to office, even if they intend to advocate for racial issues. Robert Smith (1996) warns black politicians of the dangers of cooptation, or of abandoning racial causes and becoming a stakeholder in the status quo. Finally, black politicians may find themselves unincorporated, or strategically limited by powerful political opponents who have the institutional capacity to curtail their effectiveness (see Browning *et al.* 1984). In his study of Mayor Harold Washington of Chicago, Michael Preston found that Washington was stymied in his efforts to promote the welfare of blacks by a powerful legislative chairman who controlled the votes on the Chicago Board of Alderman. Lacking a legislative majority, Washington found that Chicago aldermen felt emboldened to block his policies (Preston 1987).

Like many black politicians who toiled in lower level offices before him, President Obama confronted a number of political and structural realities which make his reticence on race understandable (though not necessarily acceptable). After Democrats lost control of the House of Representatives in 2010, he had to operate under divided government conditions in which the Republican Party, which vowed to obstruct him at nearly every turn, stalled or opposed many of his legislative initiatives.

The twin crises of an unpopular predecessor and the worst financial crisis since the Great Depression may have opened the door for Obama's electoral victory. However, the magnitude of the financial crisis was so severe that the general populace was so singularly focused on the economy that they would be less open to discussions about systemic inequality. And despite the fact that Obama's election represented a high-water mark in America's march toward racial equality, racial resentment and stereotyping remain a feature of American politics, even among some Obama supporters. Thus, America may have been ready for a black president, but not necessarily for the difficult dialogue and deliberation that needs to take place to truly eradicate racial prejudice and inequality.

In the face of such constraints, it is common for black politicians to resort to symbolic politics to compensate for their inability to deliver materially to black communities. Symbolic politics involves political efforts that cost little (either monetarily or in terms of proscribing behavior) but are valuable from a public relations standpoint. Scholars have pinpointed numerous examples of symbolic politics. Katherine Tate (2003) noted that black Democratic members of Congress managed to pass bills during a period when Republicans controlled the House of Representatives by focusing on passing proclamations and renaming highways and federal buildings. Robert Smith (1996) cites the Congressional Black Caucus' (CBC) annual introduction of an alternative budget as a prime example of symbolic legislation. Components of this budget have no hope of being incorporated into the actual budget, and CBC members do not lobby their colleagues to generate support for the budget outside of the caucus. As such, Smith argues that this expression is tantamount to a stunt.

I should note, though, that symbolic politics also can be very meaningful. Few would discount the importance of creating a federal holiday to honor Martin Luther King, for instance. More important, symbolic politics can help signal openness and access to communities which have felt excluded from the traditional process. Christian Grose (2011), for instance, notes that black members of Congress serving majority black districts are more likely to set up district offices in black neighborhoods than white members who previously served those communities. Such a gesture sends a powerful signal that they seek to be responsive to issues of concern to blacks.

How do blacks respond?

> But most of the time, Obama left it to his surrogates to defend him when it came to race. In narrowing the differences between Obama and the majority-white nation he was appealing to, the campaign simply set out to erase race as a negative. This was no accident. The formula centered on white voters to be comforted by this approach, and for black voters to be willing to look the other way. (Ifill 2009, 56)

The success of deracialization is premised on the assumption that black voters will overwhelmingly support black candidates and thus do not require the same levels of outreach that nonblack voters may require in order for black candidates to win their vote (see Albritton et al. 1996). While some black politicians in recent years have learned the hard way that one cannot completely ignore black voters (see Gillespie 2012, 225–227; Gillespie 2013; Gillespie and Demessie 2013), this axiom has its roots in ideas of Democratic electoral capture, or the concept that blacks tend to be ideologically more liberal than the average Democrat (see Frymer 1999, ch. 4). This means that in a two-party system like the United States, neither party perfectly represents black partisan interests, but the Democratic Party comes closest by far. With the likelihood of massive black voter defection to the Republican Party being minimal, Democratic candidates can feel reasonably certain that blacks will vote for them with little outreach (Tate 1994, ch. 3). (Dawson (1994, 210) points out that blacks have the option of not voting at all if they are dissatisfied with both Democratic and Republican candidates, though.)

Scholars who are critical of the Obama Administration implicitly invoke theories of electoral capture and racial solidarity when they chide blacks for not standing up more for their policy preferences. For instance, Frederick Harris contends that blacks have settled for the symbolism of a descriptively representative president and have wasted an important opportunity to push for greater substantive representation (Harris 2012).

The normative concerns of scholars like Harris are valid and worthy of public discussion. However, critics must take care to not overlook important transformations in black communities. While scholars still detect racial differences in policy preferences and voting behavior between blacks and whites (see Hutchings 2009), the mainstreaming of blacks, particularly middle-class blacks, has moderated opinion within black communities. Katherine Tate examined approximately two decades worth of black public opinion data on major policy issues. While she confirms the persistence of the black–white gap in public opinion on a wide variety of issues, she notes that the gap narrowed in the 2000s. She attributes the narrowing to blacks' increased social and political mobility. As blacks have reaped the benefits of the civil rights movement and started to integrate into mainstream America, and as black Democratic officeholding has become more common, Tate contends that blacks may have greater incentives to hold more moderate points of view. Essentially, Tate argues that the radicalism of earlier eras of blacks was born out of the extreme marginalization and deprivation of segregation. With the end of codified discrimination and the partial progress of blacks socially, economically, and politically, blacks may have become more comfortable espousing mainstream points of view (Tate 2010).

Work by David Bositis at the Joint Center for Political and Economic Studies helps to support the idea that race was still important, but less salient for blacks by the turn of the century. In a 2002 survey of black politicians and black citizens, Bositis found that younger black politicians and respondents were more likely to focus on non-racial issues than their elders. They were also more likely to support neoliberal policy positions (e.g., school vouchers) than their older colleagues. In addition, election surveys from the decade indicate that black voters typically cited generic issues like the economy or war as their most salient concerns. Before 2014 and the rise of Black Lives Matter, racial discrimination typically ranked at the bottom of those lists (Bositis 2002; 2008).

So, the complacency that Harris observed at the end of Obama's first term in office may have been a function of real black preferences to de-emphasize race. The problem with this is that racial inequality remains an intractable problem in black communities. For instance, Dawson (2011) laments the decline of civic organization in poor communities of color and challenges the dominance of neoliberal black politicians (he would count Obama as a neoliberal) who support development policies which exacerbate income inequality at the expense of the black and Latino/a poor.

The challenge for students of black politics is how to portray this dynamic. Blacks are still politically distinct in America, but they have the same kitchen-sink concerns as everyone else. Race is still important to blacks, but—at least in the early part of the Obama Administration, before the public outcry over police shootings—it may have been a secondary concern, despite the fact that race still negatively impacted blacks' life chances.

All of this suggests a tremendous pragmatism among rank-and-file blacks. This may explain attitudes toward President Obama. Given the hostile political environment in which Obama operated and a lack of concern inside and outside the black community over racial issues during the early part of his tenure, blacks may have been comfortable settling for symbolism. This may not have been normatively good, but it reflected a rough reality.

2

How he did: The racial successes, failures, and impact of the Obama presidency

> I think a lot of the biggest challenges in terms of the African American community or Latino community have to do with economics, and if we get our economics right, then in my mind that is always a mechanism to improve race relations.
>
> -President Barack Obama April 29, 2009

In only the third domestic news conference of his presidency, President Obama fielded a question from BET (Black Entertainment Television) News reporter Andre Showell about how he planned to address disproportionately high unemployment rates in black and Latino/a communities. He specifically asked if the president planned to create targeted strategies to help these particularly distressed communities. President Obama responded by saying "that every step we are taking is designed to help all people" (Obama 2009b). While the president was clearly sensitive to the plight of unemployed black and Latino/a Americans, his response reflected his commitment to non-race-specific policies. By attacking unemployment generally, President Obama hoped to gradually improve employment rates in communities of color.

Some black elites were unimpressed by this position. Two years later, frustrated with her perception that the Obama Administration had done little to address chronic unemployment in communities of color, Congresswoman Maxine Waters (D-CA) openly vented at a Congressional Black Caucus-sponsored job fair in Atlanta:

> The Congressional Black Caucus loves the president, too. We're supportive of the president, but we're getting tired. We're getting tired. The unemployment is unconscionable. We don't know what the strategy is.

We don't know why on this trip that he's in the United States now, he's not in any black community. (Waters, quoted in Muskal 2011)

Some observers speculate that President Obama was reacting to Waters' criticism in his speech at the annual Congressional Black Caucus gala dinner later that year when he told the audience, "Take off your bedroom slippers. Put on your marching shoes ... Shake it off. Stop complainin'. Stop grumblin'. Stop cryin'. We are going to press on. We have work to do" (Obama, quoted in Smith 2011; see Williams 2011).

The tension of this episode exposes an important strain undergirding the relationship between African Americans and the first black president. President Obama opted to take a more general, deracialized approached to addressing inequality. Certain critics in the African American community charged that Obama should have targeted specific policies to addressing black–white inequality. Who was right?

In this chapter, I present descriptive data which will help inform our understanding of black–white inequality. How did blacks fare relative to whites during the Obama presidency, and was the rate of that progress slower or faster compared to President Obama's predecessors? In the ongoing debate about whether targeted or deracialized approaches are the best method to reduce inequality, did President Obama's deracialized approach produce positive results? Was he able, at the very least, to partially close racial gaps?

Literature review

At the end of his book examining the influence of blacks in electing US presidents (which was published 20 years before Barack Obama's election), Ronald Walters asserted the normative idea that blacks sought political power "to achieve changes in their socio-economic condition" (Walters 1988, 206). Walters was not the first to assert that reducing inequality is a primary aim of black political participation. This idea animated W.E.B. DuBois' contribution to the debate with Booker T. Washington about the efficacy of pursuing political or economic power first. It also influences assessments of the performance of black political executives who served before Barack Obama at the state and local level.

Despite the symbolic importance of electing the first black mayors in major cities in the 1960s and 1970s, scholars have noted that those leaders were unsuccessful at improving the overall socioeconomic status of African Americans, particularly the most disadvantaged blacks. In her analysis of the first wave of black mayors, Linda Williams found that structural barriers prevented black mayors from being able to improve the socioeconomic status of their residents. Robert Smith made similar observations. On the whole, these scholars concluded that the rise of black mayors led to increased business and career opportunities for a rarefied subset of middle-class blacks, with little overall improvement in the socioeconomic standing of the vast majority of African American residents (Williams 1987, 128–129; Smith 1990).

The consequence of the inability of black elected officials to reduce inequality is a tendency to focus on a circumscribed political agenda and symbolic politics: the types of high visibility political gestures that do not require significant public expenditures or legally regulate behavior. Robert Smith noted that in lieu of addressing persistent inequality, early black mayors focused on easier projects. He observed a trend in focusing on down-town economic development and on instituting affirmative action policies in city employment (Smith 1990). Congressional scholars have made similar findings. For instance, Katherine Tate noted that black Democratic House members in the Republican-controlled 103rd Congress were more likely to successfully sponsor legislation than their white Democratic counterparts. However, a deeper examination reveals that this success was largely due to the fact that black Democrats were getting noncontroversial, symbolic bills (like resolutions honoring important black historical figures or renaming federal buildings) through the legislative process (Tate 2003).

Narrowing gaps in the Obama Administration

When Barack Obama became president, he entered an arena that was certainly different from the ones that early black mayors such as Coleman Young and Richard Hatcher or even black governors like Douglas Wilder faced. While all of these positions are executive offices, mayors, governors, and presidents do have different powers and responsibilities. However, some challenges are similar and have persisted for decades. Williams observed that early black mayors assumed power during an era of economic contraction and shrinking tax bases, which hampered their ability to introduce social programs designed to reduce economic inequality (Williams 1987, 128–129). Obama assumed the presidency during the worst economic crisis since the Great Depression. The seriousness of the economic crisis demanded immediate attention (Crotty 2012b). If Obama had intended to create targeted policies to address black disadvantage, the necessity of having to address a catastrophic financial crisis would have limited his flexibility. However, given Obama's commitment to race-neutral campaign strategies (see Frasure 2010;

McIlwain 2010, 168–169), it is arguable that President Obama had always intended to address certain types of racial inequality indirectly, as part of a larger, national program.

Assessing President Obama's performance

Scholars, journalists, political operatives, and pundits have devoted thousands of pages to analyzing Barack Obama. The best known works explain how and why Obama won the 2008 election (e.g., Heilemann and Halperin 2010; Plouffe 2010). Academic works studying the role of race in the Obama presidency focus on electoral behavior and public opinion (e.g., Tesler and Sears 2010; Kinder and Dale-Riddle 2012), or on whether Obama's election portended the advent of a post-racial America (see Logan 2012; Rich 2012).

A number of edited volumes published during Obama's first term provided preliminary policy assessments of the Obama Administration (e.g., Dye et al. 2010; Crotty 2012a; Esposito and Finley 2012; Dowdle et al. 2012; Watson et al. 2012). While these volumes are incredibly useful, these volumes rarely probed the question of how blacks fared materially under the Obama Administration. When they do focus on race, they include one or two chapters on the prospects for post-racialism (Rich 2012) or public opinion (Nunnally 2012).

Romano and Hinojosa (2012) stand out as an exception. They examined President Obama's race-specific campaign promises from 2008 and identified what they called "progressive policy promises that deal directly with issues of race in America" (Romano and Hinojosa 2012, 166). Of 508 campaign promises, they argue that only 11 promises directly addressed inequality. These included providing capital to minority-owned businesses; fully funding anti-discrimination compliance agencies like the Equal Employment Opportunity Commission (EEOC) and the Office of Federal Contract Compliance Programs (OFCCP); passing the Lily Ledbetter law, which gives women more time to sue for wage discrimination; appointing an advisor for Native American policy; equalizing sentencing guidelines for crack and powder cocaine; giving greater attention to hate crimes; passing legislation to protect voting rights; banning racial profiling; removing civil damage caps in discrimination cases and passing comprehensive immigration reform, including a path to citizenship for undocumented immigrants living in the United States (Romano and Hinojosa 2012, 167).

At the time that their chapter was published, Romano and Hinojosa contended that Obama had only partially succeeded in advancing even this modest racial agenda. The first piece of legislation that President Obama signed into law was the Lily Ledbetter Act, which extended the time period that victims can bring wage discrimination suits against their employers. In addition, they argued that the Small Business Administration had done greater outreach among minority business owners. The Obama Administration did increase funding for anti-discrimination regulatory agencies like the EEOC and the OFCCP, and President Obama did name a Native American policy advisor (Romano and Hinojosa 2012, 170).

Romano and Hinojosa argued that the Obama Administration was in the process of fulfilling or had partially fulfilled other campaign promises. The Civil Rights Division of the Justice Department did increase its staff and appeared to shift its focus back to traditional civil rights enforcement (they argue that during the Bush Administration, the Civil Rights Division focused more on religious discrimination and human trafficking). And while the Obama Administration did manage to get legislation reducing sentencing disparities between crack and powder cocaine through Congress and eliminated mandatory minimum sentences for simple drug possession, the legislation did not completely eliminate the disparities, as those convicted of possessing crack cocaine still receive longer sentences (Romano and Hinojosa 2012, 171).

Some race-specific promises remained unfulfilled—both in 2012, when Romano and Hinojosa were writing, and after President Obama left office. Racial profiling remains a problem. The Supreme Court ruling in *Shelby County v. Holder* has arguably made enforcement of the Voting Rights Act more difficult. President Obama was unable to get an immigration reform bill through Congress. In lieu of legislation, his administration did create a policy called Deferred Action for Childhood Arrivals (DACA), which allowed undocumented immigrants who were brought to the United States as children (and graduated high school or performed military service) to register to obtain temporary legal status[1] (Romano and Hinojosa 2012, 171–172). These failures do stem in part from Congress' inability or refusal to pass legislation to address these issues.

In addition to the discrimination-specific campaign promises, it is important to acknowledge that President Obama made general campaign promises which many predicted would have a disproportionate, positive impact on communities of color. The Affordable Care Act (ACA) stands as the primary example. In 2010, the year that President Obama signed the ACA into law, the National Center for Health Statistics estimated that approximately one-third

---

[1] In 2017, President Obama's successor, Donald Trump, announced a new policy to rescind the DACA program. Congress does have the ability to redefine the status of these immigrants via legislation. As this book is going to press, Congress has not passed any such legislation. We will have to wait to see if that happens.

of the 60 million Americans without health insurance were black. Half were Latino/a (Caliendo 2014, 126). Thus, it was reasonable to assume that despite the fact that Obamacare was crafted in general, race-neutral terms, it was going to disproportionately help people of color[2] (Romano and Hinojosa 2012, 176–177).

This chapter hopes to make a contribution to all of the existing Obama analyses by charting statistical measures of socioeconomic inequality over time, by race. This analysis differs from previous work on the Obama Administration in important ways. Michael Dawson supports his case that black socioeconomic disadvantage persists in the black community using data that largely ends before the beginning of the Obama Administration (Dawson 2011, ch. 4). Bruce Caswell examines socioeconomic measures such as unemployment and poverty. While he puts Obama's performance on these measures in comparative context, often comparing Obama's rates to presidents dating back to the Truman Administration, he does not break those measures down by race (Caswell 2012). In this chapter, I am going to combine both approaches. I will look at socioeconomic measures, broken down by race, over a nearly 25-year period. This will allow me to compare racial inequality over the course of Bill Clinton, George W. Bush, and Barack Obama's presidencies and determine if any observed changes in black–white inequality during the Obama Administration were part of longer-term trends or were unique to the Obama Administration.

First order findings: promises made, promises kept

First, though, it is helpful to look at candidate Obama's campaign promises. Did he make specific promises that appear to be explicitly targeted to the African American community; and if so, did he keep those promises? As a deracialized candidate, did Obama make promises that are framed in race-neutral terms but seem to be targeted to benefit blacks (and/or all minorities)?

To answer these questions, I revisit some of the data points which Romano and Hinojosa (2012) used. I looked at Politifact's list of Barack Obama's 2008 and 2012 campaign promises. Politifact, a project of the *Tampa Bay Times*, studies the veracity of the claims that politicians make in campaigns and in key policy debates (Holan 2011; Adair and Holan 2013). They tallied a list of 533 Obama campaign promises[3] and rated them according to their

---

2   I should credit one of my students, Levi Lyman-Barner, for challenging me to think more critically about this issue.

3   Some promises are related. For simplicity, I count each promise Politifact lists as a discrete promise.

Table 2.1 Descriptive statistics, Obama campaign promises by fulfillment and identity target

Description	N (%)
Promises broken	129 (24.2%)
Promises compromised	146 (27.4%)
Promises kept	258 (48.4%)
Promises addressing black concerns	31 (5.8%)
Promises addressing Latino/a concerns	26 (4.9%)
Promises addressing Asian American concerns	9 (1.7%)
Promises addressing Native American concerns	13 (2.4%)
Promises addressing women's concerns	23 (4.3%)
Promises addressing LGBT concerns	7 (1.3%)
Promises addressing senior concerns	12 (2.3%)
Promises addressing veterans' concerns	32 (6.0%)
Promises addressing the concerns of the poor	74 (13.9%)
Total	533

Source: Author calculations from Politifact (n.d.). Intercoder sample agreement rate: 91.7%

completion (Politifact n.d.). The promises ranged from "introducing comprehensive immigration reform in the first year," which Politifact codes as a broken promise, to killing Osama bin Laden, which President Obama fulfilled.[4] I supplemented this list by coding the promises according to the target constituency of the promise.

Table 2.1 includes a basic descriptive analysis of Barack Obama's campaign promises. According to Politifact, Obama fulfilled 48 percent of the promises he made in his administration. He broke 24 percent of the promises he made and compromised on 27 percent of the pledges.

Table 2.1 also includes a breakdown of the overall percentage of promises which targeted key constituencies. About 5 percent of the promises would be of interest to the Latino/a community. These promises include comprehensive immigration reform; allowing Cuban Americans to have greater contact with their relatives in Cuba; and discussing security alliances with Latin American political leaders. President Obama addressed Asian American and Native American concerns in about 2 percent of his promises each. I should note that there is overlap among these promises. For instance, a promise like comprehensive immigration reform might be of particular interest to Latino/a and Asian American constituents; as such, it was coded for both groups. Similarly, I coded the promise to diversify media ownership for all minority groups, as it was intended to benefit all underrepresented racial and ethnic groups.[5]

4 Politifact also included frivolous promises, like buying Malia and Sasha Obama a dog.
5 Another example would be the promise to increase high school graduation rates. On the surface, this promise might seem more likely to target black, Latino/a, and Native American

President Obama made promises to other constituencies too. Seven of his promises (or a little more than 1 percent of the total) addressed LGBT concerns, like ending "don't ask, don't tell" or repealing the Defense of Marriage Act. Slightly more than 2 percent of the promises targeted senior citizens. Exemplary promises include eliminating income taxes for seniors making less than $50,000/year.

Of the groups examined in Table 2.1, Obama made the most promises to women, veterans, and the poor. Twenty-three promises (or 4.3 percent) addressed women's issues. Thirty-two promises (or 6 percent) affected veterans. By far, President Obama issued more promises designed to address poverty. Seventy-four promises (or nearly 14 percent of the total) were intended to address issues of concern to the poor.

Nearly 6 percent of promises considered the interests of black communities. These promises ranged from promising wetlands protection along the Gulf Coast as part of hurricane prevention (I would argue that Hurricane Katrina was a racialized event) to establishing school STEM (Science, Technology, Engineering, and Math) programs with a particular focus on reaching out to underrepresented minorities to signing a bill outlawing voter intimidation and deceptive electioneering.

It is important to know that some of these promises to blacks were racialized, and that some would be associated with blackness regardless of their intent because of long-standing stereotyping (see Gilens 1999). Promises about voting rights, sentencing equalization for crack and powder cocaine, and pledges to rebuild New Orleans after Hurricane Katrina fit in this category. Some promises included groups besides blacks or were racially transcendent. Examples of these include the generic promise to pursue hate crimes and civil rights abuses (which Politifact distinguishes from a specific promise to add sexual orientation as a protected class to hate crimes legislation) and promises to expand broadband access in the United States, respectively. In the former example, all minority groups (racial and otherwise) would have an interest in the enforcement of civil rights (and all were coded as having an interest in this promise). In the latter example, I would contend that a promise to reduce the digital divide would be important to rural and/or black voters. (For a list of all of the promises President Obama made to blacks, see the Appendix.)

In Table 2.2, I examine the promises that candidate Obama made to key constituent groups. Here, I am interested in the status of those promises. Was

students. However, when assessing whether Obama kept the promise, Politifact pointed to a Department of Education document which touted improvements in graduation rates across racial groups, including Asian Americans. As such, I coded the promise as being of interest to Asian Americans as well.

Table 2.2 Cross-tabulation of fulfilled Obama campaign promises by target constituency

Promise status	Blacks	Latinos/as	Asian Americans	Native Americans	Women	LGBT	Seniors	Veterans	The poor
Kept	17 (54.8%)	15 (57.7%)	2 (22.2%)	8 (61.5%)	13 (56.5%)	5 (71.4%)	5 (41.7%)	21 (65.6%)	32 (43.2%)
Broken	5 (16.1%)	5 (19.1%)	4 (44.4%)	3 (23.1%)	6 (26.1%)	1 (14.3%)	2 (16.7%)	1 (3.1%)	15 (20.3%)
Compromised	9 (29.0%)	6 (23.1%)	3 (33.3%)	2 (15.4%)	4 (17.4%)	1 (14.3%)	5 (41.7%)	10 (31.3%)	27 (36.5%)
Total promises by group	31	26	9	13	23	7	12	32	74

Source: Author calculations from Politifact (n.d.).

President Obama able to keep his promises? Did he have to compromise with Congress or other political actors? Or was he unable to fulfill his promises? Recall from Table 2.1 that, overall, President Obama kept a plurality (48.4 percent) of the promises he made. When we look at the promises he made toward specific groups, we find that in most instances, President Obama kept a majority of the promises he made. He kept about 55 percent of the promises he made that would have particular appeal to blacks. This proportion is comparable to the proportion of kept promises he made that would appeal to Latinos/as (57.7 percent) and women (56.5 percent).

President Obama also succeeded in keeping promises to some other groups. Obama kept more than 60 percent of the promises he made to veterans and Native Americans. And he kept more than 70 percent of promises he made to the LGBT community. However, there were some groups that received fewer fulfilled promises than average. Obama kept only 42 percent of promises to seniors, and he broke more promises (44.4 percent) that would affect Asian Americans (the fulfilled promise rate for this group was 22.2 percent). This was largely due to the fact that President Obama failed to keep some key promises about immigration reform and voting rights. I should note that, in these instances, other groups besides Asian Americans also had an interest in these issues. The difference between Latinos/as or African Americans and Asian Americans, though, was that Obama made and kept other promises to blacks and Latinos/as.

On the surface, the Politifact findings partially corroborate Frederick Harris' (2012) contention that groups like the Tea Party and the LGBT community received more attention from the president than blacks. I do not code Politifact promises for their Tea Party content, so I will not assess that claim here. However, the Politifact data does suggest that President Obama was more successful in addressing LGBT issues than other issues, particularly black issues. It is important to note, though, that Obama made far fewer promises to LGBT Americans than he made to other groups. While, proportionally, Obama was able to achieve more of his LGBT policy agenda, he actually kept more promises to blacks (17) than he made to the LGBT community (7) in the first place.

This raises important questions about whether we should deem some promises to be more important than others. In this analysis, I have chosen to weight each promise equally. I have also followed Politifact's lead in considering each promise as discrete. I think that this is appropriate for a first-run analysis. However, future analyses may consider weighting promises differently or clustering promises together if they seem to be related to one another.

There is some value in not weighting these promises, though. While President Obama's promises to expand the legal recognition of same-sex unions or to allow LGBT Americans to serve openly in the military are undeniably high profile, these are only two of more than 500 promises he made as a candidate. Weighting these promises equally reminds us of the extent to which candidates make promises and pushes us to consider the entire universe of promises, not just the high-profile pledges.

Second order findings: two case studies

With the Politifact findings in mind, it is helpful to look closely at a few select agencies and divisions to determine how their operations evolved over the course of the Obama Administration. In this section, I look at Small Business Administration (SBA) loans to minority-owned businesses and funding for Historically Black Colleges and Universities.

SBA loans to minority businesses

Politifact lists President Obama's pledge to "increase minority access to capital" as one of his kept campaign promises (Politifact n.d.). When Politifact designates the promise as kept, though, it is not necessarily making distinctions between subgroups or indicating whether or not there is continued room for improvement. So, here, I would like to conduct a deeper examination.

I requested and received data on budget allocations for 7(a) loans by race from the SBA. This category of loans is among the most common type of SBA credit product; grantees use these loans to start or expand small businesses. There are some restrictions on the types of businesses that are eligible for 7(a) loans. Grantees should have invested their own money in the business before pursuing a loan. Not all franchise businesses are eligible for 7(a) loans. Applicants with felony records are not eligible for 7(a) loans. Finally, the SBA does not award loans to businesses engaged in illegal or prurient activity (Small Business Administration n.d.b).

I report here on allocations from fiscal years 1993 to 2015. Figure 2.1 shows the distribution of 7(a) loans to small businesses by race. Here, I look specifically at the number of loans that were approved for businesses in a fiscal year. In general, we see that the number of loans increases from the early 2000s through 2007, during the economic expansion. We see a contraction in the number of approved loans in 2008 and 2009, which would be consistent with the economic crisis facing the country at the time. After that, we see a brief increase in the number of approved loans

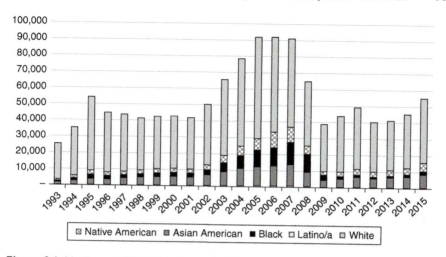

Figure 2.1 Number of SBA 7(a) loans to small businesses, by racial/ethnic group, fiscal years 1993–2015

Note: These figures exclude multi-racial firms and firms owned by Alaska Natives, which were separate categories.

Source: Small Business Administration (n.d.a).

in 2010 and 2011, and annual increases in the number of approved loans after 2012.

Proportionally, white firms received the majority of loans over the course of the time period studied. The proportion of loans distributed to white-owned firms ranges from a low of just over 54 percent in 2007 to nearly 82 percent in 1993. Proportionally, the number of loans going to Asian American-owned firms doubled over time. Where 6.3 percent of firms receiving loans in 1993 were headed by Asian Americans, that percentage was consistently in the double digits in the 2000s and up to 13.2 percent in 2015.

Black and Latino/a owned firms fared differently. Latino/a owned firms have never been proportionally represented in the distribution of SBA loans. Black owned firms only comprised 10 percent or more of the firms receiving 7(a) loans in a four-year period: from 2005–2008. Black firms even comprised a dispro-portionately larger number of loans (relative to their share of the population) in 2007 and 2008 (13.8 and 15.9 percent, respectively). However, from 2010 to 2015, the proportion of 7(a) loans going to black-owned firms plummeted, ran-ging from 2.5 percent to 4 percent of all loans in this category. Proportionally speaking, black firms won the greatest number of 7(a) loans during the Bush Administration, and the fewest number of loans during the Obama years.

We see a similar pattern when we examine this data in terms of loan award amounts. In Figure 2.2, I look at SBA 7(a) loan expenditures by race. Specifically, I look at the amount of money being allocated to firms by the

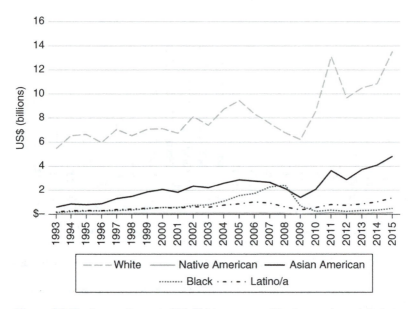

Figure 2.2 Total expenditures in SBA 7(a) loans to small businesses, by racial/ethnic group, fiscal years 1993–2015
Note: These figures exclude multi-racial firms and firms owned by Alaska Natives and Puerto Ricans, which were separate categories. An inflation-adjusted graph is available upon request.
Source: Small Business Administration (n.d.a).

race/ethnicity of the firm's owner. Here, we see some general patterns. From an absolute dollar standpoint, the SBA increased its loan allocations to firms from 1993 to 2005. Loan allocations start to decrease after that, and reach a low point in 2009, after which allocations rebound.

We know from Figure 2.1 that white firms received the largest share of 7(a) loans. Figure 2.2 shows that they also received the largest share of loan dollars allocated. In 2015, this amounted to about $13.5 billion in loan support. The pattern of Asian American loan support looks similar to the national pattern, with the total value of loans going to Asian American firms increasing through the mid-2000s, decreasing in the wake of the 2008 financial crisis and then increasing thereafter. In 2015, Asian-American-owned firms received $4.8 billion in loan support.

In contrast, black and Latino/a owned firms received less loan support, as measured by the amount of assistance they received. Latino/a firms saw the aggregate amount of their loans increase through 2006, when Latino/a firms received over $1 billion in loan assistance. That number falls to a low of nearly $360 million in 2009, but increased in subsequent years. In 2015, Latino/a firms received $1.3 billion in 7(a) loans.

In terms of aggregate dollars, black owned firms received more 7(a) loans during the Bush years. From 2004 to 2008, black-owned firms received

$1 billion to $2.4 billion in 7(a) loans. This plummets to nearly $680 million in 2009, and fell to as low as $235 million in 2012. In 2015, black-owned firms only received about $491 million in 7(a) loans.

This data has implications for future studies. There are a number of possible structural explanations to explain why black-owned businesses have not taken advantage of these programs. In a report for the SBA, McManus (2016) noted that minority-owned businesses were less likely to borrow to start a business, less likely to use private loans to expand their businesses, and more likely to believe that private loans were not an option for them. Minority-owned businesses that received loans tended to have more employees and higher revenues. This is a problem for black-owned businesses because they are disproportionately clustered in industries with the lowest revenues and fewest employees (McManus 2016, 4–10). Future studies should definitely probe whether the capital requirements to be eligible for SBA loans make it difficult for black-owned businesses to get capital. They should also look at different loan programs to see if blacks were more likely to receive different types of assistance.

Support for Historically Black Colleges

Though not mentioned as a campaign promise, examining President Obama's support for Historically Black Colleges and Universities (HBCUs) is a potential window on his engagement with black communities. Black colleges hold a special place in African American communities because of the historic exclusion of blacks from mainstream institutions of higher education. The Department of Education estimates that 14 percent of all black college graduates received their degrees from HBCUs in 2014–2015 (National Center for Educational Statistics n.d.).

Because President Obama did not run on a pro-HBCU platform, a decision to quietly increase support for black colleges could be seen as evidence of the "wink and nod" that Frederick Harris (2012) was doubtful would materialize. A "wink and nod" is the idea that deracialized black politicians implicitly try to convince black voters to support them without making promises to black communities. In exchange for their vote, blacks are supposed to trust that these black politicians will quietly deliver material benefits to them (Harris 2012, 139). Moreover, examination of executive support for black education has been an important barometer for black politics scholars since Judson Lance Jeffries cited increased support for black colleges as one of the achievements of former Virginia Governor Douglas Wilder, America's first elected black governor (Jeffries 2000).

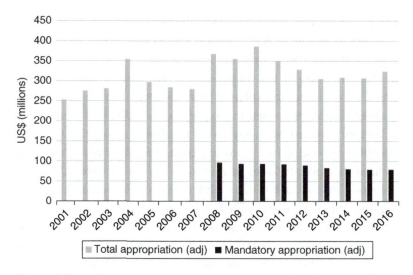

Figure 2.3 Mandatory and discretionary appropriations for Historically Black Colleges and Universities, fiscal years 2001–2016 (in October 2015 dollars)
Source: US Department of Education (n.d.a).

To look at this question further, I examined federal funding figures for HBCUs from 2001 to 2016. These figures are included in Figure 2.3, which disaggregates funding based on whether or not it was a mandatory or discretionary appropriation from fiscal years (FY) 2008 to 2016. In inflation adjusted dollars, total appropriations for HBCUs fluctuated over time. During President Bush's tenure, total appropriations grew slightly over his first term in office and then increased dramatically in FY2004. Appropriations decreased during his second term in office and spiked again in FY2008. Total appropriations increased at the beginning of Obama's first term, then decreased through FY2013 and then increased after that in FY2014 and FY2016.[6]

Mandatory appropriations decreased incrementally over the course of the Obama Administration. In inflation adjusted dollars, HBCUs received about $97 million in mandatory appropriations in FY2008. This number had fallen to about $79 million in FY2016.

6 In addition, in 2013, the *Washington Post* reported that changes in loan qualification standards for parents seeking federal loans to cover their obligations for their children's tuition adversely and disproportionately affected parents of students at HBCUs, who were more likely to use these loans to help pay their children's expenses. This, in turn, reduced the budgets at many HBCUs, which had come to rely on the revenues generated from these parental loans (see Anderson 2013; Carter 2013).

A word on other Obama initiatives

In early 2014, President Obama announced his My Brother's Keeper Initiative. This program created a public–private partnership which sought to promote positive life outcomes for disadvantaged black, Latino, and Native American young men through mentorship, job training, and educational programs. This program was perhaps Obama's most racialized and visible attempt to reach out to African Americans. The program garnered much criticism from the left, though, particularly among black feminists. They argued that a focus on poor males of color ignored the fact that these young men have sisters and female neighbors who live in the same communities and face the same risks and challenges. As such, they contended that My Brother's Keeper was well-intentioned but chauvinistic and would be better served if it targeted disadvantaged boys and girls (see Crenshaw 2014). Other critics, such as Princeton professor Eddie Glaude (2016, 68–69), further asserted that programs such as My Brother's Keeper gave insufficient attention to structural racism and the widespread cultural practice of accepting perpetual inequality. Glaude went so far as to describe My Brother's Keeper as, "a Band-Aid for a gunshot wound" (Glaude 2016, 7).

It is very difficult to ascertain the real effect of a program like My Brother's Keeper. To date, no one has released a comprehensive examination of the impact of My Brother's Keeper. Most journalistic analyses of the program are anecdotal in nature and focus on human-interest stories about individual teens who participated in the local programs which received grant support from the My Brother's Keeper initiative (see Allen 2016; Jones 2016).

The best way to assess the effectiveness of My Brother's Keeper would be to compare outcomes from participants in My Brother's Keeper programs and similarly situated young people who did not participate in the program. Ideally, My Brother's Keeper programs would have selected participants through a lottery system, which would allow researchers to examine outcomes using an experimental research design. In the absence of randomization, though, researchers can use matching techniques to identify suitable groups of non-participants to compare to participants. Future studies should seek to engage in these types of program evaluation.

Third order findings: selected inequality indicators

Now, it is important to see if there is any indication that black–white inequality decreased after President Barack Obama took office. Here, I focus on key socioeconomic indicators. The advantage of this analysis over other work (i.e., Dawson 2011; Harris 2012) is that I include statistics through most or all of President Obama's term (depending on data availability). I am most interested in the black–white gaps in these indices, not necessarily the direction of the indicators themselves. For instance, I expect that unemployment will increase for all groups during recessions. However, if blacks and whites have identical unemployment rates, this suggests the absence of inequality and evinces that there are no structural factors exacerbating unemployment in black communities.

Unemployment

I show black and white labor force participation and unemployment rates (seasonally adjusted for workers aged 16 and older) for January 1993 to January 2017 in Figure 2.4. As the graph shows, blacks have a slightly lower labor force participation rate than whites. The big difference is in unemployment rates, though. Black and white unemployment rates rise and fall in tandem based on the general state of the economy (for instance, there are local spikes in unemployment around the 2001 recession and the 2008–2009 recession). As such, the gap between black and white unemployment remains relatively constant: black unemployment is typically about twice the rate of white unemployment. If we look at the average ratio of black to white unemployment by president, President Obama does have a slightly lower ratio than Presidents Bush and Clinton. (The average black to white unemployment ratio[7] during the Obama Administration is 1.94:1, compared to 2.08:1 during the Bush Administration and 2.21:1 during the Clinton Administration.) Still, blacks were about twice as likely to be unemployed as their white counterparts during the Obama Administration, which was also the case in previous administrations.

We should note that, on average, unemployment rates for blacks and whites were higher in the Obama Administration due to the Great Recession. Black unemployment was typically 10 percent or higher during the Obama Administration through mid-2015—in fact, during the first six-and-a-half years of Obama's term (through July 2015), black unemployment was only below 10 percent in three months (April, June, and July 2015).

Figure 2.4 also shows that labor force participation rates declined for both blacks and whites in the Clinton, Bush, and Obama Administrations.

---

7 I calculate average unemployment for an administration starting in February of the first year of their term in office, since presidents only serve 11 days in January of their first year of office. That January is credited to the prior administration.

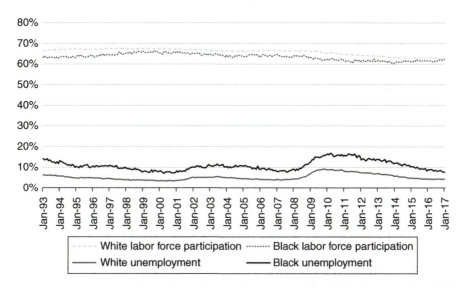

Figure 2.4 Monthly unemployment and labor participation (seasonally adjusted) by race, 1993 to 2017
Source: Bureau of Labor Statistics (n.d.), based on Current Population Survey.

About two-thirds of whites worked or were seeking work in the Clinton Administration, compared to nearly 65 percent of blacks. The white labor force participation rate drops slightly during the Bush Administration. Then, the white labor force participation rate was 66.5 percent, compared to 64.2 percent for blacks. Labor force participation rates continue to fall in the Obama Administration. On average, 63.9 percent of whites worked or looked for work during the Obama Administration, compared to 61.6 percent of blacks.

Income

Next, I look at income inequality. In Figure 2.5, I show median household income by race from 1993 to 2016. Please note that this data does not control for the number of household members who contribute to a family's income. In addition, each racial group includes households which identify with more than one race. The Census Bureau did not allow Americans to identify with more than one race until the 2000s. As such, I deemed it more consistent to not disaggregate multi-racial Americans when such data became available. Counting multi-racial Americans with their constitutive groups actually makes the measures more conservative, as multi-racial Americans' socioeconomic outcomes tend to fall between the average outcomes of the groups with which they share racial identities (see Hochschild *et al.* 2012).

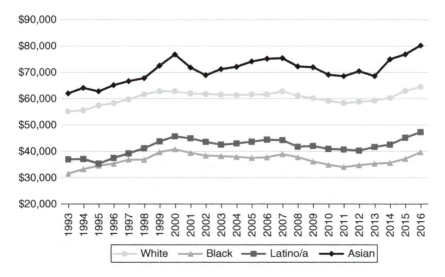

Figure 2.5 Estimated median household income (in 2015 dollars) by race, 1993–2016
Source: Proctor *et al.* (2016), 25–29; Semega *et al.* (2017), 25–29.

Figure 2.5 reveals persistent income stratification along racial lines. Whites and Asian Americans have consistently higher household incomes than blacks and Latinos/as, with Asian Americans having the highest median household incomes of all the groups examined. In general, income levels across groups tend to follow the same patterns. Incomes rose in the 1990s. In the early 2000s, white incomes decreased slightly but stayed relatively constant; Asian American incomes fell sharply in 2000 to 2002 and then started to rebound in 2003; Latino/a and black incomes fell slightly in the early 2000s and were starting to increase in the years leading up to the 2008 recession. Household income for all groups fell in 2008 and did not start to rebound for these groups until the early 2010's. After 2013, incomes rose for all four racial and ethnic groups studied here, but at different rates. Incomes for Asian American households, for instance, increased at a faster rate from 2013 to 2016 than they did for other groups (particularly from 2013 to 2014) while the increase in white household income was somewhat sluggish from 2012 to 2013 and 2015 to 2016.

Wealth is also an important measure. Above income, accumulated wealth can buffer families from financial devastation in the face of unexpected expenses. Most important, wealth can be bequeathed to future generations, helping descendants buy property, pay for advanced education, and start businesses. Scholars have noted that because of the loss of wages due to slavery and discriminatory practices that limited the appreciation of homes

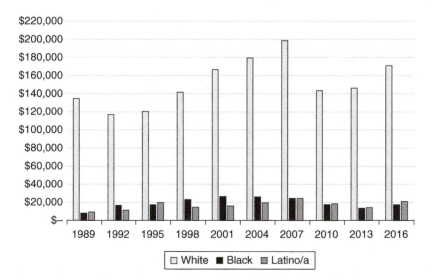

Figure 2.6 Median household wealth by race of head of household, 1989–2016 (2016 dollars)
Source: Federal Reserve Board of Governors (2017).

in predominantly black neighborhoods, blacks tend to have less wealth than whites (Conley 1999; Oliver and Shapiro 2006).

Figure 2.6 shows that wealth inequality continued to be a problem during the Obama Administration. The data I use here is from the Federal Reserve Board's Survey of Consumer Finances. The findings I present here are more conservative estimates of wealth inequalities than other measures that exist (see, for example, Kochhar *et al.* 2011). I use these data in part because they have more longitudinal data points. Even here, though, we see stark differences in wealth across racial and ethnic groups. Typically, the median household net worth of black and Latino/a families is a fraction of the net worth of white families. Black net worth increases in the early 2000s, most likely because of the economic boom which increased housing values. However, white and Latino/a net worth increases at a more rapid pace during this time period. For instance, in 1998, median white wealth was nearly $142,000, compared to about $23,000 for blacks and nearly $15,000 for Latinos/as. In 2007, just before the housing bust, median white household wealth was nearly $199,000, compared to about $24,000 for black and Latino/a households. This means that while white and Latino families experienced a double-digit percentage increase in wealth, black wealth barely increased. (And it should be noted that despite this increase in Latino/a wealth, in absolute dollars, Latino/a wealth remained modest.)

In the wake of the housing bust and economic recession of 2008–2009, net worth decreased among all groups. But because blacks and Latinos/as had less wealth to begin with, that reduction in net worth would be more acutely felt. In 2010, median net worth falls to about $143,000 for whites, but drops to about $18,000 for blacks and Latinos/as.

Since then, the rate of wealth recovery has been uneven for different racial and ethnic groups. While white wealth increased from 2010 to 2013, net worth continued to decline for blacks and Latinos/as during the same time period. Median wealth levels for all groups increased from 2013 to 2016. However, blacks lagged whites and Latinos in recouping wealth. While median net worth figures for whites and Latinos/as in 2016 were higher than they were in 2010, median net worth for blacks in 2016 was actually $200 less (in inflation adjusted dollars) than it was in 2010.

Homeownership

In Figure 2.7, I turn to homeownership data. Homeownership is the primary means by which average Americans accumulate wealth. Blacks and Latinos/as have historically had lower homeownership rates, and as such, they tend to have lower net worth. That blacks and Latinos/as were more susceptible to foreclosure during the Great Recession has been widely reported (see Hall *et al.* 2015), so I expect lower overall homeownership rates and steeper downward slopes in homeownership rates among blacks and Latinos/as starting in 2008. What I am most interested in here is whether or not those homeownership rates stabilized toward the end of the Obama Administration.

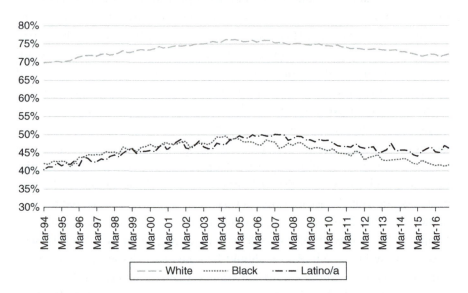

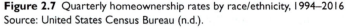

Figure 2.7 Quarterly homeownership rates by race/ethnicity, 1994–2016
Source: United States Census Bureau (n.d.).

While whites are more likely to own homes than blacks and Latinos/as, homeownership rates largely increase for all three groups from the early 1990s to the mid-2000s. Among whites, homeownership rates peak at just above 76 percent in 2004. White homeownership rates consistently fall below 75 percent after 2008 and continue to fall through 2016, where they hovered around 72 percent. At the beginning of the time period examined (March, or first quarter, 1994), Latino/a homeownership rates were just over 40 percent. By the end of the Clinton Administration, Latino/a homeownership rates approached 48 percent. The highest homeownership rate for this group was 50.1 percent, which was last recorded in the third quarter of 2007. Latino/a homeownership rates fell throughout the Great Recession; and while we see a slight rebound in 2013, it started to fall toward the end of the year and did not rebound in 2014. In 2015–2016, Latino/a homeownership rates ranged from 45 to 47 percent.

Black homeownership rates resemble Latino/a homeownership during the 1990s and early 2000s. However, the data indicate that black homeownership rates started to decline sooner and did not recover over the course of the Obama Administration. In 1994, black homeownership rates were below 43 percent. At the beginning of Bill Clinton's second term (first quarter 1997), more than 44 percent of blacks owned their homes. By the end of Clinton Administration (fourth quarter 2000), black homeownership rates were around 48 percent. After some fluctuation in the first part of the 2000s, black homeownership rates increased to their highest levels (above 49 percent) for much of 2004. They stayed in the 48 percent range for most of 2005 and 2006. We start to see the consistent decline in black homeownership rates in late 2008. There was a slight rebound in late 2011, but black homeownership rates pitched lower after that. In 2016, the last year of the Obama Administration, black homeownership rates were below 42 percent.

The comparative homeownership data is instructive. We see similarities and contrasts across groups, over time. The data clearly suggest that the Great Recession and precipitating housing crisis had a chilling effect on homeownership across the three racial/ethnic groups studied here. However, the data indicate slight differences in recovery rates across the groups. While Latino/a homeownership rates started to rebound in 2015–2016, black and white homeownership rates continued to exhibit softness. Even here, though, there were differences between blacks and whites. Despite the decrease in homeownership rates among whites, homeownership levels in this group still surpassed the homeownership rate in 1994, the beginning of the time period studied. Blacks, unfortunately, did not share the same fortune. Homeownership rates among this group, which stayed below 42 percent through 2016, were lower than black homeownership rates in 1994.

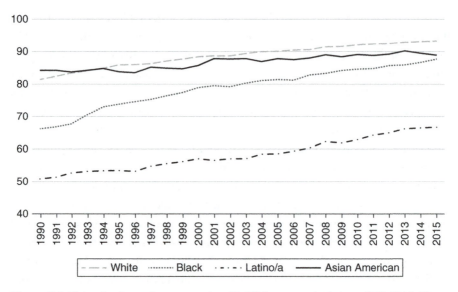

Figure 2.8 High school completion rates (age 25–29) by race and ethnicity, 1990–2015 (%)
Note: Asian American data includes Pacific Islanders.
Source: National Center for Education Statistics (2015, Table 104.10).

Education

Next, I turn to education indicators, as education is a strong predictor of future life chances. In Figure 2.8, I chart high school completion rates for adults aged 25–29 using National Center for Education Statistics data. These graduation rates include those who finish traditional high schools and those who complete GED or equivalency programs. Whites and Asian Americans have had the highest high school completion rates, with whites slightly out-pacing Asian Americans since the mid-1990s. Black high school completion rates have consistently lagged behind those of whites, but the completion rate has been above 80 percent since 2003, and the gap between black and white high school graduation rates has narrowed over time. Since 2006, black graduation rates among young people have risen slowly but steadily, hitting an all-time high of 88.9 percent (for the time period studied) in 2015.

The gap between Latino/a and white high school completion rates remained quite large. High school completion rates among Latinos/as trailed black high school completion rates by 15 percentage points or more during the entire time period studied. Moreover, while Latino/a graduation rates continued to improve through 2015, the rate of that improvement lagged the improvement rate among blacks. For instance, while black graduation rates jumped nearly 3 percentage points from 2013 to 2015, Latino/a graduation rates improved by only half a percentage point during the same time period.

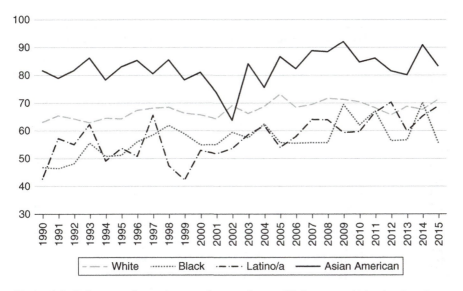

Figure 2.9 College enrollment (two- or four-year) rates (%) for recent high school graduates by race, 1990–2015
Note: Asian American figure includes Pacific Islanders through 2003.
Source: National Center for Education Statistics (2016a, Table 302.20).

In Figure 2.9, I look at college enrollment rates by race for students who graduated from high school the year before. Here, there is evidence of inconsistent progress in the Obama era. During the Clinton and Bush years, Asian American students typically enrolled in college right out of high school at the highest rates. White college enrollment increased slightly, but the enrollment rates were largely static. Latino/a college enrollment fluctuated wildly in the 1990s, and with the exception of 2005, increased during the George W. Bush Administration. Black college enrollment also fluctuated, but the general pattern is an increase through 1998, followed by relatively static enrollment rates through 2008 (with spikes in 2002 and 2004).

During the Obama Administration, college enrollment rates continued to fluctuate. White enrollment rates declined through 2012 but rose afterward. Asian American enrollment rates declined through 2013. They started to rise in 2014 but fell again in 2015. Latino/a college enrollment rates fell through the first two years of the Obama Administration. Enrollment rebounded from 2010 to 2012, fell again in 2013, and then rose for the final two years studied. Black college enrollment rates rose and fell during the entire Obama Administration. Despite peak college enrollment among recent high school graduates in 2009 and 2014, black enrollment in 2015 was almost identical to the black enrollment rate in 2008.

Table 2.3 Mean SAT and ACT scores by race, 1996–2015

	Mean cumulative SAT scores		Mean ACT composite score	
	White	Black	White	Black
1996	1,049	856		
1997	1,052	857	21.7	17.1
1998	1,054	860	21.7	17.1
1999	1,055	856	21.6	17.1
2000	1,058	860	21.8	17
2001	1,060	859	21.8	16.9
2002	1,060	857	22.6	17.6
2003	1,063	857	21.7	16.9
2004	1,059	857	21.8	17.1
2005	1,068	864	21.9	17
2006	1,582	1,291	22	17.1
2007	1,579	1,287	22.1	17
2008	1,583	1,280	22.3	16.9
2009	1,581	1,276	22.2	16.9
2010	1,580	1,277	22.3	16.9
2011	1,579	1,272	22.4	17
2012	1,578	1,273	22.4	17
2013	1,576	1,278	22.2	16.9
2014	1,576	1,278	22.3	17
2015	1,576	1,277	22.4	17.1

Source: National Center for Education Statistics (2016b); ACT, Inc. (n.d.).

There are many possible explanations for these enrollment rates, which education scholars are sure to explain in the future. Future work should study how the popularity of gap years varies across racial and ethnic lines and probe the impact of affordability on decisions to enroll in college immediately after finishing high school.

I now turn to an analysis of standardized test score data in Table 2.3.[8] It may seem unusual to look at test scores, but right after President Obama took office, there was some speculation that his ascent might have a positive effect on black students' test performance (see Dillon 2009). The data I include here are average test scores for the two major college entrance exams, the SAT and the ACT. Students taking these tests represent a rarefied subset of the student population. However, SAT/ACT scores are reported annually, unlike National Assessment of Educational Progress (NAEP) scores, which are more representative of the US student population but only released every 3–5 years. I also acknowledge that standardized test scores are an imperfect measure of student performance and aptitude and that there have been numerous studies showing that tests have cultural and class biases which disadvantage

8   The reader will note a significant increase in the average SAT score starting in 2006. In 2006, the College Board introduced a required writing component to the SAT and increased the highest possible score to 2,400, as opposed to the earlier maximum score of 1,600.

low-income students and students of color (see Jencks 1998). Because the College Board and the ACT calculate average scores by Latino/a nationality and Asian sub-ethnicity differently,[9] I omit them from this analysis.

Table 2.3 shows that very little changed in the black–white test score gap in the two decades studied. In the older (pre-2006) version of the SAT, blacks scored, on average, about 200 points lower on the SAT than their white counterparts. From 2006 to 2015, when the maximum score increased from 1,600 to 2,400 after adding a third section to the test, the average black–white gap increased from 200 points to about 300 points, which translates to a similar average gap of 100 points per section of the SAT.

This pattern also holds for the ACT. On average, black ACT scores have been five points lower than white ACT scores since 1997. The gap between 1997 and 2006 typically fell a little below five points, while the gap increased to slightly more than five points after 2007.

Health

Given the prominence of the Affordable Care Act in President Obama's overall policy agenda, it is important to track inequality on key health measures. Here, I look at life expectancy and the number of people who lack health insurance.

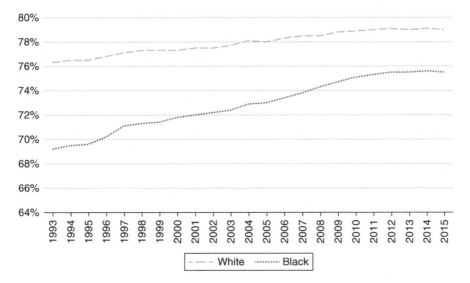

Figure 2.10 Life expectancy rates at birth by race, 1993–2015
Source: National Center for Health Statistics (2017, 116).

9 The College Board reports scores for Mexican Americans, Puerto Rican Americans and "other Latinos" separately, while the ACT separates scores of Asian Americans and Pacific Islanders.

Figure 2.10 charts changes in life expectancy rates for blacks and whites[10] over time, using data from the Centers for Disease Control (CDC). The data I show here is projected life expectancy for a person born in the year in question. For instance, the 2015 figures predict the life expectancy for a person born in 2015. As the figure shows, life expectancy has gradually improved for both blacks and whites over time. Blacks, though, still lag behind whites in terms of life expectancy.

Despite the gap in black and white life expectancy, this is one area where black–white inequalities have improved over time. A black person born in 1993, at the start of the Clinton Administration, was predicted to live 7.1 fewer years than a white person born that year. Over the course of three presidential administrations, we see that the gap shrunk significantly. Blacks born in 2015, the last year for which data was available, were only predicted to live 3.5 fewer years than their white counterparts.

It is important to compare the rate of change in life expectancy as well, as it helps to explain why the racial gap narrowed over time. The life expectancy gap is smaller largely because black life expectancy improved at a faster rate than white life expectancy. Blacks experienced the biggest improvements in life expectancy for people born between 1995 and 1997, during the Clinton Administration, and between 2005 and 2010, during the Bush and Obama Administrations. Rates were relatively stable for blacks and whites born between 2013 and 2015.

Regardless of the outcome of the Trump Administration and Congressional Republicans' efforts to change or repeal the Affordable Care Act, Obamacare (as it is known) was a key feature of Barack Obama's policy agenda. As such, it is important to see if there is even preliminary evidence that Obamacare had an effect on reducing the proportion of Americans who lacked health insurance.[11] I look at this data in Figure 2.11. A few things are of note. First, it is clear that some racial/ethnic groups were more likely to lack insurance than others. While about 10 percent of whites lacked insurance in 2008, minorities were more likely to be uninsured. About 14 percent of Asian Americans lacked insurance in 2008, as did about 17 percent of blacks. Nearly 31 percent of Latinos/as lacked health insurance. These patterns of lacking insurance stayed relatively constant, even increasing slightly, until Obamacare went into effect in 2014. It is in 2014 when we start to see the percentage of uninsured

---

10 I only chart life expectancy for blacks and whites because of the limited availability of longitudinal data for other groups.

11 Here, I am looking at the rates of insurance enrollment. I make no judgment about the quality of the insurance programs to which people are subscribed (i.e., whether people had high deductible insurance or access to physicians who accepted their insurance, etc.). Future studies should examine whether minorities were disproportionately more likely to have expensive insurance that in practice provided little real coverage.

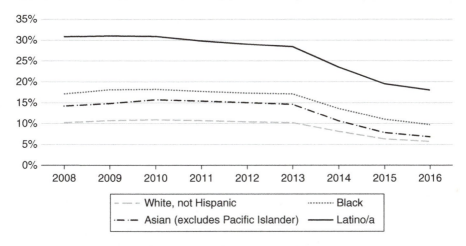

Figure 2.11 Percentage of uninsured Americans by race, 2008–2016
Source: Barnett and Berchick (2017).

Americans shrink. However, even though proportionally fewer minorities lacked insurance after 2014, the racial gaps remained. For instance, the ratio of black to white uninsurance (that is, the percentage of blacks who lack insurance relative to the percentage of whites who lack insurance) was 1.68:1 in 2008 and 1.7:1 in 2016. The inequality gap narrowed for Asian Americans (the Asian–white uninsurance ratio shrinks from 1.39:1 in 2008 to 1.19:1 in 2016), but actually grew for Latinos/as after the Affordable Care Act went into effect (the Latino/a–white uninsurance ratio was 3.02:1 in 2008, 2.79:1 in 2012, and 3.16:1 in 2016). So, while more Americans had health insurance at the end of Barack Obama's presidency, the fundamental gap in insurance enrollment rates across racial groups persisted.

Hate crimes

Finally, I turn to an examination of reported hate crimes in Figure 2.12. Here I use data from the Federal Bureau of Investigation's (FBI) Uniform Crime Report. Local police departments report hate crime incidents to the FBI, which then aggregates this information. The FBI collects data on bias crimes based on race, religion, disability, and sexual orientation. It also codes data based on whether one or many types of bias were implicated (e.g., whether someone was attacked because of one or multiple identities). For the purposes of this analysis, I only focus on single-bias hate crimes based on race/ethnicity, and I report these incidents in absolute numbers.

As Figure 2.12 shows, anti-black bias crimes were more numerous than hate crimes against other racial and ethnic groups. While the FBI recorded

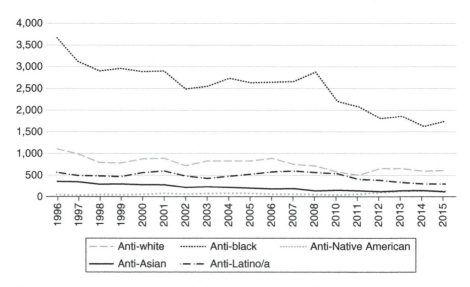

Figure 2.12 Number of single-bias hate crime incidents, 1996–2015
Source: Federal Bureau of Investigations (1995–2015). All data is derived from Table 1 of each year's Hate Crimes Report.

fewer than 1,000 hate crimes against whites, Latinos/as, Asian Americans, and Native Americans each, blacks were the target of at least 1,500 hate crimes annually during the time period studied. To be sure, blacks also experienced the sharpest decrease in the number of reported hate crimes directed toward them. While there were almost 3,700 reported anti-black hate crimes in 1996, there were 1,745 such crimes in 2015 (a slight increase from 2014, where there were only 1621 anti-black hate crimes). The sharpest decrease in reported anti-black hate crimes took place in Barack Obama's first term. While there were 2,876 anti-black hate crimes in 2008, the year Obama won the presidency, there were 1,805 anti-black hate crimes in 2012, when he won re-election.

Conclusion

After examining the various inequality statistics presented in this chapter, I conclude that, over the course of the Obama Administration, the quality of black life improved on some metrics, got worse on other dimensions, and stayed the same on yet another group of measurements. In the places where black–white inequality improved over the course of the Obama presidency (e.g., high school graduation rates, hate crimes, and life expectancy), blacks continued or accelerated gains that started years before President Obama took office. The apparent regress on some measures, such as homeownership and college attendance rates, may be attributed to exogenous shocks like the 2008–2009 recession. Future studies will need to do additional probing and process tracing to explain why black businesses received fewer loans and less money from the Small Business Administration or why funding for Historically Black Colleges decreased.[12]

What is striking about the data is its revelation of the persistence of structural inequalities that made it difficult to narrow inequality gaps on some measures. Despite the fact that black unemployment levels and rates of non-insurance subscription decrease and that black income levels increase, these improvements did not narrow the racial gap with whites.

The above statistics reflect the stark reality that structural inequality persists in American society. These statistics demand extensive study to identify the root causes of the inequality and, where fitting, the appropriate types of governmental intervention to remove the structural barriers. While I expect that there will be considerable contestation and debate about how much governmental intervention is appropriate, the persistence of gaps in outcomes for blacks and whites does warrant targeted attention.

These data points provide needed context to Harris' (2012) and Dawson's (2011) frustrations. While it is not true that nothing improved materially for blacks during the Obama Administration, one can make a credible case that there was not enough progress on some key measures like unemployment and income. The larger question is who is to blame for these sobering statistics? And perhaps most important, do blacks blame President Obama for the lack of material progress?

---

12 To be sure, the Obama Administration defended its record on small business and HBCU funding. In addition to taking credit for the general increase in the number of minority-owned businesses nationally, the Obama Administration touted an approximate 25 percent increase in the number of loans and amount of monetary support that it provided to firms in "underserved markets" (White House 2016). The Obama Administration also emphasized new programs that it developed to promote minority entrepreneurship among young men of color through the My Brother's Keeper Initiative and new regulations and a public–private partnership which provided microloans to aspiring entrepreneurs on probation and parole (White House 2016). The Department of Education also praised the Obama Administration's support of HBCUs. In an October 2016 press release, it contended that federal funding for HBCUs increased every year of the Obama Administration and that Pell Grant funding for HBCU students increased (US Department of Education 2016b). Based on the information in Figure 2.3, the funding increase was apparently not in Title III. Future studies should examine additional line items where funding for HBCUs could be housed. In addition, while the Obama Administration touted increases in Pell Grant funding as a boon for HBCU students, those increases were not specifically targeted to HBCU students (US Department of Education 2016b; Camera 2016). And despite these accomplishments, there was public dissatisfaction on other budgetary decisions which impacted HBCUs, including tougher qualification standards for the PLUS loan program for parents, which some HBCU administrators argued put strains on their financial aid budgets (see Anderson 2013; Carter 2013).

The reality of persistent inequality is staggering and sobering, and many will legitimately wonder whether President Obama exerted enough effort to tackle these issues. While some can argue that he should have done more, he did make a number of racialized and deracialized campaign promises which targeted black interests, and he fulfilled more than half of those promises. Though it is safe to say that there is more work to be done, it would be a mischaracterization to say that Obama did nothing. In the next chapter, I continue the discussion by looking deeper into the deployment of executive authority to address issues of concern to blacks.

3

Was Obama a paddling duck? Seven vignettes of substantive politics in the Obama Administration

Hollywood actors and life coaches often invoke analogies about paddling ducks to illustrate the need for composure. As the saying goes, ducks glide effortlessly on top of the water while paddling furiously beneath the surface. While some critique the metaphor from both a scientific and a philosophical standpoint (see Johnson 2012), its proponents use the image to extol listeners to work hard behind the scenes while maintaining cool, calm, and collected demeanors.

The image of the paddling duck is useful in helping to frame the discussion of President Obama's accomplishments in responding to African American political interests. The analogy seems most appropriate when describing the events leading up to the raid which killed Osama bin Laden. Obama garnered criticism for having an apparently weak foreign policy and then surprised the world by executing a successful raid to kill the mastermind behind the 9/11 attacks. What was so remarkable about the raid was that it took place in the middle of a very busy, public presidential schedule. Obama authorized the raid on Friday. Later that day, he met with civil rights activists, visited the scene of a recent tornado in Alabama, toured Cape Canaveral, and gave a college commencement address. The next day, he regaled journalists and celebrities at the White House Correspondents' Dinner. On Sunday, the day of the operation, he played golf before overseeing the operation remotely with his foreign policy team (Cooper 2010; Good 2011).

The analogy of the paddling duck also has utility for helping to frame questions about President Obama's actions with respect to racial issues. Some critics charge that President Obama did little to address racial inequality. This critique may have merit. However it may also be true that like the metaphorical gliding duck, President Obama was doing more than he appeared to be doing—he was paddling beneath the surface of the water, so to speak.

In this chapter, I examine seven cases to see if there is any evidence that the Obama Administration was paddling beneath the surface. Here, I am less concerned about outcomes. I am most interested in finding evidence that President Obama made an effort to address issues of concern to African Americans. Was the Obama Administration attempting to set the agenda on racial concerns in specific issue domains? To the extent that comparative data is available, did Obama Administration officials attend to racial issues more or less often than their predecessors?

First, I conduct a comparative analysis of the substance of executive orders in the Clinton, Bush, and Obama Administrations. Next, I examine press releases from four Cabinet departments: Labor, Education, Health and Human Services, and Justice. I examine federal reports issued in the wake of police shootings of unarmed blacks and then turn to a comparative discussion of presidential pardons and commutations.

Executive orders

President Obama's use of executive orders made front-page news throughout his time in office. In the face of Republican efforts to thwart his policy agenda, President Obama—who as a candidate expressed his aversion to unilateral executive action—pledged to circumvent legislative blockages with the use of executive orders (Dodds 2012, 343). In the summer of 2014, then-Republican House Speaker John Boehner announced plans to sue the president over this practice, contending that Obama usurped legislative authority when he used executive orders to modify the implementation of the Affordable Care Act (see Berman 2014).

The controversy surrounding the use of executive orders reflects an ongoing debate about the balance of power between the president and Congress—one that appears to be poised to continue into the Trump Administration. It also demonstrates the real power that presidents have. Most scholars agree that presidential power has expanded, not contracted, in the past century; and executive orders are one of the arrows in the president's quiver that has facilitated the expansion of presidential power.

The Constitution does not explicitly endow the presidency with the power of unilateral action. Nonetheless, Graham Dodds writes that "unilateralism is a central feature of the contemporary presidency ... Every single president has issued unilateral directives" (Dodds 2012, 343). Terry Moe and

William Howell argue that unilateral actions have emerged in response to the "ongoing practice of politics," and that their use is a natural result of the trial and error that results from putting the abstract concepts of the Constitution into practice (Moe and Howell 1999, 853). Indeed, after centuries of practice and tacit judicial consent, executive unilateral action is likely here to stay (Dodds 2012, 344).

Presidents have exercised their unilateral privileges to expand their power and to be pragmatic. Howell and Lewis note, for instance, that Executive Branch agencies created by executive orders tend to be subject to greater oversight by the president compared to agencies created by congressional statute. They view the trend of creating agencies by executive order as evidence of presidents' preferences to try to centralize power in the Executive Branch (Howell and Lewis 2002). In addition, presidents have been known to issue executive orders as a means of circumventing legislative impasses and of addressing the concerns of key constituencies. For instance, Howell and Lewis note that Franklin Roosevelt's executive order to create the Fair Employment Practices Committee (a precursor to the Equal Employment Opportunity Commission) reflected the stark legislative reality that Congress, which at the time was dominated by Southern segregationists, would not pass civil rights legislation. It was also the result of intense lobbying on the part of civil rights organizations (Howell and Lewis 2002, 1101).

Some critics contend that presidential use of executive orders is tantamount to the rise of an "imperial presidency" (see Schlesinger 2004). In reality, though, separation of powers does provide presidents with incentives to use discretion when exercising unilateral power. Congress still retains the power of the purse and can use the budgetary process to de-fund initiatives that presidents create. Also, courts can curtail presidents' use of executive orders if they overstep their bounds. Moe and Howell contend, though, that despite these checks, once executive orders go into effect, inertial factors usually privilege the president, thus reinforcing the resiliency of presidential unilateral action as a permanent feature of presidential power (Howell and Lewis 2002; Moe and Howell 1999).

Despite the limitations of checks and balances on curbing presidential power, presidents do have to consider the fact that Executive Branch politics may hamper their ability to successfully wield the power of unilateral action. Dickinson warns that unilateral action does not mean that presidents no longer have to bargain to get their desired policies. Instead of bargaining with members of Congress, they may have to negotiate with Executive Branch departments and agencies to get the policies emanating from their orders properly implemented. Even then, the staffers and bureaucrats in charge of implementing the executive order still may not follow instructions (Dickinson 2009, 757–758).

Moe and Howell imply that presidents will likely engender less controversy when they use unilateral powers to make decisions about foreign policy because the Constitution does give the president agency to act diplomatically on behalf of the country. They contend that presidents can be "bold" when they deviate from congressional preferences on foreign policy issues, but argue that presidents should be judicious in their use of unilateral power on domestic issues and opt for "incrementalism and moderation" (Moe and Howell 1999, 863–864).

In reality, though, presidents have availed themselves of what Moe and Howell called the "first mover" advantage (i.e., that presidents are uniquely situated to act first on an issue, putting the Legislative and Judicial Branches in a reactive mode in which presidents usually win because the other branches cannot or will not muster a successful counterattack). This is especially true on issues of race (Moe and Howell 1999, 855).

Race and executive orders

Many of the most prominent unilateral actions in American history have targeted racial or ethnic minorities—in good and bad ways. Moe and Howell concede that "presidents have always acted unilaterally to make law. The Louisiana Purchase, the freeing of the slaves, the internment of the Japanese, the desegregation of the military, the initiation of affirmative action, the imposition of regulatory review—these are but a few of the most notable examples" (Moe and Howell 1999, 851). Despite the fact that these actions may be subject to threats of lost congressional funding or litigation, many of these types of actions have survived the administrations which created them. In looking at the evolution of Executive Branch policy regarding employment discrimination, Howell and Lewis note that while the first anti-discrimination agency, Roosevelt's Fair Employment Practices Committee (FEPC), was funded by the president's discretionary funds (to elide the potential for congressional de-funding) and had little enforcement capability, subsequent presidents gave more power to successor agencies to combat employment discrimination (Howell and Lewis 2002, 1101–1102).

The overall logic of expanded executive power may tacitly raise the expectation that presidents should act, especially in the interest of key constituencies. That presidents have used executive orders in the past to broaden their powers suggests that while presidents are not omnipotent and have constitutional constraints on their authority, they cannot hide behind the doctrine of separation of powers when people question them about their lack of advocacy on key issues of concern. If presidents and Executive Branch departments and agencies can elide legislatures to prosecute wars and engage in surveillance activities against American citizens, then critics will argue that surely they have the capacity to institute policies that will benefit key constituency groups.

Obama, race, and unilateral action

As the first African American president, many eagerly looked to see if President Obama would take unprecedented action to help the African American community. Some saw his election as a unique opportunity to push the issue of equality and progress. However, as Chapter 1 discussed, Obama's decision to use a deracialized campaign strategy may have made him reluctant to act unilaterally on behalf of blacks. Early analyses of President Obama's executive orders evince the absence of excessive unilateral action on behalf of racial minorities. Dodds' description of Obama's first executive orders includes discussions of the president's efforts to signal support of the labor movement and LGBT causes; to endorse stem cell research; to reverse the anti-abortion directives of his predecessor; to allow for more government transparency; and to signal that his administration sought to take a different approach to prosecuting the War on Terror (Dodds 2012, 346–347). Milkis *et al.* characterize some of these directives, particularly the ones regarding labor unions and environmental policies, as overtures to Obama's base, but Dodds points out that some of these reversals are part of a time-honored tradition of partisan reversing. When the presidency switches partisan hands, it is customary for new presidents to issue executive orders regarding labor unions and the use of foreign aid for abortion (Dodds 2012, 346–347; Milkis *et al.* 2012, 66).

Still, there is little preliminary evidence that President Obama disproportionately used his unilateral powers to target communities of color. In an earlier analysis of President Obama's executive orders, proclamations, radio addresses, and signing statements, I found no statistical difference in the number of race-based unilateral actions that Presidents Clinton, G.W. Bush, and Obama each issued in their first year in office (Gillespie 2010b).

In this section, I hope to extend my 2010 analysis to include executive orders from the entirety of Presidents Clinton, Bush, and Obama's terms. The longer time period will provide a more comprehensive view of how all three presidents acted unilaterally. Despite the longer timeframe and bigger sample size, though, I predict that I will find the same pattern. All three presidents will issue race-based directives at approximately the same rate.

To test this hypothesis, I conducted a content analysis of executive orders issued by the three former presidents. I include all of the executive orders for Presidents Clinton, Bush, and Obama. Using a database of executive orders compiled by the University of California, Santa Barbara (Peters and Woolley 1999–2017), I coded executive orders for their content and targeted constituency. Did the presidential directive address (either directly or indirectly)[1] issues of concern to African Americans? Did it create new bureaucratic structures to help or hurt blacks? Was the directive a substantive order, which empowered an Executive Branch agency to enact changes affecting blacks or create a new bureaucracy with enforcement capabilities? Or was the executive order a symbolic gesture? An example of a symbolic executive order is the type of order that creates an advisory board that makes suggestions but lacks the ability to implement any of its recommendations or that has no oversight capacity in general.

I present descriptive results in Table 3.1. In absolute numbers, President Obama issued fewer executive orders than his predecessors. In general, most of Presidents Clinton, Bush, and Obama's executive orders neither directly nor indirectly addressed issues of concern to racial and ethnic minorities. However, there were some notable observations.

In the aggregate, President Obama issued a bigger proportion executive orders addressing issues of concern to African Americans than Bill Clinton and George W. Bush. While 15–19 percent of Clinton and Bush's executive orders directly or indirectly addressed black concerns, 22 percent of President Obama's orders addressed black issues in some shape or form. When I disaggregate those executive orders by whether they were racialized or used coded racial language, I find that Obama issued greater proportions of both types of orders compared to his predecessors. Because of the small number of racialized and coded orders, though, these differences are not statistically significant.

I also code black-themed executive orders for whether or not the orders were substantive or symbolic. An example of a symbolic order[2] would include

---

1 Executive orders that directly addressed African American issues (counted here as "racialized orders") included orders which created boards, committees, or offices that focused on the concerns of blacks. (They often include "black" or "African American" in their title.) Alternately, the issue focus of the order could directly relate to racial discrimination or reference familiar racialized events, like Hurricane Katrina or Ferguson or were foreign policy directives focused on Sub-Saharan African or black Caribbean nations. Racially coded orders either tangentially addressed issues of concern to African Americans or used language that could be interpreted as implicitly referencing race—positively or stereotypically. For instance, some conversations about drugs imply race. Similarly, the discussion of Motor Voter implies race without being explicit.

2 One key distinction between symbolic and substantive advisory committees would be their capacity to make change. Because task forces and working groups were comprised of high-ranking bureaucrats with implementation authority, I coded these as substantive, in contrast to symbolic committees of citizens who could only make recommendations.

Table 3.1 Executive orders addressing racial issues, by president, Clinton to Obama Administrations

	Bill Clinton	George W. Bush	Barack Obama
Orders addressing African American concerns*	55 (15.1%)	54 (18.6%)	61 (22.1%)
Explicitly racialized orders (% of total)	36 (9.9%)	32 (11.0%)	37 (13.4%)
Racially coded orders (% of total)	19 (5.2%)	22 (7.6%)	24 (8.7%)
Substantive orders (% of all black themed orders)	41 (74.5%)	44 (81.5%)	47 (77.0%)
Symbolic orders (% of all black themed orders)	14 (25.5%)	10 (18.5%)	14 (23.0%)
Orders about Africa/black Caribbean (% of total)	24 (6.6%)	28 (9.6%)	21 (7.6%)
Orders addressing concerns of other racial and ethnic minorities** (% of total)	68 (18.7%)	72 (24.8%)	80 (29.0%)
Substantive orders (% of all minority themed orders)	52 (76.5%)	59 (81.9%)	65 (81.3%
Symbolic orders (% of all minority themed orders)	16 (23.5%)	13 (18.1%)	15 (18.8%)
Total executive orders	364	291	276

Source: Author's compilation. Intercoder sample check agreement rate=88.2 percent.
**p<0.05; *p<0.1, chi-squared, two-tailed test.

orders to create advisory committees charged with making recommendations to the president on an issue of concern to blacks. An executive order charging an agency or department with implementing the recommendations of an advisory board, however, would count as a substantive executive order. I find that President Obama issued symbolic and substantive orders at a roughly similar rate compared to his predecessors. About three-fourths to four-fifths of their orders were substantive, and a fifth to a quarter of their orders were symbolic. There was also no statistical difference in the proportion of executive orders each president issued which focused on Africa or the Caribbean.

As a point of comparison, I also looked at orders that might be of interest to other racial or ethnic minorities in the United States. There is some overlap with black-themed orders. For instance, if a president issued an order targeting minorities broadly, I coded the order as being of interest to blacks and other minorities. This category also includes foreign policy orders that, because of migration patterns, may be of interest to large[3] immigrant subgroups in the United States. I find that, in the aggregate, President Obama also issued significantly more executive orders of interest to other racial and ethnic groups than

---

3 I concede that the definition of "large immigrant subgroup" is subjective. As a result, I may include or omit executive orders that other coders would code differently. I encourage future work to use different coding standards as they see fit to allow for comparison and robustness checks.

his predecessors, particularly Bill Clinton. When I disaggregate the orders according to whether they were substantive or symbolic, the differences in the ratios of substantive to symbolic orders become negligible. Obama and Bush issued roughly equal proportions of substantive and symbolic orders, while Clinton issued a slightly greater proportion of symbolic orders.

Case studies of four Cabinet departments

In this section, I dig a little deeper to see if and how selected Cabinet-level departments addressed racial issues. Here, I look at the announced achievements of four Cabinet departments to determine the extent to which these departments actively addressed issues of concern to blacks and other identity groups. Did these Cabinet departments quietly address racial issues? Were the Obama Cabinet departments more or less activist on racial issues compared to departments in previous administrations?

To answer these questions, I turn to a content analysis of press releases from units of four Cabinet departments: Labor, Education, Health and Human Services, and Justice. (I consider issues related to housing policy in another volume (Gillespie n.d.).) I look at these departments because these offices have jurisdiction over issues of concern to blacks. By looking at these departments, I can answer questions like: did the Department of Education work to create policies to help reduce the achievement gap between black and Latino/a and Asian and white students? Did the Obama Labor Department do comparatively more to address employment discrimination based upon race than previous administrations? How was race implicated in the framing and rollout of Obamacare? Did the Civil Rights Division in the Obama-era Justice Department disproportionately focus on cases involving black victims; and if so, did they do so at the expense of responding to victims from other backgrounds?

In part because of differing levels of data availability, each of these case studies examines President Obama's record on racial issues in a different relief. For instance, because I had access to Department of Labor records going back to the Clinton Administration, I can compare labor policies across the three presidential administrations. At the time I started this project, I did not have access to press releases from the Clinton and Bush Administrations for other departments. In those instances, I will report descriptive findings for the Obama Administration only.

Department of Labor: a comparison across three administrations

I start with an examination of press releases from the Department of Labor's Employment Standards Administration (ESA) office. For years, the ESA was the office that addressed issues of employment discrimination, monitored wages, enforced child labor laws, and sought punitive action against employers who violated workers' rights. In November 2009, the organizational structure of the Department of Labor changed. ESA was formally dissolved, but its separate constituent offices remained: the Wage and Hour Division (WHD); the Office of Worker Compensation Programs (OWCP); the Office of Labor Management Standards (OLMS); and the Office of Federal Contract Compliance Programs (OFCCP). Respectively, these offices have the jurisdiction to ensure that employers meet their minimum wage obligations; that workers who are eligible to receive monetary damages for workplace related injuries receive them; that labor unions operate within legal parameters; and that federal contractors follow anti-discrimination employment guidelines. These offices have the authorization to use fines and criminal prosecution to ensure compliance.

I obtained access to copies of archived press releases from the ESA and its successor offices from January 1995 to January 20, 2017 through the Department of Labor website (US Department of Labor n.d.).[4] I found 1,109 press releases in total. There are 72 press releases from the Clinton Administration, 181 press releases from the Bush Administration, and 856 releases from the Obama Administration. The sheer number of Obama-era press releases suggests three possible explanations. There is always the possibility of missing data. If that is true, future work will update the findings presented here. That the Obama Administration issued more press releases in this area could also suggest more activity during the Obama years than in previous administrations. A third possibility is that the Labor Department grew more comfortable with posting online press releases over time and started using this medium more frequently to communicate.

I first coded the press releases to determine both the type of issue that the press release announced and whether the action was targeted toward a special interest group, like minorities, young people, or veterans. I then compared the frequency of actions across administrations. I look first at the groups benefiting from DOL action at the top of Table 3.2. Here, I present the data by administration. There were significant variations in how each administration discussed minority groups and matters of concern to them. For instance, the Bush Administration was less likely to mention issues of interest to blacks in its press releases. The Obama Administration was more

---

4 Reconstructing this archive requires use of the filter function on the DOL website. For verification purposes, a list of the press releases used in this chapter are available upon request. Please note that there are only three press releases from the OLMS in this dataset after 2009. Future editions of this book will include additional press releases should they be found.

Table 3.2 Groups/issues mentioned/targeted in DOL press releases, 1995–2017

	Clinton (1995–2001)	Bush	Obama
Groups targeted in press releases			
Blacks**	3 (4.2%)	3 (1.7%)	54 (6.3%)
Latinos/as**	2 (2.8%)	4 (2.2%)	114 (13.3%)
Asian Americans**	8 (11.1%)	4 (2.2%)	45 (5.3%)
Women*	19 (26.4%)	17 (9.4%)	67 (7.8%)
Military/veterans**	4 (5.6%)	11 (6.1%)	11 (1.3%)
Young people**	19 (26.4%)	12 (6.6%)	38 (4.4%)
Immigrants	8 (11.1%)	9 (5.0%)	77 (9.0%)
Industries targeted in press releases			
Construction**	4 (5.6%)	16 (8.8%)	118 (13.8%)
Restaurant/catering**	2 (2.8%)	3 (1.7%)	116 (13.6%)
Agriculture (including forestry) and meatpacking*	13 (18.1%)	15 (8.3%)	99 (11.6%)
Garment**	8 (11.1%)	2 (1.1%)	12 (1.4%)
Energy**	1 (1.4%)	18 (9.9%)	93 (10.9%)
Health services/elder care	1 (1.4%)	7 (3.9%)	39 (4.6%)
Hotel**	0 (0%)	1 (0.6%)	27 (3.2%)
Issues discussed in press releases			
Family Medical Leave Act	2 (2.8%)	6 (3.3%)	24 (2.8%)
Wage violations**	31 (43.1%)	91 (50.3%)	276 (32.2%)
Employment discrimination**	17 (23.6%)	17 (9.4%)	85 (9.9%)
Working conditions**	24 (33.3%)	33 (18.2%)	101 (11.8%)
Total press releases	72	181	856

Source: Author's compilation. Intercoder sample agreement rate=92.5%.
**p<0.05; *p<0.1, chi-squared, two-tailed test.

likely to discuss Latino/a issues or to take action that could be interpreted as targeting Latinos/as; administration officials sometimes issued Spanish translations of press releases or required that employers who violated labor laws inform workers of their rights in Spanish. However, relative to the Clinton and Bush Administrations, the Obama-era Labor Department issued proportionally fewer press releases addressing issues about or involving veterans or military personnel. Similarly, the Bush Administration was less likely to signal that they were addressing Asian American issues or workers in their press releases, while proportionally, the Clinton Administration was most likely to do so.

The Clinton Administration reported more activity (proportionally) on labor issues about or involving women and young people. More than a quarter of the press releases examined here from the Clinton era related to women and children. The Clinton Administration settled a number of wage discrimination cases in which it was alleged that women were paid less than men for comparable work. The issue of sweatshop and child labor also figured prominently in public discourse in the 1990s (see Clark 1996). For this reason, it is not surprising that the data suggests that these issues—child labor in particular—appear to have been a priority of the Clinton Administration.

To be sure, the number of actions targeted toward racial and ethnic groups, in general, is small. In the case of the Labor Department, a good explanation for this is that many of the actions that are highlighted in the press releases involve settlements with companies that violated labor laws. Unless the identity of the victim was relevant to the violation, the press releases tended to be silent about the race, gender, or national origin of the alleged victims in these cases. Thus, it is appropriate to look beyond whether racial or gender groups are mentioned in press releases. If an administration appears to be spending a lot of time talking about its efforts to enforce labor laws in particular industries, particularly industries that are known to employ significant numbers of minorities, then that is also a clue about that administration's responsiveness to issues of concern in minority communities.

With this is mind, I coded the press releases based on the industries that were mentioned in the press releases. Often, this would come up in discussions of fines or investigations where the alleged perpetrator's business would be described. The most common industries mentioned included construction, the restaurant/catering industry, agriculture and food packaging (including a small number of forestry/landscaping businesses), and energy. With the exception of energy, all of these industries currently employ (based on the most recent Census data) disproportionately greater numbers of minorities. There are disproportionately more Latinos/as employed in construction, agriculture, restaurants, traveler accommodations (i.e., hotels), and the garment industry. Asian Americans are represented more in the garment industry. And African Americans are more likely to be overrepresented in the health services industry,[5] particularly as home health aides[6] (Bureau of Labor Statistics 2017). Because of the prominence of the sweatshop issue in the 1990s (see Clark 1996), I report numbers for the garment industry as well.

The middle rows of Table 3.2 report the breakdown for the number of press releases reporting action against businesses in particular industries. In each

---

5 In this coding, health services includes hospital and clinic workers. It does include a few cases about doctors and nurses. Most of the cases were about in-home caretakers, and employees of rehabilitation centers, nursing homes, and assisted living facilities, though.

6 Some may ask why retail was not included here, as blacks are overrepresented in retail occupations (Bureau of Labor Statistics 2017). I identified the industry categories to code based on a reading of the press releases. After looking through some of the press releases, I selected industries that appeared often in the readings. Relatively speaking, there were few actions taken against the retail industry during the timeframe studied. For this reason I omitted it. I welcome future coders to corroborate this finding by intentionally coding the dataset for evidence of government oversight of the retail industry.

of these industries, one administration was significantly more or less likely to target action towards it compared to other administrations. For instance, the Clinton Administration issued proportionally more press releases about actions it took against agriculture and the garment industry, while it was the least likely to report activity involving the energy sector (the Bush and Obama Labor Departments reported similar proportions of activity against the energy sector). Based on the press releases, the Obama Administration reported more oversight of the restaurant and catering industry and of the hotel industry. Nearly 5 percent of the press releases coded from the Obama Administration addressed issues related to workers in the health or elder care industry. This percentage is comparable to the proportion of press releases the Bush Administration issued about this industry.

Finally, it is important to consider the types of issues that are discussed in the dataset. Did the Labor Department tout its activity in combating employment discrimination? Was it enforcing labor laws that could be easily construed as benefiting women or minorities? At the bottom of Table 3.2, I examine the frequency of each administration's discussion of key issues: the Family Medical Leave Act, which was signed into law by President Bill Clinton; wage violations, a key jurisdiction of the Wage and Hourly Division; employment discrimination; and discussions of work conditions. Included under the rubric of work conditions are violations of child labor laws and punitive practices such as charging employees for their uniforms or making workers live in substandard company properties.

There was no statistical difference across administrations in the frequency of their discussions of the Family Medical Leave Act. I would have expected the Clinton Administration to discuss this more. However, given the fact that the act was signed into law nearly two years before the start of this dataset, it is possible that the increased discussion took place earlier. However, for the time period examined, the Clinton Administration appears to have been very active (relative to its successors) in enforcing employment discrimination law and work conditions. Approximately one-quarter to one-third of the press releases examined discussed these issues. In contrast, the Bush Administration issued more press releases (half of its total) about combating wage violations.

To be sure, the Labor Department under President Obama made more announcements about its activities than previous administrations. Proportionally speaking, though, the administration's activity was spread around a number of different issues, including issues not recorded here. Where more than 40 percent of the press releases in the Clinton and Bush Administrations addressed wage issues, less than a third of the Obama-era press releases dealt with that issue (though it was addressed nearly 300 times).

Table 3.3 Employment discrimination cases by race of victim, Clinton through Obama Administrations

Press releases addressing employment discrimination cases against:	Clinton	Bush	Obama
Blacks**	1 (5.9%)	2 (11.8%)	45 (52.9%)
Latinos/as**	0 (0%)	0 (0%)	23 (27.1%)
Asian Americans**	0 (0%)	1 (5.9%)	19 (22.4%)
Total press releases	17	17	85

Source: Author's compilation.
**p<0.05; *p<0.1, chi-squared, two-tailed test.

So while the Obama Administration's Labor Department sometimes addressed issues of concern to minorities and problems in industries that disproportionately employ minorities at a lower rate than his predecessors, his administration cannot be accused of inactivity on these issues. If one can judge activity by the number of press releases, the Obama Administration was extremely active on racial issues.

It is helpful at this point to compare the Obama Administration to its predecessors on if and how it addressed an explicitly racial issue across different racial/ethnic groups. In Table 3.3, I break down employment discrimination press releases by three potential victim groups: blacks, Latinos/as, and Asian Americans. As the table shows, the Obama Labor Department was significantly more active in advertising its work combating racial discrimination against members of all three racial/ethnic groups. While the Clinton and Bush Administration documents offered very few examples of employment discrimination across racial lines, more than half of Obama's press releases on employment discrimination identified a black victim; more than a quarter identified a Latino/a victim; and more than a fifth identified an Asian American victim.

To be sure, Labor Department press releases were inconsistent in how they discussed race. In many cases, particularly in the wage cases, race or ethnicity is not mentioned at all and can only be inferred when the release mentions a civil rights group or notes that it requires that remedies be provided in different languages. However, employment discrimination press releases usually did indicate the identity on which a person was disadvantaged. There is a case to be made that the Obama Administration's decision to be more explicit in its discussions of race in this context is evidence of intentionality and racial activism.

There was one incidental finding that buttresses the argument regarding intentionality. As I coded Obama-era press releases, I noted that the Labor Department often framed their advocacy of workers, particularly immigrant workers and workers in low-paying or low-skilled occupations, in terms of advocating for the "vulnerable" (see, for example, US Department of Labor 2015). Invoking the term "vulnerable" could be a sign of paternalism; however, it also suggests a commitment to advocating for the disadvantaged that is worth noting.

Department of Education: which groups got attention?

Next, I turn to an examination of Obama Administration initiatives in education. Here, my dataset is a content analysis of all of the press releases from the Department of Education from January 30, 2009 to January 20, 2017. I accessed these press releases using the Department of Education's website (US Department of Education n.d.b).[7] Because I only have access to press releases from one administration, I will not conduct a comparative analysis here. Still, it is helpful to identify (where possible) the types of issues and populations for which the Obama-era Education Department advocated. In total, there were 1,697 valid press releases during this time period.

As with the coding for the Labor Department, I am most interested in whether press releases from the Education Department openly discussed issues of concern to minority groups. Did they talk about narrowing the achievement gap? Did they target programs specifically to promote academic achievement among minorities? For comparative purposes, I code the press releases not just for overtures to blacks, but also to other racial and ethnic groups,[8] women and girls, veterans and active military, LGBT and low-income students.

Before delving into the descriptive data, it is important to note that Education Department press releases often discussed racial issues in transcendent terms. That is, they often did not reference particular groups, but did talk about issues in broad strokes, referring to "underrepresented" or "underserved" groups. Based on common parlance about underrepresented minority groups (URMs), I interpreted these adjectives to mean that the department was targeting racial and ethnic minorities (particularly black, Latino/a, and Native American populations) and/or low-income groups. Using the context of the wider press release, I made judgment calls about the meaning of these racial and class euphemisms, recognizing that these were subjective calls.

---

7 The Trump Administration has since archived the Obama-era press releases. If a researcher has difficulty accessing press releases but wants to see the dataset used for this analysis, it can be furnished upon request.

8 An outside coder and I coded the dataset, and a third student did the intercoder sample check. There are instances when the primary outside coder and I disagreed about coding. In general, she was more conservative than I in detecting the racial subtext of press releases. In reviewing the dataset, I made the editorial decision to overrule a few of her coding decisions. A third coder then coded a sample of the dataset to check both of our work.

Table 3.4 Frequencies of issues discussed in Department of Education press releases, 2009–2017

Press releases discuss:	Frequency (%)
Issues of concern to blacks	209 (12.3%)
Issues of concern to Latinos	279 (16.4%)
Issues of concern to Asian Americans	90 (5.3%)
Issues of concern to Native Americans	256 (15.1%)
Issues of concern to immigrants/language minorities±	51 (3.0%)
Issues of concern to the LGBT community	18 (1.1%)
Issues of concern to girls/women	70 (4.1%)
Issues of concern to veterans/military	33 (1.9%)
Issues of concern to the disabled	337 (19.9%)
Issues of concern to low-income Americans	560 (33.0%)
Charter Schools	118 (7.0%)
My Brother's Keeper	31 (5.7%)^
Personal responsibility frames	98 (5.8%)
Total press releases	1697

Source: Author's compilation. Intercoder sample agreement rate=95.4%.

± Unless specified, issues of concern to immigrants were not necessarily coded as being of concern to Latinos/as or Asian Americans. This category was coded partially by the content of press releases and (for early releases) based on the content of titles of press releases (i.e., whether the title specifically referenced immigrant students, or English language learners, etc.). There may be omissions in this category.

^ The denominator for this percentage was calculated from the 540 press releases that were issued from February 2014, when My Brother's Keeper was announced, to the end of the Obama Administration.

The descriptive findings are listed in Table 3.4. As the table shows, the Department of Education under President Obama paid considerable attention to issues of race. More than one in seven press releases addressed a policy, program, or goal that could be construed as targeting blacks, Latinos/as, or Native Americans. To be sure, many of these press releases discussed programs that were broadly defined as helping "underrepresented groups." It should be noted, though, that the Education Department actually did discuss programs that explicitly focused on Native American students. In addition, the Department of Education made discrete announcements that highlighted efforts to support institutions such as Historically Black Colleges and Universities (HBCUs), Hispanic serving institutions (HSIs), Asian American and Native American Pacific Islander serving institutions (AANAPISIs).

There are some differences in attention toward racial and ethnic minority groups. For instance, while Asian American issues are not neglected in these press releases, they do get less attention. This is largely due to the fact that Asian Americans are not always perceived to be underrepresented in some educational sectors and that they do not appear to be on the disadvantaged side of the achievement gap. The data also shows that the Education Department paid some attention to immigrant students and students who were learning English as a second language.

There is also no evidence that the Department of Education ignored racial issues in exchange for addressing issues of concern to other identity groups. In fact, the opposite might be true. Press releases highlighting the Department of Education's efforts to address issues related to women and girls (e.g., encouraging girls to pursue STEM fields or Title IX cases which did not specifically name male victims) only made up 4 percent of the database. Similarly, press releases addressing issues of concern to the LGBT community comprised 1 percent of the database. Veterans' concerns were only addressed in about 2 percent of the press releases.

This is not to say that the Department of Education focused on issues of concern to racial groups to the exclusion of other groups. There was considerable discussion about issues of concern to disabled students (often related to enforcement of the Individuals with Disabilities Education Act (IDEA)). Nearly 20 percent of the press releases discussed advocacy for disabled students or addressed a disability issue. And one-third of the press releases discussed low-income students. Press releases often talked about initiatives intended to help under-resourced schools in poor neighborhoods. There was also considerable discussion about college financial aid, which I coded as being of interest to low-income students in particular. One can also see in the press releases the Department of Education's efforts to regulate the for-profit college industry, even going as far as shutting down schools which it deemed were diploma mills that were short-changing students. There were two justifications for this. Often, these schools saddled students with considerable debt and few job prospects upon graduation. The Department of Education also charged these schools with taking advantage of veterans so that they could unfairly garner more federal student financial aid (see, for example, US Department of Education 2016a). In this dataset, these press releases were coded as being relevant to low-income students and, where mentioned, veterans. Race was never mentioned or implied, so I do not code for it here. However, there is a compelling case to be made that in targeting low-income students, it is difficult to not consider race as a subtext of the discussion of for-profit colleges (see McMillan Cottom 2017).

In the coding, I also took care to note a couple of key issues that would be of interest to blacks. Charter schools have long been a hotly contested topic in black communities. While many black Americans have expressed support for educational reform efforts like vouchers and charter schools, older black elected officials have resisted these efforts (see Bositis 2002). Indeed, support for vouchers has been used as a litmus test in the past for deracialized black politicians. In previous work, I have found that supporters of school reform sometimes face a backlash and have their commitment to black communities questioned (Gillespie 2012; Gillespie and Demessie 2013).

As Table 3.4 shows, charter schools were mentioned in 7 percent of the press releases from the Department of Education during the Obama Administration. Interestingly, the plurality of these press releases (54, or 46 percent) were issued in the first year of Obama's term. After that, only 7–11 press releases a year mentioned charter schools.

President Obama also delegated responsibility for the My Brother's Keeper program to the Department of Education. After Obama launched the program in February 2014, 31 press releases, or nearly 6 percent of press releases issued from February 2014 to January 2017, mentioned My Brother's Keeper. I should note here that while we typically think of My Brother's Keeper as a program for African American boys, the Education Department documents make clear that this program was intended to help boys from other underrepresented groups as well, particularly Latino and Native American boys. As such, these racial categories were also coded accordingly whenever I noted that My Brother's Keeper was mentioned.

Finally, I examined the Education Department press releases to see if the department used its platform to frame issues through the lens of personal responsibility. For instance, if a press release encouraged parents to read to their young children every night, I coded it as having a personal responsibility frame—the encouragement sounds like a public service announcement. In this dataset, there are instances where the Department of Education sought to educate the public, particularly parents, about their responsibilities to their children. Exemplary press releases would include announcements about anti-truancy efforts and discussion of financial literacy activities, whether standalone or in the context of helping families navigate the college loan process. In all, only about 6 percent of press releases included a personal responsibility frame.

The examination of the press releases from the Department of Education shows that the department was attentive to racial issues. While race was often discussed broadly, in terms of "underrepresented" groups, racial issues were not ignored in the Obama Administration. What is most interesting about the Department of Education is the evolution of the discussion of charter schools. Whereas the department was eager to talk about charter schools in the first year of the Obama Administration, there was scant discussion of charter schools in later years. This could reflect a change in attitude or a change in perception of public support for charter schools. Or it could reflect that charter schools were fully embedded as a part of administration policy early and did not need to be discussed in later years of the administration.[9] Future studies should explore this question, taking advantage of key archival data when it becomes available.

Department of Health and Human Services: a comparison of Clinton and Obama-era health care discourse

Regardless of what happens to the health care reform during the Trump Administration, most scholars will likely point to the Affordable Care Act (ACA) as one of Barack Obama's key achievements. In passing a mandate that every American acquire health insurance, Obama achieved a feat that presidents going back to the Truman Administration had failed to produce (Dawes 2016, 58).

On the surface, health care may seem like a nonracial issue. In describing the likely beneficiaries of the ACA, scholars Lawrence Jacobs and Theda Skocpol describe three archetypal beneficiaries, whom they argue are "the most economically vulnerable people in our country" but could be of any race: a single mother with a child who has a pre-existing medical condition; a single woman who stopped working to be the caretaker for an aging parent; and an unemployed, married couple who struggle with mental illness and substance abuse (Jacobs and Skocpol 2010, 131).

To be sure, economic vulnerability and race are highly correlated. And we know from Figure 2.11 that racial and ethnic minorities are more likely than whites to lack insurance. Based on this, some may ask whether President Obama conceived of health care reform as a transcendent issue and intended the passage of the ACA to be a wink and a nod to blacks. Though he would frame health care in universal terms, the fact that blacks (and Latinos/as) were more likely to be uninsured meant that this policy would disproportionately have positive impacts for communities of color. Was that intentional? Was Obama using deracialization to provide a public good to all that would benefit blacks most? After all, health care is one of the issues that Charles Hamilton, an early proponent of deracialization, argued could be framed in a transcendent way to the benefit of blacks (Hamilton 1977).

We know from Figure 2.11 that although fewer minorities lacked insurance after Obamacare went into effect, racial insurance gaps persisted in the United States. What is more important to this discussion, then, is whether or not there is evidence that the Obama Administration thought about health care reform in racialized terms and if his efforts look different than previous attempts at providing health insurance for all Americans.

9   I credit Cheryl Harris for challenging me to consider this possibility.

To answer this question, I look at press releases from the Department of Health and Human Services for the year leading up to and the year after the passage of Obamacare (2009–2010). I accessed these press releases using the Department of Health and Human Services webpage (US Department of Health and Human Services n.d.). For comparative purposes, I look at the comparable period in the Clinton Administration (1993–1994). Both presidents proposed comprehensive health care legislation in their first two years of office, and the initiative either failed or succeeded in that timeframe (Obama's bill was signed into law in March 2010; Clinton's bill failed in September 1994). I do understand that by choosing to look at the first two years of each administration (and because the Obama proposal passed six months earlier in the calendar year than the Clinton proposal failed), I incorporate more time for post-bill analysis in the Obama Administration. I justify this decision on the grounds that it is helpful here to include press releases that discuss how the Obama Administration framed the rollout of the Affordable Care Act.

I present the descriptive statistics for the Health and Human Services (HHS) data in Table 3.5. As with previous data, I compare the rates at which Clinton and Obama era officials in HHS discussed minorities or issues that could be construed as being of particular concern to them. In all, there were

Table 3.5 Issue and community foci of HHS press releases in the first two years of the Clinton and Obama Administrations

	Clinton (1993–1994)	Obama (2009–2010)
Targeted group		
Blacks*	42 (11.5%)	36 (8.0%)
Latinos/as	38 (10.4%)	36 (8.0%)
Asian Americans	16 (4.4%)	15 (3.3%)
Native Americans**	26 (7.1%)	55 (12.2%)
Women**	86 (23.6%)	58 (12.9%)
Disabled	35 (9.6%)	46 (10.2%)
Poor	72 (19.8%)	90 (20.0%)
Elderly**	82 (22.5%)	65 (14.4%)
Children**	134 (36.8%)	132 (29.3%)
Issue area		
Heathcare reform**	31 (8.5%)	137 (30.4%)
Preventative care**	67 (18.4%)	152 (33.7%)
Obesity**	2 (0.5%)	28 (6.2%)
HIV/AIDS**	39 (10.7%)	25 (5.5%)
Social Security/SSI**	22 (6.0%)	7 (1.6%)
Medicare/Medicaid	91 (25.0%)	108 (23.9%)
Welfare**	44 (12.1%)	14 (3.1%)
Total	364	451

Source: Author's compilation. Intercoder sample (1994, 2009–2010 only) agreement rate=93.4 percent.
**p<0.05; *p>0.1, Pearson's chi-square. Two-tailed test.

364 press releases in the first two years of the Clinton Administration and 451 press releases in the first two years of the Obama Administration. I coded the press releases according to whether or not they explicitly mentioned racial or ethnic groups or referenced information that could be reasonably construed as a signal to an ethnic community.

As Table 3.5 shows, racial and other identity groups were mentioned infrequently in HHS press releases. Blacks or black-interest issues appeared in about 12 percent of the Clinton-era press releases and 8 percent of Obama-era press releases. This difference is on the threshold of significance at the $p<0.1$ level. Clinton and Obama era press releases mentioned Asian and Latino/a American themes at roughly the same rate. The Obama Administration was significantly more likely to target Native Americans or discuss Native American issues in its press releases.

For the sake of comparison, I also coded the dataset to determine how often other groups were mentioned in press releases. In general, women, children, the poor, and the elderly were discussed more often in press releases than racial or ethnic minority groups. The disabled were mentioned at about the same rate as minorities; proportionally, one administration did not discuss issues related to disabilities more than the other. Both administrations were equally likely to discuss issues related to poverty. The Clinton Administration, however, was more likely to mention or discuss issues related to women, children, and the elderly.

While HHS press releases tended not to discuss identity groups, it is helpful to examine the extent to which they discussed issues of concern to these constituencies, as this is another way of signaling responsiveness that may not have been captured in the aforementioned codes. For example, while HHS press releases rarely discuss HIV/AIDS in the context of race or sexual orientation, HIV disproportionately affects black and LGBT communities. The Clinton Administration was nearly twice as likely to issue press releases about HIV/AIDS, perhaps reflecting the comparatively earlier stage of the crisis. Nearly 11 percent of the Clinton press releases discuss HIV, as do about 6 percent of the Obama press releases.

About one-quarter of all press releases address Medicare and Medicaid. (In the Obama Administration, the Children's Health Insurance Program also comes up in these discussions often.) While both administrations discussed Medicare and Medicaid with roughly the same frequency, the Clinton Administration talked about Social Security (including Supplemental Security Income) more. This may be due to the fact that, until 1995, the Social Security Administration was part of the Department of Health and Human Services (see Social Security Administration n.d.). In his first two years of office, President Clinton also introduced a plan to change welfare, a highly racialized issue (see

Quadagno 1994; Gilens 1999; Hancock 2004). Not surprisingly, Clinton's press releases were about four times as likely to mention or discuss welfare.

Table 3.5 also shows that obesity gained particular salience during the Obama Administration. Perhaps because of discussions of Michelle Obama's Let's Move campaign (and perhaps because of the increased salience of the issue generally), HHS press releases in the Obama Administration were 12 times more likely to mention obesity than press releases from the Clinton Administration. Of the 28 Obama-era press releases that discussed obesity, five also mentioned African Americans.

Prevention was an ongoing theme of HHS press releases. They provided information about how to get influenza vaccinations. They urged Americans to stop smoking. As Table 3.5 shows, prevention discussions were significantly more prevalent in the Obama Administration. Nearly 34 percent of Obama press releases discussed prevention, compared to 18 percent of Clinton press releases. Preventative care and healthcare reform were often mentioned together. More than one-quarter of all press releases mentioning healthcare reform in the Obama era also mentioned preventative care, compared to about 13 percent of Clinton-era press releases.

During their first two years in office, both Presidents Clinton and Obama introduced healthcare reform legislation. Obama's HHS talked about the legis-lation more, though. Healthcare reform—not general pronouncements about insurance or health management—is explicitly mentioned in 30 percent of the press releases from Obama's first two years in office, compared to only 9 per-cent of press releases in the same period in the Clinton Administration. Much of the disparity is due to the fact that Obama's Affordable Care Act passed, while Clinton's Health Security Act did not. Nearly three-quarters of the press releases mentioning healthcare reform came after President Obama signed the ACA into law. In contrast, HHS released only two press releases mentioning healthcare reform after Clinton's initiative failed. However, even when we compare the frequency of healthcare mentions across administrations in the pre-passage/failure stage, the Obama Administration was more likely to bring up healthcare reform. Nearly 16 percent of all of the press releases issued before the signing of the ACA mentioned reform, compared to about 10 per-cent of Clinton-era press releases from the comparable period.

To what extent did the Department of Health and Human Services frame healthcare reform as a racial issue? We know from remarks that President Obama made in an April 2009 press conference that he believed that healthcare reform would disproportionately benefit black and Latino/a com-munities (Obama 2009b). How much did HHS mention minority groups in the context of healthcare reform, and how does this compare to the Clinton Administration's framing of the issue?

In general, neither administration framed healthcare reform in the context of identity groups. Blacks and healthcare reform were mentioned simultaneously in 10 press releases across both administrations, as were Latinos/as and healthcare reform.

Only three press releases simultaneously mentioned Asian Americans and healthcare reform. Native Americans got more attention, but they were mentioned in 20 healthcare reform press releases. (Tribal governments were often listed as stakeholders in government documents.) Though race/ethnicity and healthcare reform were rarely mentioned together, when they are, it was more likely to happen in the Obama Administration and more likely to happen with Latinos/as and Native Americans. Similarly, poverty and healthcare reform, which were mentioned simultaneously in 41 press releases, were more likely to be discussed under Obama than under Clinton.

Department of Justice: change over time?

Next, I turn to an examination of the Civil Rights Division of the Department of Justice (DOJ-CRD). This unit of the Justice Department has the responsibility for enforcing the provisions of the landmark civil rights legislation of the 1960s: the Civil Rights Act, the Voting Rights Act, and the Fair Housing Act. In their press releases, the Civil Rights Division announces investigations, indictments, convictions, and settlements, among other things. Housing and employment discrimination, voting rights, and police misconduct fall under the division's purview. This dataset includes 1998 valid press releases from the Obama Administration, dating from late April 2009[10] to the end of President Obama's term in office. I accessed these press releases using the website of the US Department of Justice's Office of Public Affairs (n.d.). The website's search engine has a filtering feature which extracts the Civil Rights Division's press releases from other offices within the Justice Department.[11] I should note that it is more common in this dataset, compared to the others used in this chapter, to discuss the same case in multiple press releases. While this sometimes happened in other departments, the Civil Rights Division often used press releases to update the public on the status of a case. Thus, there could be 3–4 separate press releases about the opening of an investigation, an indictment, and a conviction that all relate to the same case. High-profile

---

10 As the book was going to press, I did discover press releases from the first three months of the Obama Administration. Future work will incorporate these releases into the dataset.

11 The press release archives often require the use of a filtering function. If a researcher cannot access the press releases but wants to see the dataset used for this analysis, it can be furnished upon request.

Table 3.6 Types of crimes mentioned in DOJ Civil Rights Division press releases, 2009–2017

Type of alleged crime/issue	Frequency (%)
Employment discrimination	339 (17.0%)
Voting rights	136 (6.8%)
Banking discrimination	59 (3.0%)
Housing discrimination	233 (11.7%)
Education discrimination	133 (6.7%)
Slavery/human trafficking (non-sexual)	47 (2.4%)
Sex trafficking/prostitution	84 (4.2%)
Other sex crimes	76 (3.8%)
Law enforcement misconduct	514 (25.7%)
Racial profiling	54 (2.7%)
Hate crimes	228 (11.4%)
Total press releases	1,998

Note: Because of overlap in coding (some press releases involve multiple types of crimes and victims), frequencies will not add to 100%.
Source: Author's compilation. Intercoder sample agreement rate=97.2%.

cases and cases with multiple defendants (with potentially different plea settlements) could garner additional press notifications. Each of these releases is counted individually in this analysis.

In Table 3.6, I present descriptive data about the frequency of certain types of crime discussions in press releases. Seventeen percent of the DOJ-CRD press releases addressed cases of employment discrimination. These cases included racial and gender discrimination, as well as discrimination against military reservists who were illegally fired as a result of their deployments.

Almost 7 percent of the press releases addressed voting rights concerns. There were a number of different voting rights issues addressed by the Civil Rights Division. The DOJ announced instances where they would be observing local and state elections. They announced cases where they were going to require jurisdictions to print ballots in different languages, in keeping with the language minority protection provisions of the Voting Rights Act. Before 2013, they also announced settlements with various voting jurisdictions in which the Department of Justice agreed (under the condition of judicial assent) to remove these jurisdictions from the preclearance requirements of the Voting Rights Act. Before the Supreme Court invalidated the preclearance provisions of the Voting Rights Act in 2013, localities that had been covered by these provisions could ask to be removed from the preclearance list if they met certain criteria, namely ten years with no voting rights complaints. The Justice Department supported many jurisdictions' efforts to remove themselves from preclearance. However, the Commonwealth of Virginia received considerable attention on this issue. In the 21 press releases that announce preclearance waivers in this dataset, 12 provide relief for Virginia counties and cities (covering 13 localities).

Nearly 12 percent of the press releases examined here discussed the Civil Rights Division's efforts to address housing discrimination. Many of these press releases discussed cases where prospective renters and homebuyers encountered discrimination because they had children. There were also a considerable number of cases where housing developers were penalized for not building accessible housing for the disabled. Still, the Justice Department did initiate investigations of housing discrimination based on race.

Nearly 60 press releases (or 3 percent) addressed banking discrimination, which includes instances of minorities receiving unfair interest rates for personal credit products. This number does include press releases which addressed discrimination in the mortgage industry.

About 7 percent of the press releases addressed cases of exploitation, either non-sexual human trafficking or sex trafficking, which disproportionately had female victims. More than 80 press releases discussed the DOJ's role in sex trafficking cases, and 47 press releases discussed cases involving other forms of human trafficking (i.e., forcing employees to work without pay and without the freedom to leave their workplace). An additional 76 press releases (or about 4 percent of the total) discussed cases involving some other form of sexual assault.

About 11 percent of press releases described the DOJ-CRD's efforts to prosecute hate crimes. I define hate crimes as any crime that was prosecuted by the Hate Crimes Unit within the Civil Rights Division. I also included other press releases which described crimes of intimidation, bias, or assault that appeared to be motivated by the victim's race, gender, religion, or sexual orientation. Crimes included acts like cross-burnings, church/synagogue/mosque burnings, kidnapping, assault, or murder. About 58 percent of the hate crime press releases identified blacks as at least one of the victims in the case. Latinos/as were named as victims in approximately 8 percent of the hate crimes press releases. Whites were named as victims in 7 percent of hate crimes press releases. An Asian American was noted as the victim in one hate crimes press release, and Native Americans were named as victims in three hate crimes press releases.

I created a special code to capture the phenomenon of attacking a group because it was multi-racial.[12] An exemplary situation would be an assailant burning a cross on the front lawn of an interracial couple. I contend that this coding decision is appropriate because these groups were attacked specifically because of their multiracial composition. In addition, it helps to elide the potential problem of a group being identified as multiracial without

---

12 People who were biracial with no other description could be included in this category. However, most of the time, this category was reserved for multi-racial groups.

identifying the specific racial composition of the group. I find that 40 press releases, or 17.5 percent of the total number of press releases discussing hate crimes, focused on crimes that targeted multi-racial individuals or groups.

The Justice Department also investigated hate crimes perpetrated against other identity groups. Religious people or groups (Christian, Muslim, and Jewish) were mentioned as victims in about 18 percent of the hate crimes press releases. LGBT identified individuals were victims in almost 10 percent of the hate crimes press releases. Women were mentioned as hate crime victims in three press releases.

Law enforcement misconduct (which includes police, correction officers, and probation and parole officers) constituted a plurality of the press releases (almost 26 percent) in this dataset. Even before the flashpoints of Ferguson, Cleveland, and Baltimore, the Justice Department was investigating and reprimanding police departments and officers across the country for bad behavior. The press releases paint a vivid and disturbing picture of police misconduct. Alleged crimes include sexual assault, identity theft, theft, shock treatment, improper use of solitary confinement, assault, murder, goading inmates into assaulting their peers, conspiracy to cover up crimes, and denying inmates access to mental and physical health care.

In Table 3.7, I look at all of the press releases (not just the hate crimes press releases) and tabulate the number of times the racial identity of a victim of a justice violation was mentioned. Please know that the race of the victim was not always mentioned. For instance, while the race of the victim is relevant to a discussion of hate crimes, housing discrimination, or a voting rights

Table 3.7 Victims mentioned in DOJ Civil Rights Division press releases, by disclosed identity group, 2009–2017

Relevant identity of victim	Frequency (%)
African American	428 (21.4%)
Latino/a	211 (10.6%)
Asian American	67 (3.4%)
Native American	41 (2.1%)
White	35 (1.8%)
Multiracial	45 (2.3%)
Religious	85 (4.3%)
LGBT	36 (1.8%)
Women	245 (12.3%)
Military/veteran	120 (6.0%)
Physically disabled	283 (14.2%)
Developmentally disabled	46 (2.3%)
Mentally ill	61 (3.1%)
Language minority	106 (5.3%)
Immigrant	209 (10.5%)
Total press releases	1,998

Source: Author's compilation. Intercoder sample agreement rate=97.2%.

violation, they might not be mentioned in cases of police misconduct unless there is a charge of racial profiling. Also, keep in mind that press releases may have discussed multiple victims or victims who had multiple relevant identities. As such, there is overlap in the tabulations.

When the race of the victim was mentioned in Obama-era press releases, they were more likely to be black. More than 21 percent of DOJ-CRD press releases mention an African American victim. Latinos/as were identified as victims in almost 11 percent of DOJ-CRD press releases. Asian Americans were identified as victims in about 3 percent of DOJ-CRD press releases. Whites, Native Americans, and multi-racial groups were mentioned in 2 percent of press releases each.

When I look at other relevant identity groups, I find that women, immigrants, and the physically disabled garnered considerable attention from the Civil Rights Division as well. Female victims were mentioned or implied in over 12 percent of the press releases examined. Sexual orientation or gender non-conformity was mentioned in almost 2 percent of the press releases. Almost two-thirds of the press releases identifying a victim as LGBT also discussed a hate crime. The DOJ-CRD reported activity on behalf of physically disabled victims in 14 percent of this dataset. Similarly, 2 percent of this dataset addressed issues related to developmental disabilities (e.g., Down Syndrome), and 3 percent of press releases addressed issues related to mental illness.

A victim's immigrant status came up in almost 11 percent of the press releases examined. The dataset includes cases of employment discrimination, racial profiling, and hate crimes directed toward people because of their national origin or immigration status. About 5 percent of the press releases highlighted language differences, and discussed the ways that people were subject to unlawful behavior because they did not speak English at all or very well. Finally, the Civil Rights Division issued 120 press releases where it discussed action it took on behalf of active duty military or veterans that it believed had been subjected to discrimination.

Given the prominence of issues related to policing toward the end of President Obama's tenure, it is important to consider the ways that the Department of Justice may have been influenced by the news cycle. Did the Justice Department issue more or fewer press releases (proportionally) about issues related to policing after Ferguson? Or Baltimore? Moreover, do we see an increase in civil rights activity in the DOJ-CRD as the Obama presidency waned? In short, is there any preliminary evidence that the Obama Administration behaved differently in the wake of Black Lives Matter or its own lame-duck status?

Figure 3.1 charts the rate of press activity (measured as the percentage of press releases per quarter) on four high-profile issues in the Justice Department's

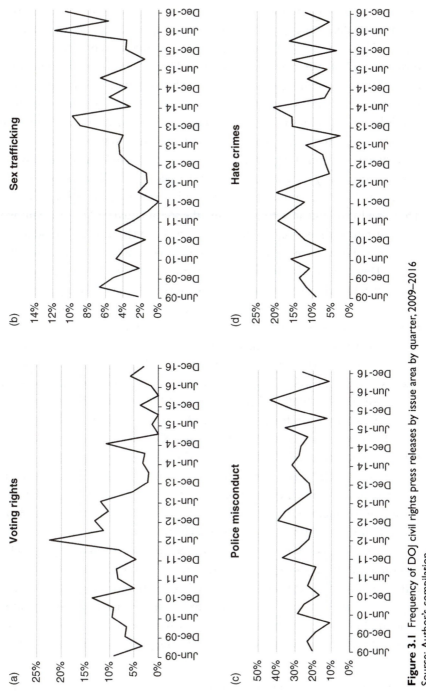

Figure 3.1 Frequency of DOJ civil rights press releases by issue area by quarter, 2009–2016

Source: Author's compilation.

Civil Rights Division: voting rights, sex trafficking, police misconduct, and hate crimes. In general, the figures reveal quarterly volatility in the percentage of press releases issued on each topic. On hate crimes (d) and police misconduct (c) in particular, some quarters witnessed sharp spikes in activity, only to be followed by a quarter with comparatively fewer reports. For instance, there are proportionally fewer press releases about hate crimes from the third quarter of 2012 to the second quarter of 2013. This does not mean that the Justice Department was not working on these types of cases. Rather, this suggests that it had more things to report in some quarters than in others.[13] In general, though, the pattern of police misconduct reporting suggests that the Justice Department examined these types of issues pretty consistently throughout the Obama presidency. In general, at least 10 percent of the press releases each quarter updated the public about ongoing investigations of police misconduct. There is a local spike in activity around the second quarter of 2015. This would be consistent with increased activity in the wake of the death of Freddie Gray, a black man who died in police custody in Baltimore, Maryland. Incidentally, the Justice Department also released information regarding its investigations into the Michael Brown shooting in Ferguson during this same time period.

There is a different pattern in the discussion of voting rights (a) and sex trafficking (b). While discussions of sex trafficking tapered off in 2014–2015, the Justice Department reported more about sex trafficking cases in Obama's second term than in his first term. When we look at voting rights cases, we see local spikes in press release activity in midterm election seasons (i.e., third quarter 2010 and third quarter 2014). As noted earlier, there was also a spike in press release activity in the summer of 2012. This is the time period where the Justice Department was waiving preclearance requirements for some counties that had been covered under the Voting Rights Act. After the Supreme Court invalidated the formula used to determine which states required preclearance in *Shelby County* v. *Holder* (570 U.S. 2 (2013)), the Justice Department started issuing fewer press releases about voting rights in general (at least until the next midterm election cycle).

In Figure 3.2, I deploy the same methodology to determine if press releases mentioned members of specific groups or issues relevant to those groups at differing rates throughout President Obama's tenure in office. Here, I am aggregating press releases which may mention the racial or other identity of a victim, but I also look at issues that may have been framed as racial issues. Again, the goal here is to see if the Justice Department appears to advocate

---

13 Future studies may also want to consider whether presidents have incentives to minimize the discussion of hate crimes around election campaigns.

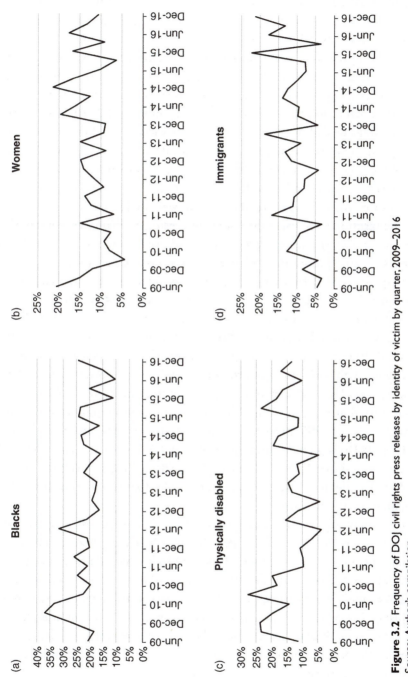

Figure 3.2 Frequency of DOJ civil rights press releases by identity of victim by quarter, 2009–2016
Source: Author's compilation.

for members of particular groups and issues of concern to them more toward the end of Obama's presidency. In this figure, I look at whether CRD press releases mention blacks or black issues, women or women's issues, the physically disabled or disability issues, and immigrants or immigration issues.

There were different temporal patterns for different groups. For instance, in the first quarter examined (second quarter 2009) in Figure 3.2b, more than 20 percent of the press releases addressed women's issues or female victims. This proportion fell to less than 5 percent by the beginning of 2010. With a couple of exceptions, though women and women's issues received more attention in subsequent quarters, these issues were typically mentioned less than 15 percent of the time in press releases for the rest of the Obama presidency.

While there was volatility in discussions of immigrants and issues related to immigration (d), the overall trend was an increase in discussions of immigrants and immigration issues over the course of President Obama's tenure in office. While immigration issues were barely discussed in the second and third quarters of 2009, more than 15 percent of press releases in the second and fourth quarters of 2016 discussed immigrants and immigration related issues.

Toward the beginning of the Obama presidency, the Civil Rights Division devoted a lot of attention to touting its efforts to improve accessibility for physically disabled Americans. In President Obama's first two years in office, the Civil Rights Division was particularly active in reaching settlement agreements with various towns around the country to improve accessibility in public spaces. This was part of a larger program, called Project Civic Access, which started at the end of the Clinton Administration and, by virtue of its internet presence, still appears to be active today (US Department of Justice, Civil Rights Division n.d.). The relatively high level of activity observed in the first quarters of the Obama Administration reflects the proportionally greater number of settlement agreements reached under that program in 2009–2010 compared to later years.

Surprisingly, blacks and black issues were the subject of proportionally more cases per quarter in President Obama's first term than in his second term. Proportionally, cases about blacks or black issues made up the greatest share of press releases in the first quarter of 2010 and in the second quarter of 2012. As I mentioned earlier, the 2012 spike is at least partially attributed to the Justice Department's waiving of preclearance for some counties covered under the Voting Rights Act. Voting rights issues in general are coded as black issues in this dataset, even when the outcome of the case might not be satisfying to some activists.

The 2010 spike can be attributed to the Justice Department's involvement in an ongoing case that dates back to Hurricane Katrina. In the aftermath of the storm, six New Orleans police officers were accused of shooting six African American storm victims (a seventh person was charged with impersonating a police officer in the vicinity and providing false testimony in defense of the police officers). Two of the shooting victims—a teenager and a man with developmental disabilities—were killed. Afterwards, the police were charged with murder and with conspiracy for allegedly contriving a self-defense story to try to justify the shooting. This case took more than a decade to resolve. Initial convictions were thrown out of court. The case was finally settled in 2016 when, in two separate sets of negotiations, the officers pleaded guilty in exchange for lighter sentences than they received in the initial trial (Maggi 2010; US Department of Justice, Office of Public Affairs 2010; Fantz and Grinberg 2016; Lane 2016).

In 2010, the Justice Department press releases covered its involvement in the case and announced the federal indictment of the officers. This case garnered attention in multiple press releases for two key reasons. First, this was a high-profile case. While it is not unusual for the DOJ to issue new press releases at each stage of a case (i.e., investigation, indictment, and settlement), notorious cases sometimes warranted additional coverage. Second, because this case involved multiple defendants, the Justice Department sometimes followed the common practice of updating the status of different defendants and persons of interests in separate press releases, especially if they were standing in separate trials.

The Department of Justice data reveals some interesting things about the evolution of civil rights advocacy over the course of the Obama Administration. African American victims and interests were not neglected by the Obama Administration. The Civil Rights Division actively prosecuted hate crimes against blacks and other groups. They also were investigating and prosecuting police misconduct cases well before the well-publicized deaths of people like Michael Brown, Eric Garner, Sandra Bland, Tamir Rice, Malissa Williams, Timothy Russell, and others. Finally, if we look at the totality of cases discussed by the Justice Department, when they disclosed the race of the victim, the victim was more likely to be African American.

This being said, there are questions about certain decisions that the Civil Rights Division made with respect to black issues that will continue to be debated. For instance, some will question the Justice Department's decision to quietly waive preclearance[14] for some counties before *Shelby County* v. *Holder*

---

14 Under the Voting Rights Act, jurisdictions with a history of voter disenfranchisement because of race or language were required to get any changes to their electoral systems (i.e., to redraw district lines, move precinct voting locations, etc.) approved by the Justice Department. The formula for determining which jurisdictions were subjected to this requirement was chosen

(570 U.S. 2 (2013)). While on the surface, it looks like the Justice Department was trying to counter what became the controlling judicial belief (as evidenced by Chief Justice John Roberts' opinion in *Shelby* and a previous opinion in *Northwest Austin Municipal Utility District No. 1 v. Holder* (557 U.S. 193 (2009), which presaged *Shelby*) that Section 4 of the Voting Rights Act was outdated (because it unfairly subjected jurisdictions to oversight for voting rights violations that had long been corrected), some might question the strategy of ceding oversight capabilities in the first place.[15] Moreover, these actions did not prevent the Supreme Court from removing this enforcement instrument (at least temporarily) from the Justice Department's anti-discrimination toolkit.

And given the national conversation around policing, some may be surprised to not see dramatic increases in the number of public statements after high-profile police shootings in 2014 and 2015. The place where we see the biggest spike in Justice Department discussions of issues of concern to blacks was early in the Obama Administration, when the Justice Department was involved in a case against police officers accused of murdering blacks in the aftermath of Hurricane Katrina. This is largely because there were multiple defendants and multiple indictments, which each garnered separate press releases.

This dataset is agnostic to how blacks might perceive the decisions being announced with respect to black issues. It merely notes that the administration chose to address an issue at all because gauging responsiveness is an important metric. This approach also nods to due process and recognizes that thorough investigations do not guarantee particular results. Moreover, this approach should empower readers to draw their own interpretations about the significance of the Obama Administration's efforts on justice issues.

With this in mind, it is important to consider that some of these black-themed press releases yielded disappointing news. In particular, the dataset included announcements that the Civil Right Division would decline to pursue charges in some high-profile cases. This, undoubtedly, was a source of frustration for some. The *Los Angeles Times*, for instance, quoted Margaret Morrow, a St. Louis woman who protested the Justice Department's decision to not file federal charges against Darren Wilson in the killing of Michael Brown. In her words, "the Justice Department 'failed us' " (Hennessy-Fiske

---

by Section 4, which was declared unconstitutional in *Shelby*. This effectively made it impossible to require preclearance.

15 I am grateful to Kareem Crayton for helping me to think through this.

et al. 2015). A fellow protester, Cathy Jackson, offered, "I don't understand how the DOJ can say this is a racist department, they were racially profiling, but on the day Michael Brown was shot, that officer didn't violate his civil rights" (Hennessy-Fiske *et al.* 2015). Others were not surprised by this outcome, noting the high burden of proof federal prosecutors would have to overcome to secure convictions against police officers. They also noted that these investigations, while not securing federal indictments, usually forced settlements and consent decrees which addressed egregious and discriminatory police practices (Williams 2016).

A comparison of policing reports from the 1960s and the 2010s

One of the other products of the increased coverage of police shootings of unarmed blacks was President Obama's decision to convene the Task Force on 21st Century Policing. He charged this task force with brainstorming ideas to help police officers reduce crime while building trust with the citizens they are charged to protect. The committee was chaired by Professor Laurie Robinson, a criminologist at George Mason University, and Charles Ramsey, then Commissioner of the Philadelphia Police. They held seven listening sessions over a two-month period in early 2015, which featured 29 panels of testimony from experts and activists in three cities. The task forced released its final report in May 2015, about six months after President Obama signed the executive order creating the committee (President's Task Force on 21st Century Policing 2015).

In addition to this presidential task force, the Justice Department also conducted thorough investigations of police practices in departments that were involved in some of the highest profile shootings: Ferguson, Missouri (Michael Brown); Cleveland, Ohio (Malissa Williams and Timothy Russell); Baltimore, Maryland (Freddie Gray); and Chicago, Illinois (Laquan McDonald) (US Department of Justice 2017).

It is helpful to compare the structure of these reports to previous government-commissioned studies which examined social unrest that was connected to episodes of police violence. A close (but not perfect) analog would be the Kerner Commission report of 1968. President Johnson convened this commission in 1967 after a number of incidences of urban unrest in the country over the previous two-year period. The most notable of these uprisings took place in the Watts section of Los Angeles (1965), Newark, New Jersey (1967), and Detroit (1967). In these and other disturbances, rumors of police brutality often foreshadowed the violence (*Report of the National Advisory Commission* 1968).

The structures of the reports provide important clues about the scope and parameters of each committee's charge. Here, I compare the topics that are discussed in each report. What they do not discuss is as important as what they do. Examining the topics discussed in each report provides important insights about how each investigative body (as a reflection of their respective administrations) chose to frame these issues when making recommendations to try to address important societal problems in which race (particularly blackness) is intimately implicated.

One of the interesting distinctions between the Johnson and Obama era reports is their scope. The Kerner Commission report was a comprehensive document which sought to gain a holistic understanding of all of the factors which contributed to the civil breakdown which led to the riots. They interviewed residents of all of the communities which they examine; developed sociological profiles of riot participants and bystanders; traced the history of racial inequality back to the colonial period; compared the experiences of American-born blacks and immigrants; and examined policing practices, among other things (*Report of the National Advisory Commission* 1968).

The scope of the Obama-era reports is more narrow. One first realizes this when they compare the size of the two commission reports (i.e., not the Justice Department reports). The *New York Times* version of the Kerner Commission report is more than 600 pages long, while the 21st Century Policing task force's report is only 116 pages long, cover to cover. Part of the reason why the Obama-era report is shorter is that it only addresses policing. If we look at the policing section of the Kerner Commission report (chapters 11 and 12 are about 36 pages), there were actually fewer pages devoted to policing in it than in the whole 21st Century Policing task force report.

To be sure, in terms of length, the Justice Department reports on its investigations into the Ferguson, Baltimore, Cleveland, and Chicago police departments resemble the Kerner Commission reports. The book compilation of the four reports is nearly 600 pages. However, each report is presented discretely. There is no attempt to provide a preface which synthesizes the findings. As such, the findings are not presented in any generalizable fashion. And as with the 21st Century Policing task force report, the focus is just on police practices (US Department of Justice 2017).

On one hand, one could look at the limited scope of the Obama-era reports as problematic. By focusing on policing, these reports ignore external, structural factors which contribute to poor police–community relations. Moreover, by focusing on policing, these reports address one important structural barrier, but do not address the economic, educational, and social structures which perpetuate inequality and make these communities particularly vulnerable to unrest.

On the other hand, though, by focusing on policing, the Obama-era reports avoided potential criticism that it was playing respectability politics. In chapter 7 of the Kerner Commission report, the commission documents socioeconomic inequality in communities that had experienced violence. While the chapter discusses unemployment rates, wage inequality and the overrepresentation of blacks in low-wage, low-skilled occupations, it also cites the phenomenon of working mothers, absentee fathers, casual sex and drug addiction (*Report of the National Advisory Commission* 1968, 260–263). By not talking about these issues, the Obama-era reports risk losing sight of the whole picture, but they also minimize the chance of sensationalizing factors which could be viewed through a culture-of-poverty lens and reduce the possibility of being charged with privileging patriarchy or personal respectability or with resorting to stereotyping vulnerable communities. For a president who was often accused of invoking personal responsibility tropes and blaming blacks for some of their problems (see Price 2016, ch. 2), this incongruous observation is important and reminds critics to ascribe greater complexity to how the Obama Administration perceived and framed important racial issues.

Presidential pardons and commutations: a comparative view

Before she became famous for her book, *The New Jim Crow*, Michelle Alexander anticipated the presidency of Barack Obama with bated breath. In the introduction to her book, she talks about being excited about the prospect of the first black president on Election Night 2008. As she left an election party, though, she saw a black man being arrested and wondered if Obama's election would be consequential for him (Alexander 2010, 2–3). In her book, Alexander argues that the American criminal justice system, which disproportionately incarcerates blacks—particularly on nonviolent drug charges—relegates them to second-class citizenship. People with felony convictions can legally be discriminated against in terms of housing, school admissions, financial aid, and employment, among other things. While she noted that candidate Obama acknowledged the structural inequity here, she also expressed concern that Obama pivoted during his campaign to endorse more "law and order" policies. For instance, Obama endorsed policing tactics which took a hard line on drugs and funneled military equipment to local police departments. He also appointed hardliners on drug issues to key posts in his administration—namely, Vice President Joe Biden and his first Chief of Staff, Rahm Emmanuel (Alexander 2010, 238–240).

To be sure, the unrest in Ferguson—and the visual imagery of police in armored vehicles policing protesters, prompted President Obama to order a review of military surplus policies, which led to his administration barring the military from giving some types of equipment to local police departments (see Peralta 2015). And we know that President Obama narrowed the sentencing gap between powder and crack cocaine in 2010 when he signed the Fair Sentencing Act into law (Crack and powder cocaine are stereotypically associated with black and white communities, respectively.). Before this law, anyone caught with 5 grams of crack cocaine received a mandatory five-year prison sentence. However, a person convicted of possessing powder cocaine would have to have 500 grams on their person to trigger the same mandatory sentence. Under the bill's guidelines, one would have to possess 28 grams of crack cocaine to get a mandatory five-year sentence (Baker 2010; CNN Wire Staff 2010).

Clearly, then, sentencing and incarceration patterns are on the front lines of the civil rights struggle. With this in mind, in this section, I examine President Obama's pardons and commutations. Other commentators have noted that the sheer number of Obama's commutations and pardons was unprecedented (see Smart 2017). Here, I seek to do a deeper dive to compare his pardon and commutation decisions to those of his predecessors. While I am interested in his actions toward drug offenders, I go beyond that discussion to compare Obama's behavior on the non-drug cases as well.

For this section, I am using a dataset of presidential commutations and pardons, using the clemency list available on the Department of Justice's website (US Department of Justice, Office of the Pardon Attorney n.d.). I should note that this dataset was compiled and coded by one of my research assistants, who also happens to have a law degree. I asked her to compile commutations[16] and pardons in the Clinton, Bush, and Obama Administrations and to code them by offense type: nonviolent drug offenses, violent offenses, white-collar crimes, and other offenses (and I deferred to her expertise on these classifications). Other offenses include crimes such as Chelsea Manning's leaking of classified government documents or Frank Ayala Martinez's conviction (whom Bill Clinton pardoned in 2001) of falsifying INS (Immigration and Naturalization Services) documents. I report the results in Table 3.8. The dataset does not identify offenders by race; however, given the prominence of sentencing discussions in current civil rights debates, this analysis is still enlightening.

---

16 "The commutations included in this dataset include stays of executions. In the one instance where someone's execution was delayed twice for the same crime, I count them once in this dataset."

Table 3.8 Presidential pardons and commutations, by type of crime, 1993–2017

	Clinton	Bush	Obama
Total number of people pardoned	396	187	212
Total number of people given commutations	64	11	1716
Nonviolent drug offenses	114	44	1790
Pardons	83 (72.8%)	36 (81.8%)	89 (5.0%)
Commutations	31 (27.2%)	8 (18.2%)	1701 (95.0%)
Violent offenses	23	8	13
Pardons	6 (26.1%)	6 (75.0%)	4 (30.8%)
Commutations	17 (73.9%)	2 (25.0%)	9 (69.2%)
White-collar offenses	215	77	130
Pardons	194 (90.2%)	74 (96.1%)	72 (55.4%)
Commutations	21 (9.8%)	3 (3.9%)	58 (44.6%)
Other offenses	123	75	296
Pardons	119 (96.7%)	74 (98.7%)	58 (19.6%)
Commutations	4 (3.3%)	1 (1.3%)	238 (80.4%)
Total persons pardoned/commuted: 2,586			

Source: Author's compilation.
Note: Some grantees had multiple types of crimes pardoned or commuted. Because of this and rounding error, N sizes may not add to the totals in the top two rows. Also the percentages presented are column percentages for the total numbers listed immediately above their respective rows.

Consistent with the findings of other researchers (see Smart 2017), it is clear that President Obama made greater use of his power to pardon and commute sentences than did his predecessors. Barack Obama issued three times as many pardons and commutations as Bill Clinton and George W. Bush combined. Moreover, as Smart (2017) notes, the overwhelming majority of those actions were clemency decisions (or commutations), not pardons.

When I break down the pardons and commutations by offense type, it is clear that most of President Obama's activity focused on commuting nonviolent drug offenses. Obama offered clemency in 95 percent[17] of the nonviolent drug offense cases. In contrast, George W. Bush pardoned 82 percent of the drug offenders to whom he showed mercy. Of Bill Clinton's changes to nonviolent drug convictions, 72 percent were pardons.

What is most interesting is Obama's sentencing and commutation behavior for other types of crimes, especially in comparison to his predecessors. In general, President Bush issued fewer pardons and commutations overall. He pardoned or commuted sentences for very few people convicted of violent

17 There is a slight discrepancy between the proportion of nonviolent drug commutations that Smart (2017) and I report. This is due to periodization. Smart ended his analysis on January 17, 2017, and this table looks at commutations for the entire Obama presidency, including those made after January 17.

crimes (eight overall: six pardons and two commutations). He pardoned 74 white-collar offenders (or 96 percent of the total number of white-collar offenders receiving sentencing relief). And among those convicted of other offenses, Bush pardoned almost 99 percent of those who received some form of sentence adjustment.

Bill Clinton's pardon and commutation patterns were mostly similar. He pardoned 90 percent of the white-collar offenders and 97 percent of the people convicted of other offenses. The one place where he was different from Bush was in his actions toward violent offenders. There, Clinton commuted the sentences of three-quarters of the cases on which he acted, while pardoning one-quarter.

Barack Obama's pardon and commutation patterns for non-drug offenses look very different. Like George W. Bush, Obama changed the status of only a few violent offenders. When he did change violent offenders' status, he, like Bill Clinton, was more likely to offer clemency. And unlike Clinton and Bush, Obama tended to commute the sentences of people convicted of other types of offenses violent rather than outright pardon them. There, 80 percent of Obama's actions were commutations. Perhaps most interesting is Obama's behavior toward white-collar criminals. Whereas Presidents Bush and Clinton pardoned over 90 percent of the white-collar criminals for whom they chose to act, Obama only pardoned 55 percent of them.

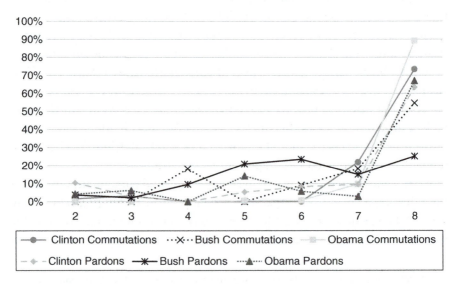

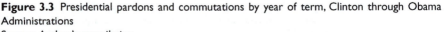

Figure 3.3 Presidential pardons and commutations by year of term, Clinton through Obama Administrations
Source: Author's compilation.

It is also important to consider the timing of these pardons and commutations. Many of Obama's pardons and commutations took place at the end of his presidency. Is that unusual? Figure 3.3 helps to answer this question. In this figure, I break down the proportion of each president's pardons and commutations (as a percentage of each president's total number of pardons and commutations) by the year in office in which he issued them. All pardons and commutations made in the second year are listed as time point 2, etc., and the values listed at the data points for each line add to 100 percent.

As Figure 3.3 shows, while President Obama issued more pardons and commutations than his predecessors, the timing and proportion of those decisions was in line with prior practice. Bill Clinton certainly waited until his last year in office to issue pardons and clemency and George W. Bush did the same thing with his commutations. The one place where there was deviation is Bush's record on pardons. His pardons were more evenly distributed throughout his time in office. After his third year in office, he issued at least 10 percent of his total number of pardons per year. This suggests that while Obama distinguished himself in terms of pardon and clemency volume, he issued similar proportions of pardon and commutation decisions in each year of office compared to previous presidents.

Conclusion

Collectively, these findings present a complex picture of the Obama Administration's efforts on issues of concern to blacks. There is evidence to corroborate the idea that on issues of race, the Obama Administration was paddling beneath the surface, so to speak. In some departments, like in Health and Human Services, the African American advocacy in the Obama Administration is subtle and inferred from the discussion of an issue (obesity) that is perceived to be of importance in black communities. Other departments, like Education and Justice, talked a considerable amount about race. To be sure, one expects to see such discussions in the Civil Rights Division of the Justice Department. However, the data evince at least some attempt to balance advocacy for black issues alongside advocacy for other groups, like the disabled.

There were some revelations in this data. With the exception of President Obama's pardon and clemency activity, there is no real evidence of a "fourth quarter surge" of activity on the racial issues examined here. More often, racial discussions were either consistent across time in a department or ebbed and flowed throughout his administration.

It is important to consider these findings in light of the larger political context. Yes, President Obama does sometimes appear to have been more active in addressing racial constituencies—including blacks—than his predecessors. Sometimes, this attentiveness was symbolic. Many times, it was substantive. Occasionally, like in the case of voting rights or police department investigations, some may take issue with how the administration approached an issue or with the outcome of an inquiry. In other instances, the action, like providing clemency for nearly 2,000 nonviolent drug offenders, is insufficient to address larger structural issues. Here, it is important to recognize the strengths and the shortcomings of Obama's approach and to be cognizant of the institutional constraints he faced (like the improbability of a Republican-controlled Congress passing more liberal drug sentencing laws).

4

The right person saying the right thing: Descriptive representation and rhetoric in the Obama Administration

Symbolic politics—the gestures, appearances, and performances politicians make to establish goodwill among their constituents—are clearly less important than the substantive laws and policies which govern actual behavior and have the potential to improve the status of African Americans. However, their significance should not be underestimated. One of the reasons for not underestimating the importance of symbolic politics is that, sometimes, the lines between symbolic and substantive politics are blurred. There are some aspects of governance which incorporate both symbolic and substantive elements. Take the creation of the federal Martin Luther King Jr. Day holiday, for instance. On the surface, a holiday is a thoroughly symbolic event. However, this holiday was created at significant cost to the federal government. Federal employees may not have to work, but they still have to be paid. And the cultural significance of naming a holiday in honor of a black civil rights leader should not be minimized.

This chapter focuses on aspects of the Obama Administration which are both substantive and symbolic. The racial backgrounds of the people presidents appoint to positions of influence should not preclude their ability to act in the interests of all Americans, blacks included. However, the representation literature does provide a justification for the importance of descriptive representation and even makes claims about the connections between descriptive representation and substantive politics. Similarly, presidential rhetoric can be deployed for symbolic and substantive purposes. It can create a powerful signal of inclusivity. It can also help set a substantive policy agenda which could have long-reaching implications for reducing inequality and for aiding the life chances of blacks and other disadvantaged groups.

Descriptive representation

Scholars of representation have long touted the importance of descriptive representation within elective bodies. Writing of the symbolic importance of gender diversity, Virginia Sapiro contends that, "More women in office will increase the acceptability of women in government" (Sapiro 1981, 712; see also Martin 1989, 168). Similarly, Jane Mansbridge notes that descriptive representation confers legitimacy on deliberative bodies by signaling to minorities that they are full participants in decision-making. She also contends that diverse representatives may recognize and respond to issues of concern to minority communities quickly and that the diversity of perspectives that people of differing backgrounds bring to policy discussions might create more robust deliberations, thus avoiding groupthink (Mansbridge 1999).

When students of African American politics study descriptive representation, they too focus on descriptive representation within the ranks of elected officials (see Bobo and Gilliam 1990; Tate 2003). However, Robert C. Smith reminds us of the continued importance of studying Executive Branch appointments when he notes that "an obvious deficiency in the literature on black political participation is the failure to study black appointed officials as well as elected officials" (Smith 1984, 370). Indeed, political appointees are extensions of the presidents who hire them. If they are descriptively diverse and empowered by a diverse president, then they may quickly recognize sources of inequality and feel particularly empowered to act on behalf of communities of color in the name of their president's administration.

In this chapter, I focus attention on two aspects of governing which combine substantive and symbolic politics: the descriptive representation of Obama appointees and Obama's rhetoric. I start with a discussion of political appointments.

Why appointments matter

James Riddlesperger and James King write that "the selection of senior-level administrators and advisors ranks among the most important decisions made by an American president" (Riddlesperger and King 1986, 691). Modern presidents appoint approximately 3,000–4,000 people to work with them in the White House, to lead Cabinet agencies and regulatory administrations, and to provide counsel on issues as varied as the arts and AIDS policy. Thus, the president's appointment and nomination power is absolutely essential to his ability to carry out his duties as president (Mackenzie 2002; Lewis 2012, 578). Indeed, Robert Smith writes, "It is only a slight exaggeration to say that on a routine, day-to-day basis, these persons [the president's appointees] run the federal government" (Smith 1984, 374).

Presidential appointees can help set the tone for how an administration will be perceived. Riddlesperger and King note, for instance, that if the president's key advisors are respected, then it might be easier for president's proposals to be given serious consideration. Conversely, a president's agenda can stall if the advisors and aides pushing the agenda lack gravitas (Riddlesperger and King 1986, 691).

A number of factors contribute to the perceived influence of top presidential appointees. Clearly, their training and expertise matter. However, presidents consider other factors as well when placing appointees (Lewis 2012, 586). In the Executive Branch, certain appointments hold greater cachet and power. For instance, an appointment to an "inner Cabinet" position (i.e., Secretary of State, Defense or Treasury and Attorney General) is considered an extremely powerful and high-profile position because of the longevity of the offices (these were the first Cabinet-level positions) and because the issue domains of these offices are traditionally considered bipartisan and essential to the functioning of government (Riddlesperger and King 1986, 692). Newer Cabinet offices are less prestigious; as a result, secretaries in these departments may have less influence. Riddlesperger and King note that secretaries in the "outer Cabinet" offices tended to play more of an advocacy than advisory role to the president (Riddlesperger and King 1986, 692). In addition to Cabinet offices, presidents select White House staffers, as well as make nominations for offices in the Executive Office of the President, regulatory agencies, and advisory commissions. These positions vary in terms of their proximity to and influence on (or independence from) the president. Senior White House staffers, for instance, are usually campaign veterans who have demonstrated loyalty to the president, while directors within the Executive Office of the President (like the Director of the Office of Management and Budget) might be accorded the same status and access to the president as an inner Cabinet secretary (see Riddlesperger and King 1986, 693).

Because of the advocacy role of outer Cabinet departments, there has been much speculation that presidents have often used outer Cabinet appointments to meet demands for descriptive representation. While Franklin Roosevelt nominated the first female Cabinet secretary and Lyndon Johnson nominated the first black Cabinet secretary, minorities and women were not nominated for inner Cabinet offices until Bill Clinton nominated Janet Reno[1] for Attorney General and later Madeleine Albright for Secretary of State; and George W. Bush nominated Colin Powell for Secretary of State and later Alberto Gonzales for Attorney General (see Smith 1984; Dolan 2001).

There is some debate over whether presidents actually have designated outer Cabinet offices to satisfy their desire to have a descriptively representative Cabinet (see Riddlesperger and King 1986, 692). Some speculate that presidents take special care to ensure that members of key constituent groups receive representation in high-level appointments as a kind of reward for their electoral support and surmise that Democrats in particular will feel pressure to appoint women and minorities because of strong Democratic backing from minority and women voters (see Barker and Jones 1994, 289–290; King and Riddlesperger 1996, 503). However, it must be noted that in recent years, even Republican presidents have had at least some racial diversity among their senior level nominees (see Dolan 2001, 213). This led Mann and Smith to conclude in 1981 that "Now it is accepted practice—indeed, it is expected—that a certain number of presidential appointees will be made from the ranks of women and minority groups" (Mann and Smith 1981, 230).

Why black appointments matter

Black presidential appointments carry special historical weight because of the glass ceiling that kept blacks out of the White House until 2008. Before the election of Barack Obama, appointments to Cabinet, sub-Cabinet, and other advisory positions were an important way for blacks to be descriptively represented in the Executive Branch.

Presidents appoint black nominees for a number of reasons. Lucius Barker and Mack Jones examined Jimmy Carter's appointments and noted that his black nominees were particularly attractive on a number of different dimensions. In addition to their professional qualifications, President Carter's high-level black nominees held high-profile positions in which they could help set policy that would be of special interest to African Americans (e.g., HUD Secretary Patricia Harris Roberts, EEOC Chairwoman Eleanor Holmes Norton, and Assistant Attorney General for Civil Rights Drew Days) (Barker and Jones 1994, 289–290).

---

1 Janet Reno was not the first person nominated to be Bill Clinton's Attorney General. Before Reno, Clinton nominated Zoe Baird and Kimba Wood for the post. Both women were forced to withdraw their nominations when allegations of their employing undocumented workers as nannies surfaced (see King and Riddlesperger 1996, 505–506).

Assessing the racial diversity of presidential appointments also has analogs to scholarly work done on early black mayors and governors. Linda Williams, for example, was highly critical of the first wave of black mayors who assumed office in large American cities in the 1970s and 1980s because they were unsuccessful in reducing black–white inequality on key socio-economic measures. As a result of their inability to address the most intract-able problems facing black communities, Williams contended that black mayors focused on the things they could control. One of the things they could control was the appointment and set-aside process. Williams noted that early, big-city, black mayors were particularly successful in increasing black representation in government appointments and in city contracts (Williams 1987, 128–129).

Mayor Maynard Jackson of Atlanta perhaps best exemplifies early black mayors' success in increasing black representation in contracting and in appointed positions. Robert Holmes found that over the course of Jackson's first two terms in office (he also served a non-consecutive third term in the early 1990s), the percentage of minority city employees increased from 42 to 61 percent. Jackson also drastically increased the number of city contracts going to minority-owned firms—from 0.0012 percent in 1973 to 27.5 percent in 1980 (Holmes 2011, 210).

Similarly, one of Douglas Wilder's marquee achievements as the first black governor of Virginia was the increase in the number of appointments of minorities and women (Jeffries 2000). In fact, Wilder forcefully defended his record of minority appointments in a keynote speech for the 2001 annual meeting of the National Conference of Black Political Scientists, taking issue with the fact that some scholars were initially skeptical that Wilder would be able to positively impact the lives of black Virginians as governor (Wilder 2001; see Jeffries 2000).

A brief history of African American presidential appointments

Blacks have been represented informally and formally among presidential appointees since the Reconstruction era. Robert Smith notes that "after the Civil War certain positions were for a time viewed as traditionally black offices, such as United States Recorder of Deeds for the District of Columbia" (Smith 1984, 371). In the early part of the twentieth century, some presidents did reach out informally to black advisors. Theodore Roosevelt sought the counsel of Booker T. Washington on issues related to race relations. Franklin Roosevelt created a more formal structure and appointed civil rights leaders such as Mary McLeod Bethune to the Bureau of Negro Affairs.

While blacks would not serve in the president's Cabinet until the Johnson Administration, earlier presidents did make some important sub-Cabinet appointments. William Howard Taft appointed William H. Lewis Assistant Attorney General in 1911. Dwight Eisenhower named J. Ernest Wilkins Sr. Assistant Secretary of Labor in 1954 (Smith 1984, 371).

Lyndon Johnson appointed the first black to a Cabinet-level position when he selected Robert Weaver to be his nominee for Secretary of Housing and Urban Development. Since then, with the exception of the Nixon Administration, there has been at least one black Cabinet secretary in each president's administration (Smith 1984, 371–372; Riddlesperger and King 1986, 697).

Studying presidential appointments

Many studies focus on the upper echelons of presidential appointments (i.e., Cabinet secretaries and undersecretaries, key White House advisors, and federal judges, including Supreme Court Justices). This study takes a different approach. Here, I look at all announced nominations from the Clinton, Bush, and Obama Administrations (at least as many as my research assistants and I could find), because as Smith put it, "these persons run the federal government" (Smith 1984, 374).

For the purposes of this book, I will only focus on the descriptive representation of presidential appointees in the three prior administrations. Previous examinations of presidential appointments examined the pedigrees of nominees and found that male and female and black and white nominees have roughly comparable backgrounds and qualifications (Smith 1984, 380; Carroll 1986; King and Riddlesperger 1996, 504; see Borrelli 2010 for a slight caveat). Since those early studies did not find marked disparities in the qualifications of nominees of different backgrounds, I will assume parity in qualifications today and encourage further investigation of this question in future studies.

In addition, I chose to focus on nominees and not just those who were confirmed by the Senate. This decision allows me to include nominees who may not have received Senate confirmation (see Martin 1991 for a similar research design). Including all nominees allows me to gauge presidential intent. This also becomes especially important when we consider that scholars and journalists have noted increasing delays in the confirmation process from posts as varied as ambassadorships to the federal judiciary (see Ornstein and Donilon 2000; Mackenzie 2002). Future studies should examine the confirmation experiences of diverse nominees as earlier work has suggested that female nominees are treated differently in Senate confirmations (see Borrelli 1997).

In addition to gauging presidential intent regardless of senatorial veto, examining the universe of presidential nominees also creates opportunities to examine the pervasiveness of diversity within a presidential administration. When Janet Martin studied the gender diversity of presidential nominees from the L. Johnson to Reagan Administrations, she found inconsistencies in the gender diversity of Cabinet and sub-Cabinet appointments. The nomination of a woman to a Cabinet-level position did not necessarily correlate with the nomination of more women to lower-level positions within the same department (Martin 1989, 164). In light of Martin's discovery, I cannot assume that the diversity of Cabinet-level nominees matches the diversity of lower-level nominees and must examine this further.

Similarly, Martin also found that presidents were more likely to nominate women at the beginning of their terms, when the media was more likely to pay attention to issues of diversity. As appointees left the administration to pursue other opportunities, their replacements tended to be less diverse (Martin 1989, 165). As a consequence of this finding, I will also compare the diversity of initial versus later Cabinet appointees to see if the same pattern persists in more recent administrations.

The literature suggests that sustained diversity among presidential appointments is a relatively recent phenomenon. Jimmy Carter was the first to appoint a significant number of blacks and women; and while the number of black and female appointees declined in the Reagan and first Bush Administrations, they did climb to record numbers in the Clinton Administration (Smith 1984, 374; Martin 1989, 163; Dolan 2001). This lends credence to the hypothesis that Democrats will be more likely to appoint blacks than Republicans because blacks are a key Democratic constituency (see Barker and Jones 1994, 289–290; King and Riddlesperger 1996, 503). As such, in the comparison of minority appointments between the Obama, second Bush, and Clinton Administrations, I would expect that Presidents Clinton and Obama would nominate a more racially diverse group of appointees than President Bush.

Partisanship notwithstanding, black political executives in lower offices have a track record of increasing the racial diversity of appointees and contractors (see Jeffries 2000; Holmes 2011, 210). I hypothesize then, that as a black political executive, President Obama would nominate a more diverse array of appointees than his immediate predecessors.

To test these hypotheses, I studied the race of nominees in Bill Clinton, George W. Bush, and Barack Obama's Administrations. The Bush and Obama

Administrations announced their nominations on whitehouse.gov. The online archive of the Clinton Library includes press announcements of the Clinton Administration nominees.[2] An outside coder compiled these nominations in a database and then coded each nominee by race and ethnicity. The coder used a combination of cues to determine race and ethnicity. In addition to crude cues such as phenotype (as presented in photographs) or surname, the coder consulted biographies, interviews, media profiles, encyclopedia entries, etc., looking for evidence of racial self-identification or membership in race-specific organizations. By triangulating sources to deduce a nominee's racial or ethnic identity, we sought to avoid the perils of relying just on phenotype or surname. That being said, this process is inherently inexact, and there may be some mistakes.

By this methodology, the coder was able to classify nearly all available nominees. There were a small number of nominees who could not be classified. These were largely Clinton appointees who do not have a web presence and/or who are no longer active in public life. In addition, I count biracial nominees among all the racial/ethnic groups with which they identify.[3]

Obama's Cabinet-level appointments

Most analyses of diversity in presidential appointments start and end with looking at Cabinet-level appointments, so this is a helpful starting point. Table 4.1 displays the diversity within each president's Cabinet (for the purposes of this analysis, I am excluding Cabinet-equivalent appointments, like EPA Administrator, UN Ambassador, and US Trade Representative).[4]

As Table 4.1 demonstrates, all three administrations had considerable levels of racial and ethnic diversity. Overall, Presidents Clinton and Obama appointed more descriptively diverse Cabinets than President Bush. However, President Bush's Cabinet was notably diverse. More than a quarter of the Cabinet

---

2 Please note that the Clinton list only includes nominees through 1994.

3 I did have a second coder check a sample of the racial codes to corroborate accuracy. They agreed about 81% of the time. After I checked the second coder's codes, I found that in cases of disagreement, I agreed with the original coder's decisions most. (Most of the differences in coding stemmed from one coder not being able to locate profiles that the other coder managed to find). While the dataset is not perfect (and likely could not be given the subjective nature of the codes), I present the findings from the original dataset here. List of appointees and the database of biographies from which we determined phenotype is available upon request.

4 I should note the diversity of Cabinet-equivalent offices in the last two presidential administrations. Before serving as Secretary of State, Condoleezza Rice served as President George W. Bush's National Security Advisor. Susan Rice served as President Barack Obama's UN Ambassador and National Security Advisor. President Obama appointed Lisa Jackson as EPA Administrator, and Ron Kirk as US Trade Representative.

Table 4.1 Cabinet appointments, by race and department, 1993–2017

President	Diverse appointments	Total Appointments
Bill Clinton	African American appointees (N=7) • Jesse Brown, Secretary of Veterans Affairs (1993–1997) • Ronald Brown, Secretary of Commerce (1993–1996) • Mike Espy, Secretary of Agriculture (1993–1994) • Alexis Herman, Secretary of Labor (1997–2001) • Hazel O'Leary, Secretary of Energy (1993–1997) • Rodney Slater, Secretary of Transportation (1997–2001) • Togo West, Secretary of Veterans Affairs (1998–2000) Latino/a appointees (N=3) • Henry Cisneros, Secretary of Housing and Urban Development (1993–1997) • Federico Peña, Secretary of Transportation (1993–1997) and Secretary of Energy (1997–1998) • Bill Richardson, Secretary of Energy (1998–2001) Asian American appointees (N=1) • Norman Mineta, Secretary of Commerce (2000–2001) Arab American appointees (N=1) • Donna Shalala, Secretary of Health and Human Services (1993–2001)	30
George W. Bush	African American appointees (N=4) • Alphonso Jackson, Secretary of Housing and Urban Development (2003–2008) • Rod Paige, Secretary of Education (2001–2005) • Colin Powell, Secretary of State (2001–2005) • Condoleezza Rice, Secretary of State (2005–2009) Latino/a appointees (N=3) • Alberto Gonzales, Attorney General (2005–2007) • Carlos Gutierrez, Secretary of Commerce (2005–2009) • Mel Martinez, Secretary of Housing and Urban Development (2001–2003) Asian American appointees (N=2) • Elaine Chao, Secretary of Labor (2001–2009) • Norman Mineta, Secretary of Transportation (2001–2006) Arab American appointees (N=1) • Spencer Abraham, Secretary of Energy (2001–2005)	34
Barack Obama	African American appointees (N=5) • Anthony Foxx, Secretary of Transportation (2013–2017) • Eric Holder, Attorney General (2009–2015) • Jeh Johnson, Secretary of Homeland Security (2013–2017) • John B. King Jr., Secretary of Education (2016–2017) • Loretta Lynch, Attorney General (2015–2017) Latino/a appointees (N=5) • Julian Castro, Secretary of Housing and Urban Development (2014–2017) • John B. King Jr., Secretary of Education (2016–2017) • Thomas Perez, Secretary of Labor (2013–2017) • Ken Salazar, Secretary of the Interior (2009–2013) • Hilda Solis, Secretary of Labor (2009–2013)	32

(continued)

Table 4.1 Cont.

President	Diverse appointments	Total Appointments
Barack Obama	Asian American appointees (N=3) • Steven Chu, Secretary of Energy (2009–2013) • Gary Locke, Secretary of Commerce (2009–2011) • Eric Shinseki, Secretary of Veterans Affairs (2009–2014) Arab American appointees (N=1) • Ray LaHood, Secretary of Transportation (2009–2013)	

Source: Author's compilation using online sources.

members over the course of his term were black, Latino/a, Asian American, or Arab American.

If we compare the two Democratic presidents, we see that President Obama did not surpass President Clinton in terms of the descriptive diversity of his Cabinet. Forty percent Bill Clinton's Cabinet appointees were descriptively diverse. Similarly, almost 41 percent of Barack Obama's Cabinet appointees were ethnically or racially diverse.[5] Despite the fact that he basically did not surpass Bill Clinton in terms of selecting a more diverse Cabinet, we would be hard-pressed to say that President Obama did not assemble a diverse team of Cabinet leaders. Moreover, if we look at attrition[6] and replacement, Barack Obama did slightly better at maintaining relatively consistent levels of racial and ethnic diversity in his Cabinet. Seven diverse Cabinet secretaries started in Bill Clinton's Administration; when he left office, there were only five diverse Cabinet secretaries. In contrast, Barack Obama started with seven diverse Cabinet secretaries and ended with six diverse secretaries.[7]

Cabinet-equivalent appointments and key White House staff

The data in the previous section showed that, proportionally, President Obama's Cabinet was as diverse as President Clinton's Cabinet. Where Obama stood out from his predecessors was in the appointment of his most senior level staff and Cabinet-equivalent appointees. If we expand the list of appointments in Table 4.1 to include senior advisor to the president, EPA Administrator, US Trade Representative, UN Ambassador, Director of the

5   For this calculation, I only count John King, who is listed twice in Table 4.1 because he is biracial, once.
6   Keep in mind that Ron Brown's departure was due to his untimely passing and not a resignation or termination.
7   To be fair, Ron Brown, Bill Clinton's Commerce Secretary, died tragically while in office. I do acknowledge the small sample size problem here. We are talking about the difference of one person.

Office of Drug Control Policy, Director of the Office of Management and Budget and National Security Advisor, we find that President Obama made four additional diverse appointments (Valerie Jarrett as senior advisor, Lisa Jackson as EPA Administrator, Ron Kirk as Trade Representative, Susan Rice as UN Ambassador and National Security Advisor). Bill Clinton appointed two more diverse candidates (Lee Brown as Director of the Office of Drug Control Policy and Franklin Raines as Director of the Office of Management and Budget). George W. Bush appointed one additional diverse appointment (UN Ambassador Zalmay Khalilzad). To be sure, Condoleezza Rice served as National Security Advisor from 2001 to 2005; however, because she later became Secretary of State, she is already included in the calculation of diverse Bush appointees. The same holds true for Bill Richardson, who also served as UN Ambassador under Clinton. If we add these other diverse appointees to the original calculation of diverse formal Cabinet appointees, we see that President Clinton had 14 unique diverse appointments; President Bush had 11 unique diverse appointments; and President Obama had 17 unique diverse appointments.

Including lower-level nominations

An examination of Cabinet secretaries and the most senior-level appointees alone is insufficient to understand the extent of descriptive diversity in presidential administrations. In this section, I turn to an analysis of presidents' announced nominations during the first five years of their terms. This carries the analysis through the first year of the second term in office, when presidents have the opportunity to replace appointed officials who will not serve in the second term. This data includes some Cabinet secretaries, but also encompasses sub-Cabinet level positions (i.e., assistant secretaries), upper-level staffing at independent agencies and commissions, ambassadorships, judicial and law enforcement appointments, and nominations to advisory boards and ceremonial committees.

In part because of the ongoing expansion of the number of available appointments, but also because of changes in reporting and technology, I have more information from the Obama Administration than I have for previous administrations, and there is missing nomination data across all three administrations. This is particularly acute in the Clinton Administration, where I only have two years of data. Furthermore, the dataset includes missing data about the racial identification of some nominees. Because of this, at times during this analysis, I will sometimes exclude President Clinton's nominees from the analysis, and I also acknowledge that this limits what can

Table 4.2 Demographic breakdown of presidential nominees by administration

	Clinton	Bush		Obama	
	First two years	First two years	First five years	First two years	First five years
Whites	711 (74.0%)	282 (74.8%)	757 (78.2%)	722 (71.3%)	1,728 (71.6%)
Blacks	117 (12.2%)	35 (9.3%)	82 (8.5%)	160 (15.8%)	331 (13.7%)
Latinos/as	47 (4.9%)	28 (7.4%)	71 (7.3%)	76 (7.5%)	190 (7.9%)
Asian Americans	20 (2.1%)	9 (2.4%)	23 (2.4%)	39 (3.9%)	130 (5.4%)
Native Americans	6 (0.6%)	2 (0.5%)	5 (0.5%)	13 (1.3%)	31 (1.3%)
Race unknown	62 (6.5%)	21 (5.6%)	31 (3.2%)	3 (0.3%)	11 (0.5%)
Total known nominees	96	377	968	1012	2413

Source: Author's compilation. Column percentages are in parentheses. Column percentages may not add to 100 percent because biracial nominees are counted twice. Please also note the timeframes covered for each president. The Clinton nominations span from January 20, 1993 to November 15, 1994. Bush's nominations span from January 11, 2001 to January 18, 2006. Obama's nominations span from January 1, 2009 to December 20, 2013. The first two years for Bush and Obama cover nominations made through January 20, 2003 and January 20, 2011, respectively.

be generalized from this data; my interpretations may change as I have further opportunities to expand the dataset.

Table 4.2 presents a demographic breakdown of the nominees we know about in each of the last three administrations based on race and ethnicity.[8] In their first two years in office, over 70 percent of each president's nominees were white. About 75 percent of President Bush's known nominees in his first two years were white, compared to 74 percent for President Clinton and 71 percent for President Obama. It is important to point out that the missing racial classification of some nominees potentially exacerbates the contrast between Obama nominees and the nominees previous presidents. We were able to classify more than 99 percent of the Obama nominees, but only about 94 percent of the known Bush and Clinton nominees in the first two years. I do not omit those candidates from the dataset. Assuming that at least some of those nominees are white, that would make the pool of known Obama candidates appear even more diverse by comparison.

Let us turn now to a comparison of each president's known minority nominating behavior. During the first two years of office, President Obama nominated proportionally more blacks to serve in his administration. Nearly 16 percent of the announced nominations we could find were of black people, compared to 9 percent for President Bush and 12 percent for President Clinton. While Presidents Bush and Obama nominated comparable proportions of

8 I am not including a separate category for Middle Eastern Americans in this table. In general, there were only a handful of nominees in each administration whom we were able to identify as having family origins in the Middle East, Afghanistan, or North Africa.

Latinos/as in their first two years (about 7.5 percent each), we could only identify 5 percent of President Clinton's nominees as Latino/a. President Obama nominated more Asian American appointees than his predecessors; and while the numbers are small, it should be noted that he nominated twice as many Native Americans as Bush and Clinton.

Zooming out to look at nomination patterns in the first five years allows us to see if there is any evidence to suggest that the pattern of frontloading diverse appointments persists today (see Martin 1989). While the absence of a Clinton comparison precludes my being able to rule out partisanship as a possible explanation for any observed differences across administrations, there is a normative value in comparing the Bush and Obama nominee pools to themselves over time. If the cumulative demographic profiles of the candidates at year five looks similar to the profiles at year two, then this suggests that the administration's behavior is consistent.

The available data suggests that frontloading may have taken place in the Bush, but not the Obama, Administration. When we look at five years' worth of nominees (as opposed to two), we see that Bush nominated more whites over time (there is also proportionally less missing data over the longer time period). For his part, President Obama nominated roughly the same proportion of whites in five years as he did in his first two years. Both presidents nominated proportionally fewer blacks over time. This was more pronounced in the Obama Administration; however, it is important to consider that even with that decrease, black nominees were still well represented. In the first five years of the Obama Administration, nearly 14 percent of the nominees examined were black. That is greater than the proportion of blacks in the US population (12.9 percent) in 2010 (US Census Bureau 2011, 3).

In the five-year period examined, both Presidents Bush and Obama nominated similar proportions of Latinos/as. The proportion of Latino/a Bush nominees largely stayed the same (and even fell slightly) when we compare five-year figures to two-year figures. In contrast, the proportion of Latino/a nominees increased slightly (by nearly half a percentage point) over time in the Obama Administration. The proportion of Native American nominees also does not change over time in both administrations. Obama distinguishes himself most from Bush in terms of Asian American nominations. After five years in office, based on the data we have at our disposal, Obama had named more than twice the proportion of Asian American nominees compared to President Bush.

Where blacks are being appointed

So far, the demographic breakdown of presidential appointments is falling into predictable patterns. In the first two years of office, President Obama nominated a more ethnically diverse group of candidates than his predecessors. Over time, his nominees continued to be diverse. In this section, I would like to dig a little deeper to examine African American nominees in particular. To what positions were they being nominated? Were they all African American interest positions? Were they all symbolic assignments?

I did some additional coding (beyond the original racial classification codes) for the black nominees included in the database. I wanted to see if the black appointees we know about were more likely to be nominated to serve in judicial posts (this includes all courts, including Washington, DC local courts and specialized courts, not just federal district and appellate courts), law enforcement positions like U.S. Attorney or U.S. Marshal, diplomatic posts (including ambassadorships, UN delegations, development banks, and Peace Corps leadership, foreign policy boards), Cabinet offices (including subsidiary agencies and boards), independent agencies and regulatory committees (like the EEOC; I also include Cabinet-equivalent agencies like EPA here), and advisory boards. I exclude nominations to the White House Staff and the Executive Office of the President because there is too much missing data for the reported numbers to be meaningful.[9]

I was also interested to see blacks if were likely to be nominated to serve in positions which are stereotypically thought to be of interest to the black community. For the purposes of this analysis, "black interest" positions include presidential advisory commissions that specifically reference African Americans (like the President's Board of Advisors on Historically Black Colleges and Universities), issues related to governance in Washington, DC,[10] issues related to drug policy, sentencing, ambassadorial appointments to African and Afro-Caribbean countries, and specific sub-Cabinet level appointments that address issues of racial equity (i.e., Director of the Office

9 There are some individuals who were nominated for more than one office. They only appear in the dataset once per each administration in which they were nominated. (Eric Holder, for instance, was nominated in multiple administrations.) However, this new coding does account for the multiple types of organizations to which a person was nominated. For instance, if a diplomat was subsequently nominated for a judgeship (this did not happen), they would be coded under both categories. As best as possible, I tried to code individuals with multiple nominations under their earliest nomination.

10 I include all of the Washington, DC appointments in the "black interest" category because historically, black members of Congress served on the Washington, DC oversight committees (sometimes by choice, sometimes not). Also, some of these appointments related directly to DC city governance. Given Washington's history as a majority and now plurality-black city, it was also important to mark these nominations as racialized. Tate notes a general perception that serving on DC themed committees is considered a form of substantive representation for blacks (Tate 2003). In general, when making coding decisions about whether a position was racialized, I used my best judgment to make those calls. I invite future researchers to conduct their own coding to corroborate my work.

Table 4.3 Placement of black presidential nominees

% of all black nominees	Clinton	Bush		Obama	
	First two years	First two years	First five years	First two years	First five years
Cabinet/subsidiary Cabinet agency nominations	69 (59.0%)	14 (40.0%)	36 (43.9%)	69 (43.1%)	131 (39.6%)
Independent agency nominations	15 (12.8%)	4 (11.4%)	12 (14.6%)	22 (13.8%)	48 (14.5%)
Diplomatic nominations	20 (17.1%)	4 (11.4%)	11 (13.4%)	28 (17.5%)	54 (16.3%)
Judicial nominations	27 (23.1%)	16 (45.7%)	28 (34.1%)	24 (15.0%)	60 (18.1%)
US attorney nominations	9 (7.7%)	1 (2.9%)	3 (3.7%)	8 (5.0%)	16 (4.8%)
US marshal nominations	9 (7.7%)	7 (20.0%)	8 (9.8%)	9 (5.6%)	16 (4.8%)
Advisory Board nominations	5 (4.3%)	0 (0.0%)	6 (7.3%)	39 (24.4%)	90 (27.2%)
"Black interest" nominations	21 (17.9%)	12 (34.3%)	23 (28.0%)	37 (23.1%)	58 (17.5%)
Total black nominees	117	35	82	160	331

Source: Author's compilation, based on available data. Column percentages will not add to 100 percent because some nominations overlap categories. Please also note the timeframes covered for each candidate. The Clinton nominations span from January 20, 1993 to November 15, 1994. Bush's nominations span from January 11, 2001 to January 18, 2006. Obama's nominations span from January 1, 2009 to December 20, 2013. For Bush and Obama, the second year ends on January 20, 2003 and January 20, 2011, respectively.

of Minority Impact or Assistant Attorney General for Civil Rights). I do not assume that every position in traditionally racialized Cabinet offices (like the Department of Housing and Urban Development) is a "black" position.

I present the findings in Table 4.3. The percentages shown here reflect percentage of black nominees (per president/time period) who were selected to serve in any given part of government. The column percentages will not add to 100 percent because not all sectors are represented here and because there is overlap in job descriptions and sectors. For instance, most diplomatic positions fall under the purview of the State Department. As such, these nominees are classified as Cabinet nominations and diplomatic nominations. Also, if a person was nominated for two different types of roles over the time period studied, they may also be coded as a nominee in multiple government sectors.

In their first two years of office, presidents nominated a plurality to majority of black nominees to serve in Cabinet departments (or in agencies that fall under the jurisdiction of a Cabinet department). This was most pronounced in the Clinton Administration, where nearly 60 percent of the known black nominees were chosen for positions in Cabinet agencies. About 40–45 percent of black nominees in the first two years of the Bush and Obama Administrations were selected for Cabinet agencies. After five years, this proportion increases slightly for black Bush nominees, but decreases slightly for black Obama nominees.

A little more than 10 percent of black nominees across all three administrations were initially chosen to serve in one of the independent agencies or commissions. Over the first five years of their administrations, nearly one in seven black nominees in the Bush and Obama Administrations was tapped to serve in an independent agency.

Democrats appeared to be slightly more likely to nominate blacks for diplomatic posts. Presidents Clinton and Obama nominated about 17 percent of their black candidates for diplomatic positions in the first two years, compared to 11 percent of black nominees in the Bush Administration. After five years in office, President Bush designated 13 percent of his black nominees for diplomatic posts, while President Obama nominated 16 percent of blacks for diplomatic posts.

In absolute numbers, all three presidents nominated similar numbers of black judges. However, because President Bush nominated fewer blacks overall, this makes up a greater share of his black nominations than the other two presidents. In the first two years in office, President Clinton put up nearly a quarter of his black nominees for judgeships. One in seven of President Obama's black nominees was for the bench. After five years, more than a third of President Bush's black nominations were for judgeships, as were 18 percent of President Obama's nominations.

Related to judicial nominations are law enforcement nominations. The database includes blacks who were nominated to be US attorneys or federal marshals. As a share of all black nominees, there were relatively few black nominees for these positions. Patterns varied across administrations, though. About 8 percent of Bill Clinton's initial African American nominations went to US attorney candidates, compared to 5 percent in the Obama Administration and 3 percent in the Bush Administration. While President Bush only nominated three black US attorneys in his first five years of office, President Obama nominated 16 blacks. Proportionally, Bush nominated more blacks to the US Marshal Service than either Clinton or Obama. While only 5–8 percent of black nominees in the Clinton and Obama candidate pools were for the marshal service, 20 percent of black nominees in the first two years of the Bush Administration were for the marshal service, as were 10 percent of black nominees in the first five years.

So far, the profile of black nominees suggests that President Bush nominated more of his black candidates for judicial and law enforcement posts, while Presidents Clinton and Obama nominated more diplomats (proportionally). The last two rows of Table 4.3 allow us to look at the more symbolic side of the appointments process. Were blacks nominated for advisory positions where they might have less power to implement changes? And were blacks being nominated to serve in positions that arguably represented racialized interests?

Based on the available information, it appears that President Obama nominated many black people to serve in an advisory capacity. About one-quarter of all his nominees over two and five years were chosen to serve on advisory boards or commissions. To be sure, these boards vary in their scope, but the common bond is the advisory nature of the work they do. The proportion of blacks nominated to serve on advisory committees in the Obama Administration far outstrips the proportion of blacks tapped to serve on such committees in the Clinton and Bush Administrations. Four percent of the known black nominees in Clinton's first two years were chosen for advisory commissions, as were 7 percent of nominees in years three to five of the Bush Administration. This dataset does not include any black nominees to an advisory committee in Bush's first two years in office. To be sure, this does not mean that President Bush did not nominate anyone to advisory committees. The larger dataset includes dozens of advisory board nominees, just not black nominees.

Finally, the last row of Table 4.3 identifies nominees by whether their proposed appointment addressed specifically racialized issues. In all three administrations, a nontrivial number of black nominees were selected for racialized positions within the administration, such as a black interest advisory board or a substantive role that pertained to a civil rights issue. Eighteen percent of black nominees in the Clinton Administration were chosen for racialized positions, as were 34 percent of Bush nominees by the end of the second year, and 28 percent by the end of the fifth year. In President Obama's first two years of office, nearly a quarter of all black nominations were for black interest positions. Over five years, this proportion falls to 17.5 percent.

Because of the missing data issues, the conclusions I draw here are more impressionistic. However, based on the data I have at my disposal, it appears that, on the whole, President Obama nominated a more racially diverse group of public servants than his predecessors. While the diversity of Cabinet officers in the Clinton and Obama Administrations were roughly comparable (with Bush not being far behind), Obama nominated citizens from many different racial and ethnic backgrounds to serve across his government. Based on the available data, Obama nominated more black, Asian American, and Native American officials. In absolute numbers, he nominated more black US attorneys. That said, Obama was also more likely to nominate blacks to advisory positions, and he continued a tradition of nominating blacks to serve in "black positions" in his administration.

Future studies should continue to examine the descriptive diversity of presidential administrations. There is a need to build out this dataset to ensure that it accounts for every nominee. In particular, more work should be done to identify all the staff in the West Wing and in the Executive Office of the President/White House Office and all of the nominees in the past quarter century. Once those numbers are established, it is important to carry the analysis further to examine the ways that these staffers sought to address racial concerns and whether or not they succeeded or were ambitious enough.

Robert Smith warned years ago that descriptively representative appointees might not necessarily feel an obligation to address racial issues (Smith 1984). Given the number of blacks serving in advisory capacities, it is unclear that these blacks were in positions of power to be able to implement any advice they may have provided to the Obama Administration. And while Chapter 3 gives a sense of the level of racial activity taking place in some Cabinet agencies, we also know from Chapter 2 that these activities did not lessen inequality on the measures we examined. While future studies should continue to explore the connection between descriptive representation and policy outputs, this preliminary evidence suggests that descriptive representation alone, while important, cannot fix inequality.

Rhetoric in the Obama Administration

One of the big fears about black politicians who win elections by transcending race is that they will be hamstrung in the face of unfortunate racial incidents that divide Americans along racial and ethnic lines. Can candidates who claim to transcend race actually address racial disparities and speak truth to power in the face of real racial grievance? In this section, I explore presidential rhetoric in two key public performance venues: State of the Union Addresses and press conferences. Was President Obama more forthright in speaking about racial issues than his predecessors? When talking about racial issues, was he more or less likely to resort to platitudes? Was he more likely to acknowledge that there might be valid systemic explanations for persistent racial inequality? Did he articulate more cogent responses to racial issues because of his experiences as a black person in America?

Rhetoric as a form of representation

There are important connections between rhetoric and representation. Speeches, political statements, answers to press questions, etc. are one way that politicians can articulate their values and issue priorities. They can also use statements to signal responsiveness to important constituencies. By raising an issue, politicians imply its value and suggest that it is worth addressing. Daniel Gillion (2016, 3) argues that dialogue, a form of rhetoric, is an important part of the policy-making process, as it helps to set the agenda. For instance, he noticed that after President Clinton started his "National Dialogue on Race" in 1997, respondents to the Gallup poll were more likely to name race relations as one of the most important issues facing the country today.

Bringing up racial issues in speeches also sends important signals about inclusivity and responsiveness. It could also serve as the fuel driving the engine which makes descriptive representation work. For instance, Mansbridge defends descriptive representation on the grounds that it confers legitimacy on a deliberative body and that it helps minority citizens feel vested in their government. She also predicts that descriptive representatives will be more nimble in responding to crises that directly affect their ethnic communities because they are probably more intimately aware of the underlying causes of those crises and can respond without first having to be briefed about the context (Mansbridge 1999). These advantages do not operate in silence. Implicit in Mansbridge's defense is the idea that descriptive representatives will use their positions to talk about or to raise issues of concern to their communities.

Based on Mansbridge's theory, one would expect that a black president would be particularly nimble and vocal when addressing racial issues. According to her, a black president should be intimately acquainted with the problems facing black communities and would not need special briefings to familiarize himself with the issues at hand. Moreover, his cultural background should inform an immediate response to racial crises (Mansbridge 1999). Mansbridge, then, would predict that President Obama should be able to articulate quicker, more cogent responses to racial eruptions than his predecessors.

Conversely, President Obama's decision to use deracialization as a campaign strategy might temper his enthusiasm to bring up race. One of McCormick and Jones' concerns with the use of deracialization as a campaign strategy was that it might constrain a politician's ability to act on behalf of black interests once elected. In their view, deracialization was an implicit campaign promise to not engage racial issues once in office. Their normative concern was that the strategy attracted an important subset of voters who valued descriptive representatives but had no desire to advance blacks' substantive causes. More important, they feared that if deracialized politicians chose to address a racial schism, they risked destroying the electoral coalition that propelled them to office. If they took the side of their coethnics, they risked alienating non-coethnics who believed that they transcended their ethnic community; and if they took the side of non-coethnics, they risked alienating the coethnic voters who made up a base constituency (McCormick and Jones 1993).

Moreover, Melanye Price (2016, 2–3) reminds us that the content of racial speech matters. In her textual analysis of key Obama speeches, Price finds that President Obama had a tendency to use certain rhetorical tropes: personalizing racial stories; invoking Martin Luther King or the mid-twentieth-century civil rights movement; and taking the posture of mediator between blacks and whites while pushing listeners to find common ground across the racial divide. Most important, Price notes that President Obama's rhetoric often included some kind of exhortation to personal responsibility, or as she calls it, "Black blame" (Price 2016, 35). This type of framing often diverts attention from discussions of systemic inequality. And while Price concedes that blacks often warmly received President Obama's rebuke (and may have been able to reconcile the calls for personal and structural remedies to inequality), it may have had the unintended consequence of being perceived differently to nonblack audiences who may not have been primed to understand that discussions of personal responsibility do not have to come at the expense of acknowledging systemic racism (Price 2016, ch. 1).

With this in mind, I turn to a study of the content of presidential speech in two selected venues: State of the Union Addresses and presidential news conferences. I compare the content of President Obama's speeches to those of his immediate predecessors to see if he referenced racial issues with a similar frequency. I also look at how President Obama, along with Presidents Clinton and Bush, talked about race. Was the language explicit or implicit? Were they talking about racialized or transcendent policies? After examining those speeches, I turn to a reading of news conference transcripts. Here, I focus on how presidents addressed racial crises and talked about racial issues contemporaneously.

Looking at Obama's comments: State of the Union Addresses

First, let us look at State of the Union Addresses (and addresses to joint sessions of Congress in the president's first year of office). Here, I want to see if presidential rhetoric about race changes across administrations. To answer this question, I had an outside coder read State of the Union Addresses for all of the Clinton, Bush, and Obama Administrations. The coder noted the number of paragraphs in which explicitly black issues (i.e., civil rights, voting rights, racial profiling, achievement gaps) or blacks themselves were mentioned. She then coded the number of paragraphs which referenced race in coded

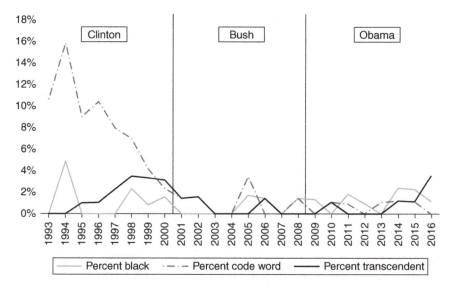

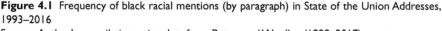

Figure 4.1 Frequency of black racial mentions (by paragraph) in State of the Union Addresses, 1993–2016
Source: Author's compilation, using data from Peters and Woolley (1999–2017).

language, like "minority," "underserved," "disadvantaged," etc. Finally, she noted the number of paragraphs which appealed to racial transcendence or exhorted Americans to come together despite their differences.

These frequencies (standardized as a percentage of the total paragraphs in each speech) are depicted in Figure 4.1.[11] As the figure shows, President Obama was similar to President Bush in that he rarely mentioned race in his State of the Union Addresses. This finding is consistent with Gillion's (2016, 48) finding, using a larger dataset, that Obama generally talked about race less than his Democratic predecessors. To be sure, President Obama mentioned race in some form in all of his addresses—unlike President Bush, who did not talk about race at all in 2003, 2004, and 2007. However, his racial comments were confined to a small number of paragraphs, usually between 1 and 3 percent of the total number of paragraphs. In contrast, race and racial issues come up frequently in President Clinton's State of the Union Addresses, especially in his first term. I should note, though, that most of President Clinton's language consisted of using racial code words. Ten percent or more of the paragraphs in his 1993,

11 The coding here reflects the more conservative coding of my outside coder. When conducting (2) intercoder checks of a sample of the State of the Union Addresses, I learned that I tended to find more frequent racial discussions across the board than my coders. The general findings were similar–we tended to more prevalent racial discussions in the Clinton Administration than in subsequent administrations–but there were variations in some of the years checked. To be as conservative as possible in my interpretations, I used the findings of the original coder.

1994, and 1996 speeches obliquely referenced race through coded language. Keep in mind that during this time, Clinton is promoting his welfare reform and anti-crime initiatives.

These findings warrant a deeper content analysis. To explore this further, I uploaded all of Presidents Clinton, Bush, and Obama's addresses into Voyant, a text analysis software tool. Voyant not only creates word clouds, but it also tabulates the most frequently used words.

Figure 4.2 juxtaposes word clouds for Presidents Clinton, Bush, and Obama. As the figure shows, issues of race did not predominate discussions in the three previous presidents' State of the Union Addresses. Welfare, which can be construed as a racialized issue, did emerge as an oft-mentioned theme in Bill Clinton's addresses. This is not surprising given Clinton's successful effort to overhaul the welfare system. It is also not surprising to see words like "terrorism" and "Iraq" rise to prominence in George W. Bush's State of the Union Addresses, especially after the 9/11 attacks and the subsequent invasion of Iraq. When we look at word frequencies, we see that President Obama often mentioned economic terms, like "jobs" or "economy." This, too, is expected, given the implosion of the global economy that coincided with his election.

Table 4.4 explores frequent word choices in greater detail. In the table, I note the frequency with which certain words appear in the text of State of the Union Addresses. I focus on a few keywords here, assuming these words are less likely to have other, irrelevant connotations. I do acknowledge that some of these words do have different meanings. Hopefully, the data in Figure 4.1 helps to provide that context. Also, please note that I only considered keywords that appeared in a speech more than twice. The categories and relevant keywords are as follows:

- **Young people/schools**: Here, I include terms such as *children, kids, baby, young*, as well as references to *schools, education, mentors, sons, daughters, and brothers (to capture potential references to My Brother's Keeper)*, etc.
- **Family issues**: This includes any references to *families, parents* and *leave*, as it could reference family leave proposals.
- **Immigrants**: This includes any mention of *immigrants, immigration*, or *citizen(ship)*.
- **Jobs**: This includes any references to *jobs* or *unemployment*.
- **Poverty**: Here, I include any references to the *poor, poverty, welfare*, and *earned*, as this includes references to the Earned Income Tax Credit, which was targeted toward working poor families.
- **African diaspora**: This includes references to Africa or Afro-Caribbean countries. Keywords here are *Africa, African*, or *Haiti*.

Clinton (1993–2000)

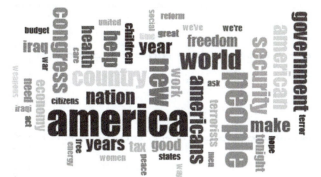

Bush (2001–2008)

Obama (2009–2016)

Figure 4.2 Most frequent words used in State of Union Addresses by president, 1993–2016
Source: Author's compilation, based on text analysis using Voyant software and State of the Union
Address transcripts from the UCSB Presidency Project.

Table 4.4 Frequency of identity group words used in State of the Union Addresses, 1993–2016

		Number of times the president mentions:									
		Young people/ schools	Family issues	Immigrants	Jobs	Poverty (including welfare and EITC)	African diaspora	Race/discrim- ination	Crime/ criminals/ police	Respon- sibility	Cities
B. Clinton	1993	34	16	0	24	11	0	0	6	6	4
	1994	50	33	0	34	24	0	0	40	4	4
	1995	52	34	25	19	18	3	0	16	15	7
	1996	53	42	11	15	11	0s	0	34	4	9
	1997	94	28	13	14	15	0	0	8	4	0
	1998	70	29	9	16	15	0	3	8	7	8
	1999	68	26	0	9	4	0	4	14	12	3
	2000	96	38	4	10	15	3	4	15	7	0
G.W. Bush	2001	38	15	5	4	0	0	0	3	5	3
	2002	12	3	9	13	0	2	0	6	2	2
	2003	13	3	9	0	0	7	0	8	0	0
	2004	47	18	5	13	0	0	0	17	0	0
	2005	19	10	6	7	2	0	0	0	10	6
	2006	19	3	9	6	0	2	0	8	4	0
	2007	23	4	13	4	3	2	0	0	0	0
	2008	29	6	13	5	0	2	0	0	6	0
B. Obama	2009	47	11	2	19	0	0	0	0	10	3
	2010	19	17	6	29	0	0	0	0	4	5
	2011	61	12	3	31	0	0	9	0	6	0
	2012	20	7	5	42	0	0	0	0	10	4
	2013	62	20	9	47	4	0	3	3	3	0
	2014	50	23	7	45	3	0	5	0	0	0
	2015	30	42	0	28	3	0	0	0	0	0
	2016	21	8	7	20	0	2	0	0	0	0

Source: Author's compilation, based on text analysis using Voyant software and State of the Union Address transcripts from the UCSB Presidency Project (Peters and Woolley 1999–2017).

- **Race/discrimination**: Here, I include usages of the words *race* and *discrimination*.
- **Crime/criminals/police**: This includes references to *crime, criminals, drugs, police*. I exclude reference to violence to avoid conflation with terrorism issues.
- **Responsibility**: I include any references to *responsibility*, as they often invoke personal responsibility in racial and nonracial ways.
- **Cities**: I include references to *cities* and *streets* here.

Some of these references are explicitly racialized. Immigration, for instance, is racialized and commonly associated with Latino/a and Asian populations. Some of these issues, like crime, poverty, and urban issues, are indirectly racialized because of common associations with blackness. Responsibility references could point to personal responsibility frames, which could also be construed as racial codes for instructing blacks about how to behave.

Table 4.4 shows that, in general, young people and issues related to them were referenced far more directly in State of the Union Addresses than minorities generally. References to young people and education were referenced at least ten times in every State of the Union examined. In contrast, words commonly associated with immigration (like, "immigrant" or "citizenship") were omitted from six State of the Union Addresses, including one Bush, one Obama, and three Clinton addresses.

Jobs and unemployment were a common theme in State of the Union Addresses. Not only were those words used in all but one State of the Union Address, they were often mentioned dozens of times in the same speech. In contrast, poverty-related words were barely mentioned in George W. Bush's addresses, but were commonly mentioned in the Clinton years, as he overhauled the national welfare system and introduced the Earned Income Tax Credit.

Race and racialized issues were inconsistently mentioned throughout the years examined. Clinton mentioned crime, criminals, and police most, especially in 1994, as he was pushing his crime legislation. President Obama only used these words in 2013. The presidents barely referenced Africa or Afro-Caribbean countries, and barely mentioned the words "race" or "discrimination."

Thus, the analysis of State of the Union Addresses corroborates existing research which found that President Obama was reticent on discussing race. Among the three immediate former presidents, President Obama was more similar to President Bush than President Clinton in terms of his frequency in talking about blacks and black issues. However, while President Clinton talked about black issues more, he talked about them indirectly and in the context of controversial, highly racialized issues like crime and welfare.

Responding to race in press conferences

State of the Union Addresses are carefully staged, highly formal events. It is helpful to juxtapose the frequency of racial discussions in those events with the frequency of racial discussions in other, more informal venues. As such, I turn to an examination of presidential rhetoric in press conferences. Compared to a formal address before Congress (like the State of the Union), news conferences are a more casual event in comparison. While the president often makes formal, scripted remarks at the beginning, the rest of the conversation is unscripted, and presidents have to think on their feet. Indeed, presidents may unwittingly reveal truths about themselves and their priorities with an ill-considered slip of the tongue.

To that end, I looked at news conference transcripts from the first Bush to the Obama Administrations. I include George H.W. Bush in this analysis so that I can capture reaction to the 1992 Los Angeles riots, which will be a nice juxtaposition to discussions of unrest in Ferguson, Missouri and Baltimore, Maryland. All of these uprisings were precipitated by allegations of police brutality against an unarmed black man. Using the Presidency Project database (Peters and Woolley 1999–2017), I collected transcripts of all of the presidential news conferences from the start of the George H.W. Bush presidency to the end of Barack Obama's term in office. I conducted keyword searches of prominent racialized word stems (i.e., "black," "Africa," "racis-," "Caribbean" or "civil right-") and then read the discussion around those words to determine if the conversation truly captured a racialized discussion. The unit of analysis here is the press conference; so, any press conference mentioning a racialized issue would be coded 1 for that particular issue.

In undertaking this analysis, I hope to answer the following questions. First, I want to see how often each president addressed racial issues in their press conferences. Related to that is the question of whether presidents initiated conversations about racialized topics in their opening statements or whether they were prompted by journalists to address racial issues. To explore that more, I will look specifically at the questions journalists ask the president. Finally, I am interested in the content of the discussion of race. Did the president frame racial controversies as isolated incidents, functions of personal failings, or evidence of systemic problems in American society?

In Table 4.5, I outline the basic descriptive statistics for the universe of news conferences. Here, I coded news conference transcripts for any overt mentions (by any news conference speaker) of blacks, African Americans, African or Afro-Caribbean nations, or racism in the United States (I excluded discussions of "minority" rights in a global context because the notion of minority rights in a discussion of foreign policy could also include nonracial

Table 4.5 Racial conversations in presidential news conferences, 1989–2017

Administration	News conferences addressing African or African American issues	News conferences addressing international black issues	News conferences addressing domestic black issues	Total news conferences
George H.W. Bush	43 (31.4%)	26 (19.0%)	21 (15.3%)	137
Bill Clinton	66 (34.2%)	48 (24.9%)	30 (15.5%)	193
George W. Bush	67 (31.9%)	59 (28.1%)	13 (6.2%)	210
Barack Obama	67 (41.1%)	58 (35.6%)	19 (11.7%)	163

Source: Author's compilation, using data from Peters and Woolley (1999–2017).

identities). I found that most news conferences did not include explicit discussions of African or African American issues at all. When they did happen, such discussions were more likely to occur during Barack Obama's presidency. Approximately 41 percent of his news conferences included some discussion of blacks or African diasporic issues. Black or diasporic issues came up in nearly 34 percent of Bill Clinton's news conferences, 32 percent of George W. Bush's news conferences, and in 31 percent of George H.W. Bush's news conferences.

Most of the discussion of racial issues in presidential news conferences in the previous four presidential administrations discussed foreign policy issues concerning Africa, Brazil, or the Afro-Caribbean. This is particularly notable with Presidents Clinton and Obama. Bush was more than four times as likely to discuss black issues in an international context as a domestic context in any given news conference; and President Obama discussed international issues related to the African diaspora in nearly three times as many press conferences as he discussed domestic issues of concern to blacks.

International crises and diplomatic trips helped to contribute to the huge disparities in discussions of international versus national issues that may be of concern to blacks. Presidents often hold news conferences during the course of trips abroad. When presidents visit African or Caribbean countries, they not only hold news conferences but tend to discuss bilateral relations between the United States and the country they happen to be visiting. Presidents Clinton, George W. Bush, and Obama all made high-profile trips to African countries in their terms in office, and they held multiple news conferences with African heads of state over the course of these trips (Presidents George H.W. Bush and Barack Obama also visited the Caribbean). This partially explains the large number of press conferences in which presidents fielded questions about diaspora-related issues. Presidents also tended to field questions about policies toward African and Caribbean nations as a result of natural disasters, political crises, or exogenous political events. For instance, President George H.W. Bush was often asked about the dismantling of apartheid in South Africa because Nelson Mandela was freed from prison during his term in office. The overthrow of President Jean Bertrand Aristide of Haiti and the rise of Mohammed Farrah Aideed in Somalia increased the salience of African and Caribbean issues during the Clinton Administration. President Obama was asked to address the 2010 Haitian earthquake, Al Qaeda affiliated groups in Sub-Saharan Africa, and, more recently, the Ebola crisis in West Africa. For his part, President George W. Bush was often asked to discuss his PEPFAR plan, which provided half a billion dollars in foreign aid to help reduce the rate of HIV infections in Sub-Saharan Africa. In his news conferences, President Obama discussed his aid program called Power Africa. Its goal was to spur economic development by improving access to electricity on the continent (Obama 2015b).

Despite the many similarities in terms of the types of racial discussions presidents have in news conferences, President Obama still stood out from his predecessors. Overall, he fielded questions about black issues in more press conferences than his three immediate predecessors did. While the overall differences are not statistically significant, that he fielded foreign policy questions about Africa or the black Caribbean is statistically notable, especially in comparison with the first President Bush. And though domestic racial issues came up more often in press conferences for the first President Bush and President Clinton, the relatively few George W. Bush news conferences in which these issues were discussed is also statistically notable.

The content of presidential responses to domestic racial issues

I am particularly interested in how presidents responded to instances of domestic racial conflict. As racial issues become salient in the news cycle, journalists often press presidents to take a position on racial issues. The positions that presidents take are enlightening. Do they evade the question? Do they affirm support for civil rights? In their articulation of civil rights challenges, do they frame those challenges in individual or structural terms? A deeper reading of some of these news conference exchanges will help to shed light on these issues.

George H.W. Bush

President George H.W. Bush fielded his first question about a domestic racial question within a week of taking office. In a January 27, 1989 news conference, a reporter asked President Bush about his administration's commitment to affirmative action in response to the Supreme Court's decision in *City of*

Richmond v. *J.A. Croson* (488 U.S. 469 (1989)). In this case, the high court invalidated Richmond, Virginia's minority set-aside program on the grounds that it was not narrowly tailored to meet Richmond's compelling interest to compensate for previous discrimination. Bush was quick to affirm his continued support of affirmative action:

> It didn't kill all set-asides, and it didn't kill off affirmative action. I have been committed to affirmative action. I want to see a reinvigorated Office of Minority Business in Commerce. I want to see our SBA [Small Business Administration] program go forward vigorously. And so, I would say that decision spoke to one set of facts – in Richmond, I believe it was – but I will not read into that a mandate to me to stop trying on equal employment and on affirmative action generally. (Bush 1989a)

Bush would continue to affirm his support for affirmative action in late 1990 when his administration reversed course on a policy change to a federal minority scholarship program. A staff lawyer in the Department of Education quietly dismantled a federal minority scholarship program on the grounds that it would not pass constitutional muster. When President Bush found out about the change, he apparently ordered a reversal of the policy. In a December 18 news conference, he expressed his support for affirmative action and claimed that he had worked out a way to continue minority scholarships.[12] While he was not sure if revisions to the program would shield it from court challenges, he hoped the changes would ensure the survival of the scholarships (Bush 1990a).

Despite Bush's support of affirmative action, he famously vetoed the 1991 extension to the Civil Rights Act on the grounds that the act as passed was a "quota bill." Bush actually went on the offensive in an October 25, 1991 news conference, using his opening statement to defend his veto of the Civil Rights Act and touting his negotiations with Congress to create a more acceptable version of the bill:

> After extraordinary debate and negotiation, we have reached an agreement with Senate Republican and Democratic leaders on a civil rights bill that would be a source of pride for all Americans. It does not resort to quotas, and it strengthens the cause of equality in the workplace. Both the administration and the Congress can present this

12 In a March 3, 1990 news conference, Bush also spoke favorably of the Annenberg family's $50 million donation to the United Negro College Fund. In his comments, Bush noted that he had personally donated to the UNCF, too (Bush 1990b).

legislation to the people of America as a new standard against discrimination and for equal opportunity …

I remember standing out there in the Rose Garden with Attorney General Thornburgh more than a year-and-a-half ago, to make an unshakable commitment to the Nation's civil rights leaders that I wanted a non-quota civil rights bill that I could sign. And assuming there are no changes in the bill as agreed to last night, we now have such a bill. And my promise will be kept, and I will enthusiastically sign this bill. (Bush 1991a)

The issue of quotas also came up when Bush nominated Clarence Thomas to the Supreme Court. Bush defended his nomination against queries from reporters about whether Bush had nominated Thomas because he was black. "I would strongly resent any charge that might be forthcoming on quotas when it relates to appointing the best man to the Court. That's the kind of thing I stand for, not opposed to," he said (Bush 1991b). Earlier, though, he acknowledged that Thomas' background was a plus:

I don't feel there's a quota; I don't feel that I had to nominate a black American at this time for the Court. I expressed my respect for the ground that Mr. Justice [Thurgood] Marshall plowed, but I don't feel there should be a black seat on the Court or an ethnic seat on the Court, if that's what your question is. I would reiterate, I think he's the best man. And if credit accrues to him for coming up through a tough life as a minority in this country, so much the better. So much the better.

I love what he said at the end; it proves he can do it, get the job done. And so, that does nothing but enhance the Court, in my view. But I just really want you to know, we looked at this list with an idea of really finding the best, and I think that's what we did. (Bush 1991b)

Bush's framing of Thomas' qualifications was interesting. In the above quote, Bush touted Thomas' background of being a disadvantaged minority. It is hard to tell whether Bush thought Thomas had been disadvantaged because of his race or because of his race and class (in his introductory remarks, President Bush noted that Thomas had been raised by his grandparents and had worked his way through school) (Bush 1991b).

In other press queries, Bush endorsed individualist and personal responsibility frames to discuss racial issues. On September 18, 1989, a reporter asked President Bush to comment on recent, high-profile incidents of racial violence. Earlier that year, a young banker had been brutally raped and beaten while jogging in Central Park in New York City. At the time, young black and Latino teenagers were arrested in the attack (they have since been exonerated). That summer, a group of whites beat a young black man, Yusef Hawkins, to death in the Bensonhurst section of Brooklyn. The reporter asked if these incidents were part of a larger trend of racial violence in America; Bush demurred and contended that he did not see the need for federal intervention to reduce racial violence: "I don't feel that there's a new trend of racial hostility. But when these regrettable incidents occur, I think that all of us should unite in speaking out against them. But I don't think there's a Federal statute that is going to take care of an incident of that nature" (Bush 1989b).

In 1992, in the wake of the Los Angeles riots, reporters asked President Bush about his assessment of urban policy and the Great Society. Bush responded that he believed that the Great Society programs had failed, and he pushed for more market-based solutions to poverty. When asked specifically about Los Angeles, Bush traced the problems that led to the riots back to the dissolution of the family (he was asked to identify non-structural factors which contributed to the rioting):

> I remember when Tom Bradley, the Mayor of Los Angeles, came to see me before the outbreak there. He joined a lot of other mayors in telling me that the number one concern that the mayors have – all of them had it, Republican, Democrat, liberal, conservative – was the dissolution and the decline of the American family. We've got to find ways to help strengthen the family. One of them is through the education program; one of them through neighborhood activities; one of them is through the kind of private sector involvement that we've been talking about through our Points of Light and that Peter Ueberroth is now trying to bring to bear on the solution to the problem.
>
> So that's the approach we'll be taking. But I'm very anxious to hear, before I make final decisions, from the local people as to what they think. One of the things that I mentioned in my speech to the Nation was the concern I felt and the concern that Mayor Bradley felt about the attacks on the Korean community. These people were peaceful people, and they were all assaulted. We've got to do something about it. I don't have an easy answer to it, but you put your finger on something that I think we have to find answer to. And somehow in the field of strengthening the family and in the field of ownership and in the field of the dignity that comes with having a piece of the action lies the answer. (Bush 1992)

Bill Clinton

The first time Bill Clinton had to respond to a domestic racial question that he could not elide was in May 1993, when he had to confront criticism that his nominee for Assistant Attorney General, Webb Hubbell, had been a member of an all-white country club (Clinton 1993a). In June 1993, Clinton touted his efforts to be responsive to members of the Congressional Black Caucus (CBC), who had expressed concerns that budget cuts would hurt the poor and blacks:

> I have set out principles: $500 billion in deficit reduction; a deficit reduction trust fund for all the tax increases and spending cuts, at least $250 billion in spending cuts, although I would like some more cuts and some less taxes. Seventy-five percent of the burden has to fall on upper income people, and we ought to keep the incentives for growth and for empowerment of the working poor and the incentives to move people from welfare to work.
>
> Those are the things that I want to see in the final bill. And what I have assured the Black Caucus—and let me say, I have talked to, oh, probably 15 of the members in the last week or so just in that caucus and many other Members of the House—is that the principles that I outlined are still there and that we'll do our best to articulate those as the Senate deals with this bill.
>
> But the real test will be what happens in the conference and what the final bill looks like that the House and the Senate will vote on. And again, I'm quite encouraged that we'll get a bill out that they'll feel good about. They made it clear to me what they felt most strongly about. And the two things above all were the earned-income tax credit for the working poor, which is an important part of our welfare reform incentive, and the empowerment zones for the depressed urban and rural areas. (Clinton 1993b)

Clinton's relationship with the CBC figured prominently in other discussions. Reporters' questions evinced a belief that the CBC held clout and attempted to hold Clinton accountable on issues of concern to African Americans. Press questions also showed CBC activity and advocacy on international and domestic issues. Take, for instance, the following exchange with a reporter:

> Question: "Mr. President, many African-American leaders have expressed their anger or extreme disappointment with the way you handled the Lani Guinier nomination and with the way you handled the Haiti situation. In addition, the Congressional Black Caucus has said it is very angry with the fact that they voted for your budget package and cast some very politically difficult votes, only to have you negotiate a watered-down package in the Senate. How would you assess your relationship right now with blacks? And what are you doing to mend fences

with the Congressional Black Caucus so that they will not vote against the conference report on the budget package?"

The President: "Well, first of all, I did not negotiate that bill that the Senate passed. That is just inaccurate. I did not do that. And I think you know what I liked about the House bill, and you know where I have been on the issues, and you know what the principles are I've enunciated ...

Secondly, and quite to the contrary when members of the Black Caucus came to see me and asked me to pursue sanctions in the United Nations against Haiti that included oil, I examined it, and I agreed to do it. They were the first people who asked me to do it. And very shortly after the meeting I agreed to go forward. But they know, the ones who follow the Haitian developments, that even before that I offered to have the United States participate in a multinational peacekeeping force to restore democracy and to restore President Aristide, and that he rejected that. They know that's a fact.

Thirdly, I don't think my commitment to civil rights is very much open to question. And I think my actions as President and the appointments I've made and the things I've stood for document that. And I believe that over the long run the Black Caucus and the Clinton administration will continue to be very close. And I've talked to any number of them personally, recently." (Clinton 1993c)

It is interesting to note that Clinton did not defend his former nominee, Lani Guinier, who was decried as a "quota queen" in the press before she withdrew her nomination to be Assistant Attorney General for Civil Rights (see Levine 1993).

Clinton also had the opportunity to respond to salient racial issues in the news. When allegations emerged that campaign officials for Governor Christine Todd Whitman in New Jersey allegedly paid black ministers not to encourage their parishioners to vote, Clinton condemned the activity (Clinton 1993d).

Like President Bush, President Clinton was asked to diagnose the source of social inequality in the United States. The query directed toward President Clinton was framed in light of the publication of Charles Murray and Richard Herrnstein's controversial book, *The Bell Curve*:

Question: "Mr. President, notwithstanding the problems all around the world, there are pernicious social problems here in the United States. And many of these problems, in many views, are breaking down along racial lines. Indeed, some people say that the progress of the sixties has been upset and overturned, that the great divide between black and white is worsening, widening. And lately, there is a new book out that suggests that these problems, these conflicts may be inherent, and we may be doomed to them. What do you think about race as it applies to the social problems? And what can you do, what can a government do to try and fix some of it?"

The President: "Well, if you're asking me first of all about Mr. Murray's book, I haven't read it. But as I understand the argument of it, I have to say I disagree with the proposition that there are inherent, racially based differences in the capacity of the American people to reach their full potential. I just don't agree with that. It goes against our entire history and our whole tradition.

I also think if you—let's just take the social problems. And I guess— I don't want to overly digress; I know a lot of you have a lot of questions, but this is a huge deal. I don't know if you saw the piece in the *Wall Street Journal* not very long ago where black Americans and white Americans were polled about the social problems generally, crime, family breakdown, drugs, gangs, violence, welfare dependency, the aggregate of them, overwhelming majorities agreed that these were the great problems of our country. And they've been developing for 30 years now. Then, overwhelming majorities agreed that we needed to reform the welfare system to move people from welfare to work. The great divergence came when one group said that this was caused because of the loss of economic opportunity, and the Government had a responsibility to rebuild it. And the other group said, no, this is caused by an escalating amount of personal misconduct, and people needed to change their personal behavior. In other words, the Government can't do anything about it.

I would like to make the following points: I think both groups are right and both groups are wrong, number one. Number two, there's not as much racial difference here as you think there is. And let me try to illustrate it by starting at the second point.

The out-of-wedlock birth rate in the aggregate in the United States is today about 30 percent. It is higher for African-American young women—that is, a birth where there was never a marriage—than it is for white young women, but it is rising faster among whites than among blacks, markedly faster. And it seems to be far more tied to poverty and lack of education and lack of being connected to the future than to race. Number two, it is plain that we are dealing with both the loss of economic opportunity and a changed set of social mores, a changed sense of what is right and wrong, what is acceptable and unacceptable. And I believe we need to change both.

What can the Government do about it? What can the President do about it? First, we can try to bring this economy back. In 1994, we've had more high-wage jobs created in our economy than in the previous 5 years combined. This is the first year when over half of the jobs coming into our economy are above average wages. Number two, as all of you know, I have signed laws to create community development banks and empowerment zones in our inner cities to try to get investment back there, to give hope to people who have been left behind, to try to do the economic mission. But having said that, to try to rebuild a society that has been pressured both in our inner cities and our isolated rural areas for a generation now—we're talking about 30 years of serious pressure—is going to take a concerted effort that starts with parents and churches and community groups and private business people and people at the local level. The Federal Government cannot be the salvation of that. We have to rebuild the bonds of society.

And everybody has a role to play. That's why—I want to compliment— Deputy Secretary Kunin is here, Governor Kunin from the Department of Education. We signed the Elementary and Secondary Education Act today; we're kicking off the college loan program—yesterday—we're kicking off the college loan program today. One of the things in that act that Secretary Riley fought so hard for was the so-called character education provision, so that the schools can explicitly work with their communities and agree about what values need to be transferred to children through the schools and promote them.

This is a very serious and complicated issue. I think it is a quick fix to try to break it down by race. I believe that the evidence is clear that what we ought to be working on is a way for every kid in this country to live up to the fullest of their potential. And that potential is quite extraordinary, and they will do quite well without regard to race if we can attack these problems." (Clinton 1994)

There are notable similarities between George H.W. Bush and Bill Clinton's responses to the sources of social problems. Clinton repudiated the claims of biological inferiority that many people believe Murray and Herrnstein were proffering in their book. He also articulated an understanding of both structural and cultural explanations for persistent inequality, opting to take a both/ and approach to understanding and addressing the issue. Clinton invoked the common tropes about personal responsibility being necessary to reduce inequality (including sexual propriety) and also included neoliberal structural remedies such as public-private partnerships, tax benefits, and new banking opportunities.

And like President Bush, President Clinton fielded questions about affirmative action. In October 1994, Clinton was asked to weigh in on a Piscataway, New Jersey court case in which a white teacher alleged reverse discrimination when she lost a job opportunity to an equally qualified black candidate. Clinton defended affirmative action here because both teachers were deemed equally qualified and because there was a need for additional diversity in Piscataway, which had a large minority school population (Clinton 1994). By March 1995, however, Clinton was touting his efforts to "mend but not end" affirmative action:

> Question: "Thank you, sir. I'd like to ask you a question, if I might, about affirmative action. I know your administration is now reviewing all of those affirmative action regulations, but there's some concern that this might be the prelude to a backing off of those policies. In fact, Jesse Jackson earlier this week expressed the opinion that maybe if you did, he might even run against you. But my question, really, on that issue is, what about the many Americans who really feel they have been punished by affirmative action? And I'd like to get your comments on that."
>
> The President: "Let me tell you about the review I've ordered and comment on the affirmative action thing. First of all, our administration is against quotas and guaranteed results, and I have been throughout my public career. I have always been for trying to help people develop their capacities so they could fully participate. And I have supported things—when I was a Governor, I supported, for example, minority scholarship programs—in my public life, I have done that.
>
> I want to make a couple of comments here. First, I have asked for a review of all the Federal Government's so-called affirmative action programs because I think it's important that we analyze, number one, what they do and what— a lot of times people mean different things when they use affirmative action. For example, I take it there is virtually no opposition to the affirmative action programs that are the most successful in our country, which are the ones adopted by the United States military, which have not resulted in people of inferior quality or ability getting preferential treatment but have resulted in an intense effort to develop the capacities of everybody who joins the military so they can fully participate and contribute as much as possible and has resulted in the most integrated institution in our society.

So I want to know what these programs are, exactly. I want to know whether they are working. I want to know whether there is some other way we can reach any objective without giving a preference by race or gender in some of these programs. Those are the three questions we need to ask.

And let me make a general observation. I asked myself when this debate started, what have we done since I've been President that has most helped minorities? And I think that— I would say that the things we have done that have most helped are things that have benefited all people who needed them: expanding the Head Start program; expanding the college loan program; expanding the earned-income tax credit, the working families tax credit which has given an average tax cut of $1,000 to families with incomes under $25,000; the empowerment zones—and one of them, one of the empowerment zones went to an all-white area in Kentucky, but the disproportionate impact was on people who'd been left behind in our cities; and one thing that the rescission package would take away, the community development banks— which I think would be a terrible mistake— which is designed to empower people through the free enterprise system to make the most of their own lives ...

Meanwhile, I urge all of you to read the history—in light of the other, the political comments you made—to read the history of how these affirmative action programs got started and who was on what side when they began. It's very interesting to go back through the last 25 years and see all the twists and turns.

The American people want an end to discrimination. They want discrimination, where it exists, to be punished. They don't want people to have an unfair break that is unwarranted. We can work this out, and I'm determined to do it" (Clinton 1995).

President Clinton was also forced to respond to unfortunate incidents of racial violence in the news. In March 2000, Clinton responded to queries of his administration's handling of police shooting incidents, particularly the case of Amadou Diallo, an unarmed African immigrant who was shot at 41 times by New York City Police in 1999 (for context, the police officers involved in Diallo's shooting had been recently acquitted at the time of this exchange (see Fritsch 2000)):

Question: "Mr. President, three unarmed black men have been shot and killed by police in New York City in the past 13 months. Do you believe that the New York Police Department has a racial problem, and does that department require Justice Department oversight?"

The President: "Well, I believe there is a Justice Department review of the practices in the department, which I think has been a matter of public record for some time. And in the Diallo case, there was a specific reference to a review of the action there for possible civil rights violations. I think the important thing I'd like to say is, first of all, there's a lot of evidence that in city after city where the crime rate has dropped—and the crime rate's gone down a lot in New York; it's gone down a lot in every major city in America—there is now ample evidence that the crime rate can go down, and the tenor of community police relations can go up. And it's largely a matter of the right sort of training, the right sort of policies, and consistent effort there.

On the specific cases, I think I should say no more, particularly in view of the latest incident, which was tragic. There is a good U.S. Attorney in New York, and I have confidence that whatever decision is appropriate will be made as all the facts come out, and that's what's being done here.

But I think that the focus ought to be everywhere on having the right kind of training and the right kind of policy direction to say that we're going to bring the crime rate down, and we're going to bring the quality of police community relations up. The two things are not inconsistent. In fact, I think, generally they reinforce one another, and I think that that's what we all ought to be working for in New York and everywhere else in the country" (Clinton 2000)

Clinton's response to the question was vague, as was his discussion of systemic practices which may have led to Diallo's death (admittedly, the ongoing DOJ investigation may have contributed to Clinton's reticence). Clinton basically affirmed the idea of community policing and suggested that better training of police and better community relations would help address the situation. He avoided an explicit discussion of the role that bias may have played in the police shootings.

George W. Bush

Shortly after his second inauguration, journalist April Ryan of American Urban Radio Networks asked President George W. Bush to articulate his approach to civil rights. He endorsed a market-driven, rising-tide-lifts-all-boats, somewhat vague approach to achieving civil rights:

Civil rights is a good education. Civil rights is opportunity. Civil rights is homeownership. Civil rights is owning your own business. Civil rights is making sure all aspects of our society are open for everybody. And we discussed that yesterday. And I believe that what I said was important, that we've got to shed ourselves of bigotry if we expect to lead by example. And I'll do the very best I can as the President to make sure that the promise—and I believe in the promise of America—is available for everybody. (Bush 2005a)

Ryan continued to press President Bush about his market-driven approach to reducing racial inequality, especially in the wake of Hurricane Katrina. In October 2005, she had the following exchange with President Bush:

Question: "Thank you, Mr. President. Mr. President, the Bible speaks of good will towards 'the least of these.' With that, how are you going to bridge the divide of poverty and race in this country beyond economics and homeownership, that after Hurricane Katrina and also the Bill Bennett statements? And also, how can the Republican Party gain the black vote—more of the black vote in 2008, after these public relations fiascos?"

The President: "Well, first of all, I happen to believe that economics has a lot to do with bridging divides. You mentioned poverty, and there is a divide in our country when it comes to wealth. And one way to bridge that divide is to encourage economic growth, vitality, jobs that pay well, and small business. You can't divorce bridging divides, April, from economic vitality; you just can't. It's a part of how we enable people to realize dreams—by having a growing economy.

Secondly, I don't think you can divorce bridging divides from ownership. In other words, I think it's essential that people own something if they're going to have a stake in the future of the country. I think part of the divide occurs because some people own a home and others don't. I think there's something so powerfully healing about a society in which more and more people have ownership.

Thirdly, education is a vital part of bridging divides. As you know, I came to Washington intent upon challenging a system which, in my view, too often gave up on children; that said, 'Let's don't measure, and let's just move them through.' It's a system that let a lot of families down, but more importantly, let a lot of children down. I think education is one of the keys to addressing the issue of divides in our country. So the No Child Left Behind Act, which challenges what I've called the soft bigotry of low expectations, is beginning to make good results. You know why? Because we measure.

I think it's important for us to continue to allow faith-based programs to interface with people to help them have hope. One of the most important initiatives I laid out was the mentoring program for children whose parents may be in prison.

And so you address the racial divide in a variety of ways. And, obviously, the tone matters, from leadership. It matters what leaders say. It matters that somebody, first of all, understands there's a problem and is willing to talk about it. And I will continue to do so as the President."

Question: "What about 2008 and the Republican Party?"

The President: "2008? My head is not there yet. I'm right here in 2005."

Question: "The Republican Party is trying to gain more of the black vote——"

The President: "Just got to keep asking for the vote. First of all, the Republican Party should never take a vote for granted, and neither should the Democrat Party. And therefore, that means you've got to go out and work hard for the vote and talk about what you believe. And I try to do so, with not a lot of success, although I improved. But I was disappointed, frankly, in the vote I got in the African American community; I was. I've done my best to elevate people to positions of authority and responsibility—not just positions, but positions where they can actually make a difference in the lives of people. I put people in my Cabinet; I put people in my sub-Cabinet. I've elevated people from all walks of life, because I believe there's a responsibility for the President to reach out. And so it's not a matter of tone; it's also a matter of action—and just got to keep working at it, April" (Bush 2005b)

The exchange is enlightening for many reasons. Bush was clearly comfortable talking about his PR efforts among black voters. Tasha Philpot (2007) has shown that Bush's efforts to be more descriptively inclusive and to mobilize black voters may have contributed to a higher black Republican vote share in 2004. Beyond that, though, it is not clear that Bush could articulate a strong civil rights plan. He talked about promoting ownership among blacks, touted the No Child Left Behind Act as a means to reduce the achievement gap, and extolled the efforts of his faith-based initiative to reach out to black communities. His overall discussion of systemic racism is cursory and shallow, though. And he did not discuss Katrina, though he was asked to do so.

In addition to Hurricane Katrina, President Bush also had to address the exogenous shock of the Jena Six. In 2007, six black teenagers nearly beat a white classmate to death at a high school in Jena, Louisiana that had experienced a series of racial incidents. Civil rights advocates came to the defense of the black teenagers, arguing that the teenagers faced steeper penalties for their behavior on account of race. When asked for his interpretation of the events, President Bush offered that he sympathized with the charged emotions that the situation had engendered and that the Justice Department was monitoring the situation (Bush 2007).

Barack Obama

President Obama fielded his first personal race question on March 24, 2009. In that question, he was asked whether he felt that he was being judged unfairly on account of his race (Obama 2009a). Indeed, one of the distinctions between Barack Obama and his predecessors was that he was asked more than a dozen times to personally reflect on his racial experiences, and even the racial experiences of relatives.[13]

In April 2009, when Andre Showell of BET asked him the now famous question about targeting certain economic policies toward minority communities who had been disproportionately affected by the Great Recession, Obama adopted a rising-tide-lifts-all-boats posture:

Well, keep in mind that every step we're taking is designed to help all people. But folks who are most vulnerable are most likely to be helped because they need the most help. So when we passed the Recovery Act, for example, and we put in place provisions that would extend unemployment insurance or allow you to keep your health insurance, even if you've lost your job, that probably disproportionately impacted those communities that had lost their jobs.

And unfortunately, the African American community and Latino community are probably overrepresented in those ranks. When we put in place additional dollars for community health centers to ensure that people are still getting the help that they need, or we expand health insurance to millions more children through the Children's Health Insurance Program, again, those probably disproportionately impact African American and Latino families simply because they're the ones who are most vulnerable. They've got higher rates of uninsured in their communities.

13 Other presidents did receive personal race questions, but by my estimation, they were neither as frequent nor as personal as the questions President Obama received. President Obama was asked to contextualize his Africa policy as a person of African descent and to reflect on his sister's racial experiences in Germany, among other questions. In contrast, the other presidents received questions about their personal reactions to seeing the aftermath of ethnic cleansing in Rwanda (Clinton) or their their thoughts on the movie *Driving Miss Daisy* (G.H.W. Bush). George W. Bush was asked to reflect on the significance of Barack Obama's election.

So my general approach is that if the economy is strong, that will lift all boats, as long as it is also supported by, for example, strategies around college affordability and job training, tax cuts for working families as opposed to the wealthiest that level the playing field and ensure bottom-up economic growth. And I'm confident that that will help the African American community live out the American Dream at the same time that it's helping communities all across the country. Okay? (Obama 2009b)

In June 2009, after the Council of Economic Advisors Chair indicated that targeted programs might be necessary to address high rates of black unemployment, President Obama reaffirmed his commitment to a transcendent approach to economic recovery. To that end, Obama's comments endorsed attacking systemic differences with the proposal of public–private partnerships:

Well, look, the – first of all, we know that when – the African American unemployment rate, the Latino unemployment rate, are consistently higher than the national average. And so if the economy as a whole is doing poorly, then you know that the African American community is going to be doing poorly, and they're going to be hit even harder. And the best thing that I can do for the African American community or the Latino community or the Asian community, whatever community, is to get the economy as a whole moving. If I don't – hold on one second; let me answer the question – if I don't do that, then I'm not going to be able to help anybody. So that's priority number one.

It is true that in certain inner-city communities, the unemployment rate is – was already sky high even before this recession. The ladders available for people to enter into the job market are even worse. And so we are interested in looking at proven programs that help people on a pathway to jobs.

There was a reason why right before Father's Day I went to a program here locally in Washington called Year Up, which has a proven track record of taking young, mostly minority people, some of whom have graduated from high school, some maybe who've just gotten their GED, and trained them on computers and provide them other technical skills, but also train them on how to carry themselves in an office, how to write an e-mail – some of the social skills that will allow them to be more employable. They've got a terrific placement rate after this 1-year program. If there are ways that we can potentially duplicate some of those programs, then we're going to do so.

So part of what we want to do is to find tools that will give people more opportunity. But the most important thing I can do is to lift the economy overall, and that's what my strategy is focused on. (Obama 2009b)

When asked again about targeted programs in December 2009, Obama offered education reform as a targeted approach to address entrenched economic inequality along racial lines (Obama 2009c).

President Obama responded to his share of exogenous racial shocks over the course of his presidency. He had his first opportunity in July 2009, when he famously criticized the Cambridge, Massachusetts Police Department for arresting his friend Henry Louis Gates in what appeared to be a case of racial profiling (Obama 2009d). While on a trip to Malaysia in April 2014, a reporter asked President Obama to comment on the inflammatory racial comments made by former Los Angeles Clippers owner Donald Sterling. Obama explained the situation to his Malaysian audience and then criticized Sterling. President Obama also affirmed his administration's support of black farmers who had won judicial relief and a financial settlement against systematic discrimination in agricultural support in the *Pigford* cases (Obama 2014a).[14]

Ferguson does not come up as a topic of discussion in a presidential news conference (not a daily press briefing) until December 19, 2014, after a St. Louis County, Missouri grand jury refused to indict Darren Wilson in the death of Michael Brown. President Obama's response was prompted by a question from April Ryan of American Urban Radio Networks, who asked the status of racial inequality. Obama touted his administration's successes in increasing high school graduation and college enrollment rates across racial groups. Yet he acknowledged the places of persistent inequality, like the wealth gap. In the wake of the deaths of Michael Brown and Eric Garner, who was killed by police in Staten Island, New York, he also talked about the systemic problems in the relationship between black communities and the police. He touted his creation of a policing task force, promised to implement as many of their recommendations as he could, and called upon state and local authorities to do their part to address the issues related to policing that were under their purview (Obama 2014b).

In a previously scheduled joint press conference with Japanese Prime Minister Shinzo Abe, President Obama addressed the unrest in Baltimore shortly after protests against the death of Freddie Gray turned violent. This press conference garnered national attention because, to the chagrin of some,

14 These are three appellate cases, from the DC Circuit Court of Appeals: *Pigford v. Glickman* (206 F.3d 1212 (2000)), *Pigford v. Veneman* (355 F.Supp.2d.148 (2005)), and *In re Black Farmers Discrimination Litigation* (also known as *Pigford* II) (856 F.Supp.2d 82 (2013)).

President Obama referred to rioters as "criminals and thugs" (Obama 2015a). The CBC took issue with such a characterization, but President Obama would not apologize for his choice of words (Jackson 2015; Lillis 2015).

What is overlooked in the brouhaha over President Obama calling a group of young black men thugs was his diagnosis of the problems which led to Baltimore. His exegesis fit Price's (2016) pattern of Obama trying to play all sides—incorporating personal responsibility, identifying a root of systemic racism, and exhorting Americans to self-examination and reconciliation:

> What I'd say is, this has been a slow-rolling crisis. This has been going on for a long time. This is not new, and we shouldn't pretend that it's new.
>
> The good news is, is that perhaps there's some newfound awareness because of social media and video cameras and so forth that there are problems and challenges when it comes to how policing and our laws are applied in certain communities, and we have to pay attention to it and respond …
>
> Now, the challenge for us, as the Federal Government is, is that we don't run these police forces. I can't federalize every police force in the country and force them to retrain. But what I can do is to start working with them collaboratively so that they can begin this process of change themselves …
>
> I think it's going to be important for organizations like the Fraternal Order of Police and other police unions and organizations to acknowledge that this is not good for police. We have to own up to the fact that occasionally there are going to be problems here, just as there are in every other occupation. There are some bad politicians who are corrupt. There are folks in the business community or on Wall Street who don't do the right thing. Well, there's some police who aren't doing the right thing. And rather than close ranks, what we've seen is a number of thoughtful police chiefs and commissioners and others recognize, they [sic] got to get their arms around this thing and work together with the community to solve the problem. And we're committed to facilitating that process …
>
> We can't just leave this to the police. I think there are police departments that have to do some soul searching. I think there are some communities that have to do some soul searching. But I think we, as a country, have to do some soul searching. This is not new. It's been going on for decades.
>
> And without making any excuses for criminal activities that take place in these communities, what we also know is that if you have impoverished communities that have been stripped away of opportunity, where children are born into abject poverty; they've got parents—often

because of substance abuse problems or incarceration or lack of education themselves—can't do right by their kids; if it's more likely that those kids end up in jail or dead than that they go to college; in communities where there are no fathers who can provide guidance to young men; communities that—where there's no investment, and manufacturing has been stripped away, and drugs have flooded the community, and the drug industry ends up being the primary employer for a whole lot of folks—in those environments, if we think that we're just going to send the police to do the dirty work of containing the problems that arise there without, as a nation and as a society, saying, "What can we do to change those communities, to help lift up those communities and give those kids opportunity?" then we're not going to solve this problem. And we'll go through the same cycles of periodic conflicts between the police and communities and the occasional riots in the streets, and everybody will feign concern until it goes away, and then we go about our business as usual.

If we are serious about solving this problem, then we're going to not only have to help the police, we're going to have to think about what can we do—the rest of us—to make sure that we're providing early education to these kids; to make sure that we're reforming our criminal justice system so it's not just a pipeline from schools to prisons; so that we're not rendering men in these communities unemployable because of a felony record for a nonviolent drug offense; that we're making investments so that they can get the training they need to find jobs. That's hard. That requires more than just the occasional news report or task force. And there's a bunch of my agenda that would make a difference right now in that.

Now, I'm under no illusion that out of this Congress we're going to get massive investments in urban communities, and so we'll try to find areas where we can make a difference around school reform and around job training and around some investments in infrastructure in these communities and trying to attract new businesses in.

But if we really want to solve the problem, if our society really wanted to solve the problem, we could. It's just, it would require everybody saying this is important, this is significant, and that we don't just pay attention to these communities when a CVS burns and we don't just pay attention when a young man gets shot or has his spine snapped. We're paying attention all the time because we consider those kids our kids and we think they're important and they shouldn't be living in poverty and violence. (Obama 2015a)

It is important to note here that Obama's "everyone is to blame" frame is technically inclusive. Yes, he invoked personal responsibility rhetoric and the culture of poverty thesis, against which some critics will surely balk. However, he was equally critical of police and police cultures which tend to obstruct reform. He also made a clear articulation of the structural issues which beset poor communities, making them more susceptible to police surveillance and violence.

The other thing that was interesting in Obama's comments was his invocation of federalism. He made it clear that there were limits to his executive power. If police departments were to be truly transformed, Obama contended that they would have to change at the grassroots. He pledged that the Executive Branch would do what it could to play a supporting role (he made no promises for Congress), but he argued that the heavy lifting would have to involve the active participation of state and local government, too.

Another interesting observation in President Obama's press conference responses was his invocation of the American racial experience in international contexts. For instance, in a June 30, 2015 news conference with then Brazilian President Dilma Rousseff, Obama noted the United States and Brazil's shared history of having been slave societies (Obama 2015b). In framing American opposition to ISIS, Obama contrasts the caliphate's parochialism with America's (and Western society's) diversity. While the transcripts clearly connoted religious pluralism, they also sometimes mentioned racial diversity as well (see Obama 2015c; 2015d). He cited the American experience with racial segregation and other forms of discrimination as a cautionary tale to separatist movements [like Brexit] in a post-election press conference in November 2016 (Obama 2016a). And in a July 25, 2015 news conference with Kenyan President Uhuru Kenyatta, Obama invoked the black civil rights struggle to urge Kenya to liberalize its policies toward the LGBT community:

> And as an African American in the United States, I am painfully aware of the history of what happens when people are treated differently, under the law, and there's—were all sorts of rationalizations that were provided by the power structure for decades in the United States for segregation and Jim Crow and slavery, and they were wrong.
>
> So I'm unequivocal on this. If somebody is a law-abiding citizen who is going about their business and working in a job and obeying the traffic signs—[*laughter*]—and doing all the other things that good citizens are supposed to do and not harming anybody, the idea that they are going to be treated differently or abused because of who they love is wrong. Full stop. (Obama 2015e)

Obama also invoked diversity as a counterweight to xenophobia when discussing trade policy with Canada and Mexico:

And so working together to find effective ways, not to close off borders, not to pretend that somehow we can shut off trade, not to forget that we are, ourselves, a nation—nations of immigrants and that diversity is our strength, but rather to say, yes, the world is big, and we are going to help shape it, and we're going to value our openness and our diversity, and the fact that we are leaders in a global supply chain, but we're going to do so in ways that make sure everybody benefits—that's important work that we're going to have to do together. And I know Justin [Trudeau] shares that commitment just as I do. (Obama 2016b)

At the same press conference, he described free trade as a boon to American minority-owned businesses (Obama 2016b).

A word on news conference questions

The previous analyses, while helpful, only present preliminary, cursory snapshots of the ways presidents engage African American issues in news conferences. The keyword searches could have inadvertently overlooked racialized discussions that did not include the aforementioned keywords. To mitigate against that type of omission—and against unintended coding error in Table 4.5—I conduct a more comprehensive analysis of news conference questions across all four administrations. This not only allows a deeper dive into the data, but it also serves as a robustness check for the previous analyses.

In this part of the analysis, I focus on the questions journalists ask the president about racialized issues. While presidents, like anyone in an interview situation, can try to steer a conversation toward their preferred talking points, the reality is that most presidents probably will not talk about an issue unless they are prompted to do so by a question. These questions are important for a variety of reasons. As a first draft of history, journalist queries document the salience of issues in any given period of time. In addition, questions can be used as a barometer of the soundness of proposed policies. As former Clinton Press Secretary Mike McCurry explained, press briefings are useful because "good, tough questions can help expose some of the flaws in the policy. If the policy is not sharp and clear, the questions in the briefing room make that abundantly clear very quickly" (McCurry, quoted in Ryan 2016, 75).

While presidential news conferences are slightly different from the regular press briefings run by press secretaries, such question-and-answer events can be an important site to interrogate a president's racial policies—if reporters are actually asking the questions. Thus, it becomes necessary to consider the extent to which presidents were queried about African American issues. We need to consider the possibility that some presidents (like President Obama) may have been asked to comment on racial issues more than other presidents. To that end, a research assistant and I compiled a dataset of every news conference question asked during the first Bush through the Obama Administrations, using the database of news conference transcripts archived on the UCSB Presidency Project website (Peters and Woolley 1999–2017). The research assistant compiled an original dataset of questions from the Clinton, G.W. Bush and Obama Administrations. While the intercoder sample check showed an acceptable rate of agreement, I continued to refine the coding after the fact and added questions from George H.W. Bush's term in office.

This dataset provides more detail than the coding in Table 4.5, which omits any discussion that did not include the word stems, "Africa-," "black," "racis-," "civil right," or "Caribbean." The dataset includes all questions clearly directed to the president or answered by the president. It omits questions that were answered by other people (foreign heads of state, and in a few rare instances, American political nominees and appointees). By focusing on questions that were specifically directed to the president or that the president chose to answer, this eliminates potential racial discussions that were initiated by other heads of state. I define African American interest questions as questions that specifically addressed issues related to Africa, Brazil, or the Afro-Caribbean, civil rights, explicit racial incidents, and racially coded policies like welfare, Great Society programs, Hurricane Katrina, domestic drug policy (particularly in the 1990s), and urban policy. In total, this dataset includes over 8,500 questions.[15]

The coding results are listed in Table 4.6. In general, reporters asked presidents very few questions about black issues. Over the course of the four administrations examined here, Bill Clinton received the greatest proportion of questions (196, or about 9 percent of the total number of questions he

---

15 The unit of analysis here is the question as it is posed. If a reporter combined multiple questions into one query, it counted as one question. The transcripts note that sometimes presidents cut journalists off before they are able to ask their full question. If they follow up with the remainder of their question, I count it as part of the original question. If a reporter asked a follow-up question or probed to get a president to answer a question he just avoided, I counted it as a new question. Compound questions were less prevalent in the first Bush Administration. This partially explains why there are more questions from his administration than from subsequent administrations, He also held more news conferences.

   While I have tried to be systematic in defining questions, these delineations are judgment calls, and other coders might define questions a little differently. This dataset is available upon request, and I encourage replication.

Table 4.6 African American interest questions in presidential news conferences, 1989–2017

Administration	News conference questions to the president about African or African American issues	Total questions
George H.W. Bush	206 (6.3%)	3,281
Bill Clinton	196 (8.8%)	2,220
George W. Bush	73 (4.0%)	1,839
Barack Obama	65 (5.5%)	1,179

Source: Author's compilation, using data from Peters and Woolley (1999–2017).

received). George H.W. Bush received the greatest number (206, or 6.3 percent) of black interest questions overall (he also fielded the greatest number of questions). Proportionally, reporters asked George W. Bush the fewest questions about black issues (73, or 4 percent) Barack Obama received 65 questions about black issues, which constituted 5.5 percent of the total number of questions he received over the course of his presidency.

The press conference transcripts sometimes list the identity and affiliation of the reporter asking the question. Reporters are identified in 180 of the 540 questions which I coded as being of interest to African Americans.[16] Of these 180 questions, 55 of them were asked by black reporters.[17] By herself, April Ryan of the American Urban Radio Networks, who is arguably the most senior black reporter in the White House Press Corps today, can be identified as having asked 34 questions. To be sure, nonblack reporters do ask racial questions, and black reporters ask questions that are not race-related. However, the fact that a nontrivial portion of all of the questions related to African American issues that were asked in a 28-year period at the White House could be attributed to one black reporter demonstrates the importance of descriptive representation among journalists, too. One of the things Ryan points out in her memoir is that while she is not the only black journalist who has regular access to the White House briefing room, African America media organizations are scarcely represented. Her news organization has consistently had a White House correspondent for 40 years, but other black news organizations have not had the same presence (Ryan 2015, 61–62). As we consider presidents' responsiveness to issues of race, we must consider the extent to which presidents are asked to account for their handling of racial

---

16 I link reporters to questions based on transcripts. Sometimes, presidents call on reporters by name. Other times, presidents use the reporter's name in their response. If there is a follow-up question, I assume that the original reporter asked the follow-up question, too, unless the transcript suggests that reporters were talking over each other or speaking out of turn. At times, these were subjective calls; I acknowledge that other coders may make different decisions.

17 I determined the race of reporters by looking at their online profiles.

issues as much as we consider the extent to which they take the initiative to speak out on racial issues. And we also have to consider the ways that the descriptive diversity of those called to hold the president accountable (and the news organizations they represent) may correlate with their inclination to ask tough questions about racial inequalities.

General observations

A comparison of presidential rhetoric and the framing of responses to questions about racial issues reveals some similarities and differences between the presidents. All four recent former presidents provided unsatisfactory answers about the balance of systemic and individualized explanations for persistent inequality. Presidents Clinton and Obama talked about systemic approaches more, but they still placed considerable emphasis on either personal responsibility or in avoiding targeted remedies to address entrenched racial inequalities.

The biggest distinction between President Obama and his predecessors is personal. Reporters asked him to reflect on his personal racial experiences when his predecessors were not subjected to such questioning. This distinction is understandable given the historic nature of Barack Obama's presidency, but asking such personal questions amplifies the symbolic importance of the first black president, not the substantive importance. This finding is not dissimilar from Price's (2016) assertion that Obama derived authority from his personal narrative. One of the interesting things to think about here is the extent to which Obama assumed this authority and initiated the personal narrative and the extent to which others (in this case, reporters) projected that authority onto him by asking him to contextualize political strategy and/or policy proposals with his personal experiences.

Conclusion

When Barack Obama was running for president, the *New York Times* ran a human interest story on Obama, the University of Chicago Law School professor. The article describes Obama as charismatic yet enigmatic. His colleagues complained that he did not socialize or engage intellectually with them; and former students observed that he was so good at arguing both sides of an argument that they never knew exactly what he thought (Kantor 2008).

After winning election, Obama was sometimes dubbed "the professor-in-chief." It was not always meant as a compliment. Freddy Gray of Britain's *Spectator* perhaps described the moniker best as, "He's too academic, too nuanced; too eager to understand both sides to be an effective leader" (Gray 2012).

It is arguable that Obama's intellectual nuance dovetails nicely with his commitment to racial transcendence. As the data in this chapter shows, Obama maintained a rhetorical commitment to transcendence throughout his term in office. In keeping with Gillion's (2016) findings, he did not talk about race much during State of the Union Addresses. And when we look at his responses to questions about racial issues—even the heart-wrenching issues about police brutality that emerged toward the end of his tenure—I find that Obama remained nuanced to the end.

To be sure, that Obama spoke out forcefully about racial issues is evidence of their salience. Even a deracialized politician like him had to confront those issues. While there might be many people who agree with his approach to these questions, there will be critics who will use Obama's responses as evidence of his inability to take a strong side. What perhaps is most interesting, though, is Obama's invocation of federalism in responding to questions about police shootings. It is as though he was priming his audience to temper their expectations.

The big question that emerges from these findings is whether these types of responses were satisfactory to rank-and-file black voters. Sure, they voted him back into office in near-record numbers, but did they quibble as they cast their ballots? We will discuss tempered expectations more in Chapter 6. The next chapter, however, addresses more explicitly symbolic politics.

5

The political power of symbolic representation: Artistic performances and commencement speeches from presidential couples

Little of beauty has America given the world save the rude grandeur God himself stamped on her bosom; the human spirit in this new world has expressed itself in vigor and ingenuity rather than in beauty. And so by fateful chance the Negro folk-song – the rhythmic cry of the slave – stands to-day not simply as the sole American music, but as the most beautiful expression of human experience born this side the seas. It has been neglected, it has been, and is, half despised, and above all it has been persistently mistaken and misunderstood; but notwithstanding, it still remains as the singular spiritual heritage of the nation and the greatest gift of the Negro people.

-W.E.B. DuBois, The Souls of Black Folk

In *The Souls of Black Folk*, W.E.B. DuBois observed that despite the historic degradation of African Americans in the United States, black popular culture, particularly black folk music, stands out as one of the most important cultural contributions that the United States has made to the world (DuBois 1996, 178). DuBois' early twentieth-century observation reflected a prescient awareness of the centrality of blacks in American culture writ large. More recent scholars have charted the ways in which blacks have contributed to American arts and letters and the ways in which black culture was (mis) appropriated in the creation of American culture. Watkins, for instance, examined the contributions of black comedians to American comedy (Watkins 1994). Bean *et al.* noted, in a bit of irony, that "Blackface minstrelsy is now recognized as America's first original contribution to world theater—a dubious honor, certainly" (Bean *et al.* 1996, xi). Indeed, in good ways and bad ways, "Afro-American impact upon wide areas of American expressive culture has become increasingly obvious" (Levine 1977, 444).

There has been a long-established link between arts and politics in the United States. Harriett Lane, who served as White House Hostess for her unmarried uncle, James Buchannan, invited artists to White House dinners in a conscious effort to raise the profile of the arts (Caroli 2010, 44). Eleanor Roosevelt publicly displayed her support of civil rights when, after the Daughters of the American Revolution refused to allow black opera singer Marian Anderson to give a concert at Constitution Hall, Roosevelt resigned the group and arranged for Anderson to sing at the Lincoln Memorial (Lusane 2011, 263).

In this chapter, I explore the symbolic importance of the White House's cultural engagement. Two important embodiments of this are artistic performances and speeches to young people. I measure this by examining the types of musical art and artists showcased in the White House's *In Performance* series, which airs nationally on PBS a few times a year. To measure rhetoric more symbolically (because nothing the president says can be truly apolitical), I study the content of commencement addresses. I look not only at the words of the president, but incorporate the words of their wives as well. Given the symbolic importance of the role of first lady, it is important to see if presidential consorts adopt the rhetorical frames of their spouses. And in the case of Michelle Obama, it is important to first determine if she talked about race more than her husband and, if so, to ponder the significance of that fact for understanding the Obama Administration's approach to addressing racial issues.

Black performers in the White House

Clarence Lusane reports that Harriett Lane was responsible for inviting the first outside black artist (i.e., a black performer who did not work for the White House in an enslaved or free capacity) to perform at the White House in 1860. "Blind Tom" Wiggins was an enslaved, visually impaired 11-year-old musical genius who could play music by ear after one hearing. Wiggins' performance was notable for its lack of controversy, which stood in sharp contrast to the uproar that a dinner visit from Booker T. Washington would elicit more than 40 years later (Lusane 2011, 155–156, 159–164, 228–229). Lusane speculates that Wiggins' enslaved status and disability elevated him to the level of "oddity" and neutralized the threat of his talent (Lusane 2011, 164).

After the Civil War, black performers were not foreign to White House functions. Lusane writes, "While some presidents preferred only white entertainers, many sought a variety of musicians and singers to perform before foreign dignitaries" (Lusane 2011, 259). The Fisk Jubilee Singers made their White House debut in 1872. Opera singer Marie Selika Williams performed for Rutherford B. Hayes in 1878. Violinist John Henry Douglass, a grandson of Frederick Douglass, performed for Presidents McKinley and Taft. In the twentieth century, numerous black opera singers performed for presidents. Jazz performances became more common in the second half of the twentieth century. Jacqueline Kennedy hosted the first jazz mini-concert for children in 1962 (featuring the Paul Winter Sextet, a white group). Duke Ellington performed at the White House in 1965. Sarah Vaughn was moved to tears after her performance for President Lyndon Johnson (Lusane 2011, 260–266, 334, 338–339).

Presidents have used artistic performances to highlight America's cultural contributions and for propaganda purposes. The State Department often sent jazz musicians abroad on cultural exchanges and used jazz music on the Voice of America radio network to mobilize insurgence against enemy regimes. When Jimmy Carter held what was the largest state dinner to date to celebrate the signing of the Camp David Accords between Israel and Egypt, he selected black opera diva Leontyne Price to perform as a representation of American cultural achievement (Lusane 2011, 335–338, 265).

White House performances by black artists have certainly evolved from the days of Blind Tom Wiggins. Whereas Wiggins may have drawn the attention of the White House because of his master's decision to market him as a circus-like curiosity (see Lusane 2011, 156), black White House performers today symbolize the pinnacle of American cultural achievement. To what extent are black performers and art forms represented among the most recent White House performances? To answer that question, I turn to an analysis of White House performances from the Reagan to the Obama Administrations.

In this chapter, I will not look at all artistic performances at the White House to avoid the risk of   inadvertently omitting important performances from my analysis. Instead, I look at invited performers[1] to the *In Performance at the White House* series, which PBS airs in collaboration with the White

---

1   I define "performers" here as anyone who appears to have a singing, acting, or hosting role in the show. In one episode, I happened to find a discrepancy in the performer's list for one episode. My original data source omitted someone included in the IMDB database list as a star of the episode. Based on the profile, this person appears to be a composer. Without viewing a video of the performance, it is difficult to determine whether he actually performed or was merely acknowledged. In the end, I chose to leave him out of this analysis.

House. This dataset includes performances from 1981[2] to 2016. As Nancy Reagan explained at the outset of her husband's term in office, the producers and presidents involved in the program intended for the series to be a way to highlight the artistic achievements of the United States. The program also has an implied secondary purpose of showcasing up-and-coming talent (Thomas 1981). Since 1978, every administration has participated in the series,[3] and the show themes have varied from Broadway to ballet to blues (White House Historical Association n.d.).[4]

The *In Performance* series presented itself as an ideal dataset for a number of reasons. By cross-referencing information from TVGuide.com and WETA (the station which produces *In Performance*), I was able to confirm that 49 episodes aired from 1981 to 2016. *TV Guide* published a list of performers in all of the episodes, and online archives of television listings confirmed the accuracy of the *TV Guide* list. Where *TV Guide* omitted airdates, these alternate listings filled in the gap (Terrace 2013, 198; WETA 2013; *TV Guide* 2014).[5]

After compiling the list of performers, I then coded the performers by race. Since many of these performers are well known, biographies are readily available. For the less-known performers, I consulted various online sources (i.e., Wikipedia, IMDB.com, personal webpages; later episodes have webpages devoted to them which include artists' lists and accompanying photographs) to confirm their racial identification. I coded biracial artists according to all of their identities, but for practical purposes, since my primary racial dummy variables are black and Latino/a, if a biracial artist has black and white or Latino/a and white ancestry, they are coded as black or Latino/a.[6]

I also chose to only include individual performers in the dataset and to exclude ensemble groups. While the racial composition of contemporary or

---

2 WETA started airing the *In Performance* series in 1978. Because I cannot find the performance lists from all five of the Carter Administration performances (see WETA n.d.; White House Historical Association n.d.), I start with the Reagan Administration. I have tried to be as comprehensive as possible with this dataset. However, there are two missing episodes in this universe, besides the episodes from the Carter Administration.

3 As this book goes to press, PBS has not yet produced an episode of In Performance with President and Mrs. Trump.

4 There are a number of special episodes in this series. George W. Bush had one show where he featured the artistic achievement of the White House Kitchen. A few episodes feature tributes to winners of the Gershwin Prize in American Song. I should note that the Library of Congress selects Gershwin Prize winners.

5 I did notice one discrepancy. I saw that the performer list excluded Tessanne Chin from the April 7, 2014 episode ("Women of Soul"), so I added her to the dataset.

6 Jazz musician Esperanza Spalding stands out as someone who would be coded as both black and Latina. I should note here that there are only four artists with Asian ancestry in this dataset (Ken Noda, Karen Olivo, Lang Lang and Tessanne Chin). Two of these artists (Olivo and Chin) are also of mixed race and are counted among the black and Latina artists in this dataset accordingly.

Table 5.1 Descriptive statistics of show characteristics, In Performance, 1981–2016

	Reagan	G.H.W. Bush	Clinton	G.W. Bush	Obama
Culturally black-themed episodes	2 (11.8%)	0 (0%)	6 (60.0%)	2 (50.0%)	8 (53.3%)
Culturally Latino/a-themed episodes	0 (0%)	0 (0%)	0 (0%)	0 (0%)	1 (6.7%)
Total episodes	16	4	10	4	15
Black performances*	16 (29.1%)	5 (27.8%)	19 (54.3%)	11 (52.4%)	75 (53.6%)
Latino/a performances	1 (1.8%)	0 (0%)	1 (2.9%)	0 (0%)	14 (10.0%)
Black performances in nonblack-themed episodes	9 (16.4%)	5 (27.8%)	5 (14.3%)	3 (14.3%)	21 (15.0%)
White performances in black-themed episodes	2 (3.6%)	0 (0%)	6 (17.1%)	1 (4.8%)	11 (7.9%)
Total performances	**55**	**18**	**35**	**21**	**140**

Source: Author's compilation. Column percentages (calculated separately for episodes and performances) are in parentheses, unless otherwise indicated.
* A performance is defined as the solo billing of a featured performer. This does not mean that the performer did not appear as part of a duet or perform alongside other acts. However, they were advertised as a solo performer and not part of a group act.

small ensembles is relatively easy to determine, larger, older groups with more transient membership are much harder to code. For instance, I cannot tell the racial composition of every member of the Marine Corps Orchestra in 1983. Finally, I must note that some artists (i.e., Beverly Sills, Aretha Franklin, etc.) appear in multiple episodes. Because the unit of analysis is the artist, these artists will appear in the dataset for each performance (hence, the use of the term "performance" instead of "performer" or "artist").

Table 5.1 includes basic descriptive statistics for the episodes and the individual performances. Some administrations participated in more episodes than others. The Reagans participated in 16 episodes.[7] Both Bush Administrations participated in four episodes each. There were 10 episodes produced during the Clinton Administration, and the Obamas participated in 15 episodes.

Series episodes revolved around themes, and some themes highlighted cultural art forms that are strongly connected to black or Latino/a communities. In this dataset, I count episodes focusing on genres like jazz, the blues, and gospel as black-themed episodes, and episodes focusing on Latin music as Latino/a-themed episodes. As Table 6.1 shows, black-themed episodes have

7 I count performances as an interaction of the performer and episode. For example, the Reagan Administration produced a three-part salute to Broadway. It was unclear whether it was all taped on the same day, but since the episodes aired separately, I count them as discrete episodes. Performers who appeared in multiple episodes would have each performance per episode counted separately

been featured in the series since its inception. Since the Clinton Administration, at least half of the episodes highlighted a black musical or art form. There was not a Latino/a-themed episode, though, until the Obama Administration.

In the bottom half of the table, I use individual performances (or the race of the person giving the performance) as my primary unit of analysis.[8] This includes artists, hosts, and anyone with a speaking role other than the president or first lady. Some episodes featured more performers than others. This is particularly true for the Obama Administration, which averaged more than nine solo performers per episode (in contrast, the Reagan Administration episodes featured an average of about 3.4 solo artists per episode). The percentages listed in the bottom half of the table are based on the total number of performances appearing in each president's universe of *In Performance* episodes. A little more than one-quarter of the performances commissioned by Presidents Reagan and G.H.W. Bush were by black artists. More than half of the performances featured in the Clinton, G.W. Bush, and Obama Administrations were black. The more recent presidents have also been more likely to invite nonblack artists to participate in black themed shows (i.e., John Mellencamp participating in a civil rights movement music special or trumpeter Phil Driscoll participating in a gospel special). Among the last three presidents, Bill Clinton stands out. In his series of *In Performance* episodes, six of his performances by whites—or more than a third of all of the performances by a nonblack artist (n=16) were featured in a black-themed episode of *In Performance*.

The descriptive data reveal a number of important trends. First, it is important to note that blacks are not underrepresented in these performances. At least 25 percent of every president's invited solo acts in *In Performance* featured African American artists. There do appear to be temporal/generational differences and differences in the themes of shows to which black artists are invited. First, the baby boomer presidents (Clinton, G.W. Bush, and Obama) invited far more blacks than their predecessors. This suggests generational differences and/or changes in American mores which made it more acceptable to showcase large numbers of black artists at the White House. Second, the earlier presidents had fewer black-themed shows, but they still invited black artists to participate in nonblack-themed performances. In contrast, the more recent presidents have tended to invite black artists to participate in episodes showcasing black musical forms.

The descriptive data suggests that there are no statistical differences between the Clinton, G.W. Bush, and Obama Administrations in terms of

---

8 Some performers have been invited back to the White House for multiple episodes. Each performance is counted separately.

Table 5.2 Logistic regression results, probability of black performer appearance by administration and show theme, *In Performance at the White House*, 1981–2016

	Coefficient (SE)		
	Model 1	**Model 2**	**Model 3**
Constant	0.143 (0.204)	−0.741 (0.350)**	−0.748 (0.370)**
Pre-1991 performance	−1.050 (0.381)**	−0.431 (0.413)	
Obama Administration performance			−0.034 (0.383)
G.W. Bush Administration performance			0.170 (0.505)
G.H.W. Bush Administration performance			−0.207 (0.473)
Reagan Administration performance			−0.500 (0.486)
Black-themed episode		1.615 (0.372)**	1.639 (0.390)**
Pseudo R-Squared	0.0364	0.1289	0.1299
N		269	

*p≤0.10; **p≤0.05. Standard errors shown are robust standard errors clustered by *In Performance* episode.

showcasing black artists. President Obama does stand out, though, for his inclusion of Latino/a art forms into his programming. There also appear to be differences between the 1980s administrations and the more recent administrations. Partisanship is not the likely explanation, since George W. Bush is a Republican.

To test these observations further, I use logistic regression analysis in Table 5.2. The unit of analysis here is each invited performance. I use the race of an invited performer (i.e., whether he/she is black) as my dependent variable, and presidential administration as my independent variable. I code each administration as a dummy variable and use the Clinton Administration as my comparison variable. To test my hypothesis that there may be a temporal/generational divide, I also create a control variable for performances that took place on or before 1991 (the last G.H.W. Bush Administration special was in 1991). I also include a dummy variable for whether a performance was embedded in a black-themed episode (i.e., showcasing a black art form or honoring a black artist).[9] Because artists appeared with other artists in specific episodes, I also present robust standard errors, which cluster artists around the episode in which they appear.

I present three models. The first equation is a simple bivariate model where pre-1991 performance is the independent variable. I find a significant and

9   There was a 1996 episode featuring Linda Ronstadt and Aaron Neville. I assume that this episode features duets that the two did together for an adult contemporary/soft rock album. As such, I do not count this episode as black-themed.

negative correlation; performers were about 65 percent less likely to be black on or before 1991 than after. The addition of other variables to the model, though, renders this variable (or the equivalent control variables for each administration) insignificant. In models 2 and 3, I also take into account whether the theme of the episode in which a performer appeared was black-themed. Whether I operationalize time by date (pre- or post-1991) or by administration, black performers were significantly (more than five times) more likely to appear episodes devoted to celebrating black artists or black cultural art forms.

In the final analysis, then, the theme of an episode appears to matter more than the president sponsoring the performance or the time in which he served. It just so happens that, since the 1990s, presidents have sponsored more black-themed cultural programming for public television, and this has given black artists a strong platform to showcase their talent – stronger, even, than in the 1980s, when black artists were already well represented among the performers invited to participate in *In Performance*.

Because Barack Obama's predecessors had already scaled up their inclusion of black artists in cultural programming on PBS, there was very little that he could do to surpass the level of black symbolic representation in the case study that I have presented here. He does deserve credit, though, for being more attentive to featuring Latino/a artists and art forms—though one could easily argue that the production of one Latino/a themed television episode is insufficient.

Commencement speeches

Just as presidents may feel greater political latitude to boost the cultural achievements of minorities because of the inherently symbolic nature of performance, might they take greater liberties talking about race, culture, and difference in graduation speeches, which are not strictly political? And given the fact that first ladies also participate in the commencement process, can they leverage their symbolic office to be more forthright than their husbands on racial issues?

The purpose of commencement addresses has evolved over time. In the early days of American higher education, commencement speeches often served as opportunities for graduating students to demonstrate what they had learned in their studies. Over time, commencements moved away from showcasing oral recitals from students to showcasing invited speakers, who, especially in the last generation, provide an inspirational message to the graduating class (Fabry 2016).

While there is historical evidence of politicians giving commencement addresses as early as the seventeenth century, the tradition of US presidents giving commencement addresses starts in earnest after World War II.

Presidential keynotes can include political content and policy announcements (Lyndon Johnson's articulation of the need for affirmative action in his 1965 commencement address at Howard University is a notable example of a commencement address serving as a policy speech), but they are also expected to inspire graduates and provide advice for practical living (Johnson 1965; Bialik 2016; Fabry 2016).

First ladies started participating in the commencement ritual in the early to mid twentieth century. Newspaper evidence suggests that Eleanor Roosevelt addressed high school graduates as early as 1937 (Perez-Rivas 1999). Jacqueline Kennedy returned to Vassar, where she had first enrolled in college, to deliver the commencement address in 1963 ("Jackie Kennedy Returns" 1963). Nancy Reagan addressed graduating medical students (Associated Press 1987). Since the early 1990s, when Barbara Bush served as first lady, media coverage of commencement addresses by first ladies has increased. If you enter the term "'first lady' commencement speech" into the Proquest Newspaper database, which collects articles from five national newspapers, the standard analytics of the search results will show a marked increase in the number of articles mentioning those words after 1990. This suggests that commencement speeches have become a routine activity for first ladies in the last generation.

The increase in the frequency of commencement addresses by first ladies reflects the heightened public profile of the president's wife in the postwar period generally. Eleanor Roosevelt was among the first prominent examples of an activist first lady, but historians point to Lady Bird Johnson as solidifying the trend of first ladies advocating for a policy platform while their husbands serve (Carlin 2004, 293; Caroli 2010).

In addition, first ladies sometimes act as powerful surrogates for their husbands and reach out to constituencies that are resistant to the president. For instance, when Lyndon Johnson signed the Civil Rights Act into law and angered many white Southerners, he sent Lady Bird Johnson to the region to campaign for him because he was unwelcome in the South. Barry Goldwater won half of the Southern states in 1964, but scholars credit Mrs. Johnson's efforts with securing Democratic victories in the other half of the region (Carlin 2004).

Because a first lady is not an elected official, she also sometimes has greater latitude to advocate for controversial issues. For instance, Franklin Roosevelt was reluctant to support strong civil rights legislation out of fear of alienating the Southern, white wing of his New Deal coalition. In contrast, Eleanor Roosevelt was an outspoken champion of civil rights (see Breitzer 2003, 162; Blair 2005, 66–69). Diane Blair notes that in some ways, Eleanor Roosevelt could say things that her husband could not say about civil rights—even if he agreed—because her reputation for candor allowed President Roosevelt to strategically distance himself from his wife. While we can only speculate about Mrs. Roosevelt's impact on her husband's favorability ratings within the black community, Blair reports that black leaders did approach her to serve as intermediary between the civil rights community and her husband. She also contends that Eleanor Roosevelt heavily influenced the civil rights rhetoric and advocacy of her husband's vice-president and successor, Harry Truman (Blair 2005, 69, 76).

Michelle Obama's symbolic and rhetorical role

Over the course of her husband's meteoric national rise, Michelle Obama served as her husband's surrogate and validator. At the beginning of Barack Obama's presidential campaign, when there was open speculation that black voters would not relate well to his exotic racial background and upbringing (see Coates 2007), Michelle Obama's personal story bound him to a traditional African American narrative and gave him a sense of authenticity. Rachel Swarns writes that Mrs. Obama's:

> forebears would witness the agonies of bondage and the jubilation of Emancipation. They watched the hopes and rights that flowered during Reconstruction fall apart in the racial violence that followed. They joined the vast march of African Americans who moved west and north, transforming themselves from farmers and sharecroppers into city people ... Their children and grandchildren would be poised to charge through the doors forced open by the civil rights movement ... They were pioneers, on the forefront of integration, who made themselves at home in predominantly white neighborhoods and studied in predominantly white schools. With their votes, they helped elect the first generation of African American politicians in Illinois. (Swarns 2012, 10–11)

When people were not sure of Barack Obama's commitment to advocating for racial issues because of his biracial background and tendency to frame racial disparities in deracialized terms, Michelle Obama served as a kind of racial arbiter and lent her husband an air of cultural legitimacy. Jodi Kantor notes that during her husband's first campaign for state senate, Michelle Obama insisted on holding a fundraiser at a local black history museum (instead of a bar) to send a counterstereotypical image of black class and couth (Kantor 2012, 85). She also proved to be an able if implicit racial surrogate during canvassing. Kantor writes, "And for the first time in his political career but not the last, she helped him connect with other people ... when Michelle knocked on doors on his behalf, neighbors instinctively understood that she, and therefore he, was one of them" (Kantor 2012, 19). Michelle Obama continued to play that role, even into her husband's 2008 presidential campaign. A decade after Obama's first political campaign, Ronald Walters wrote that he viewed Barack Obama's marriage as a signal of his commitment to the black community: "Here, he [Obama] begins the cultural presentation with strong assets ... he married a Black woman" (Walters 2007, 22).

After assuming the title of first lady, Mrs. Obama continued to explicitly and implicitly address issues of race and/or class. While helping to unveil a statue of Sojourner Truth at the US Capitol, Michelle Obama openly referenced her heritage as the descendant of slaves (Swarns 2012, 13). She reportedly agreed to sit for the cover of *Vogue* magazine—over the objections of white aides—so that young black girls could see someone who looked like them on the cover of a high fashion magazine. And according to Jodi Kantor, Michelle Obama was more likely to accept a speaking engagement if the group "somehow represented underdogs, the kind that had never been visited by a first lady before. She had little interest in lending her presence to the powerful, in speaking at Ivy League graduations" (Kantor 2012, 92).

Indeed, some people contend that Mrs. Obama's embrace of childhood obesity as a signature advocacy issue was in fact a way for the Obamas to unobtrusively inject race into policy discussions in a non-threatening way. There were obvious synergies between Mrs. Obama's "Let's Move" campaign and President Obama's health care initiative, though the East and West Wings denied the connection. Both sought to improve health outcomes and reduce the incidence of chronic diseases (Kantor 2012, 140–141). It just so happens that the chronic diseases related to obesity of deepest concern (i.e., diabetes, high blood pressure, and heart disease) also tend to disproportionately affect communities of color. Some journalists openly speculated that Mrs. Obama's anti-obesity campaign was an attempt to address racialized health disparities in a non-threatening way.[10]

Based on previous work on first ladies, it would seem as though first ladies have greater latitude to openly discuss race and advocate for racialized issues. Hence, I would expect first ladies to discuss race more than their husbands in public comments. Because of her unique position as the first black first lady (and because of her track record of addressing racial issues when working on behalf of her husband), I would expect Michelle Obama to discuss race more often than previous first ladies.

---

10 I credit Nia-Malika Henderson (then at *The Washington Post*, now at CNN, for prompting me to think about this issue).

To test this hypothesis, I examine the content of commencement addresses from the Clinton, second Bush, and Obama Administrations. This set includes transcripts of commencement addresses delivered by both the presidents and first ladies. WhiteHouse.gov has archived commencement addresses for President and Mrs. Bush and President and Mrs. Obama. The Clinton Presidential Library provided transcripts for President and Mrs. Clinton. For this analysis, I use 125[11] commencement addresses delivered from 1993 to 2016.

I will devote a future volume to a comprehensive comparative analysis of modern first ladies. Commencement addresses are a good starting point for this analysis and appropriate to include in this chapter for a number of reasons. First, the data is readily available for all three administrations. Second, the fact that presidents and first ladies deliver commencement speeches allows for comparisons between presidents and their spouses that one just cannot make with other types of speeches. Presidents make many explicit policy speeches; their spouses typically do not. Finally, commencement addresses are prime opportunities for speakers to encourage young graduates to pursue idealistic goals like eradicating poverty or promoting racial harmony.

I go into this analysis with a certain number of expectations. First, I expect that presidents will be more likely to talk about substantive policies. While commencement addresses are often inspirational, presidents often use speeches to help advance a policy position. Lyndon Johnson, for instance, made the case for affirmative action in a 1965 commencement address at Howard University (Johnson 1965). However, the fact that commencement addresses are also an opportunity to impart wisdom to impressionable young adults gives speakers the opportunity to draw on their personal experiences to help young people navigate a new and uncertain world. It is in this context that speakers—including those who live in the White House—can address racial issues or draw upon their personal experiences.

An outside coder and I read the speeches and coded them (on a binary scale), looking for discussions of domestic and international policy and specific mentions of issues of race, class, and gender. We also made note of the type of audience to which the presidents and first ladies were speaking. Presidents and first ladies have addressed a wide variety of audiences, from high schools and community colleges to Ivy League and other elite

---

11 This number includes one address that Hillary Clinton delivered to a Queens, New York high school in 2000 for which I do not have a transcript. I include this speech in the demographic analysis, but exclude the address from the content analysis for obvious reasons.

universities. The demographics of these schools vary. Some schools are perceived as majority white and elite. Other schools attract a more diverse or working-class student body.

I need to first determine the types of school audiences presidents and first ladies address and whether those audiences vary by race, level of education (secondary or post-secondary), or academic prestige. Table 6.1 presents that data. Three important patterns emerge. Because of their role as Commander-in-Chief, presidents are more likely to deliver commencement addresses at service academies (i.e., West Point, Annapolis, the Air Force Academy, etc.) than their wives. Bill Clinton and Barack Obama gave eight speeches at service academies each, while George W. Bush spoke at nine service academy graduations. In contrast, Hillary Clinton was the only first lady who spoke to a service academy (the Merchant Marine Academy).[12] First ladies are also more likely to speak at middle and senior high school graduations. The proportions range from more than one-fifth (Hillary Clinton) to about one-third (Laura Bush and Michelle Obama).

One of the more interesting findings is that the Obamas spent more time giving commencement addresses at majority black schools. I include two tallies of black institutions in Table 5.3. The first tally is for Historically Black Colleges and Universities (HBCUs). Between them, the Obamas delivered ten commencement addresses at HBCUs, with Mrs. Obama delivering seven of these speeches. In a second tally, I aggregate black colleges with majority or plurality black K-12 schools. President Obama made one-fifth of his commencement speeches to black audiences (HBCU or K-12), and Mrs. Obama delivered almost half of her speeches before black audiences. In contrast, the Bushes only made one commencement speech to a majority or plurality black audience, and the Clintons delivered five speeches. Most notably, Michelle Obama only delivered one commencement address at an elite school – in this case, Oberlin College – the entire time she served as first lady.

In Table 5.4, I turn to an analysis of the content of commencement addresses delivered by presidents and their wives.[13] Some patterns emerge which correspond to our observations in Table 5.3. For instance, the presidents are more

---

12 Michelle Obama also made an appearance at a West Point graduation. However, because she was not the main commencement speaker, that speech is not included in this dataset.

13 The outside coder coded the commencement addresses through 2013, and I coded the remainder of the dataset. To check for consistency in coding, I did code a small random sample of the earlier commencement addresses and subsequently studied the transcripts to determine the reasons for the disagreement. This led me to change some of my codes, which yielded an agreement rate of 82.4%. This is within an acceptable range (See Hodson 1999, 51; Hancock 2004, 170). The numbers in the table reflect the original codes.

Table 5.3 Commencement addresses by speaker and school type, 1993–2016

School type	Bill Clinton	George W. Bush	Barack Obama	Hillary Clinton	Laura Bush	Michelle Obama	N
Middle/high school	1 (4.2%)	1 (4.3%)	4 (16.7%)	5 (22.7%)	3 (33.3%)	8 (34.8%)	22
Community/jr. college or technical school	1 (4.2%)	3 (13.0%)	2 (8.3%)	1 (4.5%)	1 (11.1%)	0 (0%)	8
Public college	7 (29.2%)	5 (21.7%)	5 (20.8%)	9 (40.9%)	1 (11.1%)	10 (43.5%)	37
Private college (non-Ivy+)	2 (8.3%)	3 (13.0%)	0 (0%)	2 (9.1%)	2 (22.2%)	2 (8.7%)	11
Elite college* (Ivy+)	5 (20.8%)	2 (8.7%)	3 (12.5%)	3 (13.6%)	2 (22.2%)	1 (4.3%)	16
Service academy	8 (33.3%)	9 (39.1%)	8 (33.3%)	1 (4.5%)	0 (0%)	0 (0%)	26
Historically black college	2 (8.3%)	0 (0%)	3 (12.5%)	1 (4.5%)	0 (0%)	7 (30.4%)	13
Majority black school (HBC + K-12)	2 (8.3%)	0 (0%)	5 (20.8%)	3 (13.6%)	1 (11.1%)	11 (47.8%)	22
Total speeches	24	23	24	22	9	23	125±

Source: Author's compilation.
Note: Row totals represent the total number of speeches delivered to that type of audience. One speech was made to a foreign college. While it was included in the total number of commencement speeches, it is not included in any of the crosstabs. Percentages are calculated based on the total number of speeches listed in the bottom row.
* I define elite colleges as Ivy League/Seven Sister schools, as well as schools that rank among the top 25 liberal arts colleges and universities (respectively) in the latest *US News and World Report* rankings. I do make one exception for Oberlin College, which ranked #26 in the most recent liberal arts college rankings but ranked in the top 25 at the time of the commencement speech in this dataset.
± The row totals will not add to the column total. Schools listed in the last two rows are also listed in the previous rows where applicable. The public college count is for civilian schools only, though.

likely than their wives to discuss war in their speeches (which likely correlates with their greater propensity to address officers graduating from service academies and with the realities of war in the Bush and Obama Administrations; note, though, that President Obama was the least likely of the presidents to mention war in a speech). Of all the speakers, Bill Clinton was the one most likely to address the economy. Laura Bush, a former teacher, mentioned education in all nine of her commencement addresses. And despite the fact that Bill Clinton started Americorps, the Clintons mentioned volunteerism and (civilian) community service with the least frequency.

Hillary Clinton does vie with Barack and Michelle Obama, though, for mentioning issues of identity. President Obama was the most likely to mention gender equality in his speeches, but Hillary Clinton and Michelle Obama mentioned the subject in about half of their speeches, too. Mrs. Clinton was the most likely of all the presidents and their consorts to invoke the subject

Table 5.4 Commencement addresses by speaker and speech theme, 1993–2016

Speech theme discussed	Bill Clinton	George W. Bush	Barack Obama	Hillary Clinton	Laura Bush	Michelle Obama	N
War	19 (79.2%)	18 (78.3%)	16 (66.7%)	12 (57.1%)	4 (44.4%)	6 (26.1%)	75
Economy and jobs	23 (95.8%)	13 (56.5%)	18 (75.0%)	15 (71.4%)	6 (66.7%)	15 (65.2%)	90
Education	23 (95.8%)	18 (78.3%)	20 (83.3%)	19 (90.5%)	9 (100%)	19 (82.6%)	108
Health care	11 (45.8%)	10 (43.5%)	9 (37.5%)	8 (38.1%)	4 (44.4%)	9 (39.1%)	51
Volunteerism/ community service	12 (50.0%)	19 (82.6%)	16 (66.7%)	13 (61.9%)	7 (77.8%)	18 (78.3%)	85
Gender equality	3 (12.5%)	6 (26.1%)	15 (62.5%)	11 (52.4%)	2 (22.2%)	12 (52.2%)	49
Diversity	13 (54.2%)	0 (0%)	13 (54.2%)	17 (81.0%)	4 (44.4%)	16 (69.6%)	63
Civil rights	17 (70.8%)	4 (17.4%)	18 (75.0%)	16 (76.2%)	0 (0%)	20 (87.0%)	75
General life advice	23 (95.8%)	22 (95.7%)	20 (83.3%)	18 (85.7%)	9 (100%)	21 (91.3%)	113
Total speeches	24	23	24	21*	9	23	124*

Source: Author's compilation

Note: Row totals represent the total number of speeches in which the theme listed in the row was mentioned. The percentage totals reflect the column totals.

* A transcript is missing for one Hillary Clinton speech, so it has dropped from the analysis. For this reason, these totals are different from the totals listed in the previous table.

of diversity. And Michelle Obama and Hillary Clinton were the most likely to specifically reference civil rights or inequality, followed closely by Barack Obama.

There are a few places where the dataset indicates that President and Mrs. Bush did not discuss racial issues. President Bush did not discuss issues related to diversity, and Mrs. Bush did not discuss issues related to civil rights. This does not mean that race was totally absent from their commencement rhetoric. Rather, their discussions of race tended to not be framed in the context of the issues for which my coder and I were looking. For example, President Bush may have talked about his PEPFAR plan to provide AIDS drugs to Sub-Saharan Africa, but we do not code that as a statement about diversity or civil rights. Similarly, if Mrs. Bush mentioned a volunteer project that focused on rebuilding New Orleans after Hurricane Katrina, my coder marked that as a volunteer issue and not a civil rights issue based on how she discussed the effort (though in a speech at Vanderbilt University, Mrs. Bush does make a vague reference about how moving to the Gulf Region with the purpose of aiding the rebuilding is an act of justice (Bush 2006)). I recognize that other coders might make different decisions, and I invite future researchers to continue to explore commencement rhetoric.

It is also important to see if the presidents and their wives discussed traditional commencement themes. Table 5.4 does show that these speakers did not shirk from the traditional platitudes. Nearly all of the speeches included some form of personal advice to the graduates (Barack Obama and Hillary Clinton were the least likely to do so, but even they did so in at least 80 percent of their speeches).

Discussion and conclusion

Televised musical performances and commencement addresses may seem like marginal considerations in the wider project of assessing the impact of a presidential administration on improving the status of a minority community. However, considerations of what happens at these types of events should not be neglected. The content of these activities sends strong messages about who presidents seek to include and exclude from their definition of America, and they provide clues about the personal affinities and priorities of presidents. While one should not try to surmise the majority of a president's agenda from their symbolic gestures, the weight of these displays should not be completely discounted.

In terms of artistic performances, the Obamas were building on a solid foundation of presidents curating diverse forms of musical artistry in the *In Performance* series. While early broadcasts of the series featured greater proportions of white artists, minority artists—particularly black artists—and musical forms were never absent from the series and started to be even more prominently featured in the series during the Clinton Administration. Even with this increased black presence emerging decades before the they took office, Barack and Michelle Obama still managed to highlight greater diversity in this series (in absolute numbers, though not in significantly higher proportions).

I observe a similar pattern in the commencement addresses. While the Obamas were not the first first couple to discuss diversity (Hillary Clinton was notably vocal), they were more likely to discuss racial issues. In general, the findings suggest that Democratic presidents and consorts tend to be vocal on issues related to diversity and civil rights.

Moreover, the findings on staging are important. Unlike their predecessors, the Obamas clearly made an effort to accept commencement invitations from HBCUs. This clearly evinces an attempt at symbolic politics.

It is important to consider the implications of these findings. In subtle ways, the Obamas presented a more diverse tableau and raised issues on the national agenda that merited additional discussion. Given their racial backgrounds, they brought a personal authority to the discussion.

To be sure, others have pointed out that the Obamas, particularly Barack Obama, wielded this authority as a double-edged sword. Some would point to President Obama's 2013 commencement address at Morehouse College as an example of Obama's practice of invoking personal responsibility narratives. Starting with a speech that Obama made as a candidate in Chicago on Father's Day 2008 in which he upbraided abstenee black fathers, critics have noted that Obama tended to go out of his way to rebuke blacks. They contend that he did this to pander to nonblack audiences who needed reassurances that he could take blacks to task (see *Tell Me More* 2008). The problem with these performances is the way those comments reify stereotypes about blacks (see Gillespie 2012) and seem unwarranted, especially in the case of commencement addresses to audiences of high-achieving college graduates (see Coates 2013; Dionne n.d.).

These criticisms are important to consider. However, it is also important to examine the ways that President Obama's comments resonated in the larger black populace. I turn to this discussion in the next chapter.

6

The substance of hope: Public opinion and black attitudes toward the Obama presidency

In November 2013, actress Kerry Washington's hosting appearance on *Saturday Night Live* drew considerable attention because of criticism that at the time, the show lacked black female diversity. While the writers and cast mined that controversy for comic gold (the show's cold open featured Washington being forced to portray Michelle Obama, Oprah Winfrey, and Beyoncé (almost) in a matter of minutes) (*Saturday Night Live* 2013a), they also produced an often overlooked skit, entitled, "How's He Doing?" In that sketch, Washington and black male cast members Kenan Thompson and Jay Pharaoh portray pundits on a black-themed television show talking about President Obama's performance and whether they, as black Americans, would continue to support him:

> Host (**Kenan Thompson**): OK, welcome to "How's He Doing," the show where the black voter takes a frank, honest look at President Obama and asks "How's he doing?" It's Sunday at 6 AM.
>
> Well, we're closing in on a year since Barack Obama's re-election and it's been a difficult month for the President. The most recent Gallup poll puts his approval rating at a disappointing 42% amongst all voters. But perhaps the more troubling number for the President – his approval rating among black voters has dropped to a startling 93.6%. Joining us to discuss the president and his waning support is our non-partisan panel. Ronnie Williams is a writer for *Ebony* magazine and Alice Rogers Smith is a political science professor at Spelman College.
>
> **Alice Rogers Smith** (**Kerry Washington**): Yes we can, and yes we did. Twice [with a small fist pump].

Host: Alright, alright. Simply put it has not been a good month for the president. A bumpy rollout for Obamacare and a NSA wiretapping scandal that won't go away.

Ronnie Williams (Jay Pharoah): Not a good month.

Smith: Troubling times.

Host: Alright, well, the question is: has there been in a time in the past month where you wish you would have voted for Romney?

All three characters: [Laughs and high fives between the host and Williams]

Williams: I mean, hell no!

All three characters: [Laughs].

Host: I'm sorry. I always like to start with a joke. So, why do you think so many people are upset with the faulty Obamacare launch?

Williams: Well, I believe white people are mad because white people have an expectation that everything will work perfectly right away.

Smith: It's true. Have you ever seen a white person at a hotel when the room isn't ready? They act like there's been a death in the family.

Williams: Now, as a black person, my expectations are more in line with reality. For example, in my neighborhood when you go to the drive-thru, they start by telling you what they don't have. "Welcome to Jack in the Box. We are out of bread." I'm like, "come on, Dawg …"

Host: Anyway, we move now to "What would it take?" Our weekly segment where we ask, "What would it take for Barack Obama to lose your support?" Would Barack Obama lose your support if he left the Christian Church and converted?

Smith: Converted to what?

Host: Islam.

Smith: As-salaam alaikum, Barack.

Host: Judaism?

Smith: Mazel tov, Baruch.

Host: Scientology?

Smith: All hail Zenu, my Thetan brother!

Host: What about Orthodox Judaism? You know, he wears the hat and the long coat and everything.

Williams: The coat and everything? I mean, he'd just look like he's in Run DMC; so that's cool.

Host: Right, right. Well, what if he becomes an atheist?

Smith: No, no, no, no, no. I do not think I could trust a Godless man.

Host: So does he lose your support?

Smith: He does not.

Host: OK, Vladimir Putin challenges Barack Obama to a game of five-on-five basketball with world supremacy hanging in the balance.

Williams: Ok, ok.

Smith: Big mistake, Mr. Putin.

Host: Alright, Barack gets to choose his four favorite players of all time to join his side.

Williams: OK. Here we go. New Dream Team. Alright.

Host: Larry Bird?

Williams and Smith: OK.

Smith: Steve Nash?

Williams and Smith: OK.

Host: Christian Laettner?

Williams and Smith: [Puzzled looks] Christian Laettner?! Hmmmm. OK.

Host: And Brett Favre.

Williams and Smith: No! No!

Williams: No, he's not even a basketball player. You can't take the Favre over Lebron!

Host: Does he still have your support?

Smith: He does.

Williams: Yes. (*Saturday Night Live* 2013b)

This skit presents a stylized, humorous version of an important debate in the study of African American politics. The black characters declare their undying support for President Obama, even as his administration makes logistical and national security blunders which garnered widespread condemnation. When the host probes his guests to see if anything could cause them to waver in their support for the president, he learns that there was nothing President Obama could do to deter his ardent supporters—even when they clearly disagreed with him or questioned his decisions. And when questioned about the merits of their decision to support the president, the panelists were quick to defend their choice by saying that they had realistic (or perhaps low) expectations (*Saturday Night Live* 2013b).

The week this sketch aired on NBC, the Gallup presidential approval rating among blacks was actually 86 percent, not the 96.3 percent figure which Kenan Thompson's character propounded (Gallup n.d.b). What the sketch accurately captured, though, was the reality that President Obama's approval rating among African Americans remained remarkably stable and high throughout his presidency.

So far, we have seen that the Obama Administration had a mix of successes and failures in terms of improving the lives of black people. On the whole, while there is evidence that the Obama Administration tried to address issues of concern to African Americans, the material lives of blacks were not substantially different at the end of Barack Obama's presidency than when he first took office. On the bright side, there is evidence that Barack and Michelle Obama made symbolic overtures to blacks and black issues.

In this chapter, I turn to public opinion to examine the reaction of blacks to President Obama's performance. Using qualitative and quantitative data sources, I find evidence of satisficing and of a black rally effect. In other words, blacks acknowledged the shortcomings of the Obama Administration and did not agree with him in lockstep. However, they supported some of his initiatives and took pride in his presidency. Moreover, the idea of a black rally effect connotes the idea that blacks supported a coethnic president they believed to be beleaguered by a racially resentful opposition. These considerations help to explain stratospheric support for President Obama within the African American community.

Literature review

In his searing critique of the Obama Administration, Frederick Harris lamented the Faustian bargain that he believed black voters had made to get Barack Obama elected president. In the chapter titled "Wink, Nod, Vote," Harris argued that there exists "a silent agreement—a wink-and-nod—between race-neutral black candidates and black votes. This agreement entails black voters giving race-neutral black politicians a pass on discussions about racial inequality in exchange for the candidates' successful elevation to high-profile political offices" (Harris 2012, 139). Harris' concern was that blacks were trading meaningful attention to issues of community concern for descriptive representation. In the end, he worried that black issues would never get addressed while the policy preferences of other identity groups received significant, substantive consideration (Harris 2012, 175–178).

In addition to these concerns about whether President Obama gave substantive concerns about blacks their due, Michael Dawson (2011) argued that despite the symbolic importance of electing the first black president, Barack Obama's election revealed deep inadequacies in black civil society. While blacks did organize around the opportunity to make history and select a compelling, charismatic politician to break an important glass ceiling, black communities often lacked the organizational capacity to create and sustain the types of transformative movements that are necessary to solve the intractable inequalities that disproportionately plague communities of color.

Harris and Dawson ask important normative questions about the purpose of black politics. From their perspective, the purpose of black politics is to use power to alleviate socioeconomic suffering in black communities (see also Walters 1988, 206). Descriptive representation, while often a means to the end of putting sympathetic people in power to address issues of suffering, is a secondary goal. Thus, Harris (2012) and Dawson (2011) express deep concern that blacks had become so preoccupied with the symbolism of descriptive representation that they forgot to hold those descriptive representatives accountable for boosting the socioeconomic status of blacks as a whole.

Normative goals aside, it is important to gauge the state of black public opinion on the state of race, their expectations about the role of government in ameliorating inequality, and their perceptions of President Obama and his role in this project generally. Previous studies present a complex picture of the state of race and black opinion on racial issues. On the one hand, there is convincing evidence that the long-observed racial gap in public opinion persists, despite all the discussion in public discourse of Obama's election ushering in a "post-racial" era. Vincent Hutchings (2009) compared public support for policies designed to help blacks overcome racial inequality using American National Election Study data from 1988 and 2008 and found that black–white differences in support for racially ameliorative policies had changed little over the 20-year period. In addition, when he narrowed his analysis to include only Obama voters, white Obama supporters were still less supportive of race-conscious remedies than their black counterparts. So, despite strong desires to push the envelope on racial inclusion, the general will to aggressively address racial inequality may not have been present in the 2008 electorate, despite Barack Obama's campaign success.

While blacks continue to express strong preferences for race-conscious remedies to inequality, there is also evidence to suggest that black views may have moderated. In her book *What's Going On?* Katherine Tate argued that greater black integration into the economic and political (i.e., Democratic Party) mainstream helped to temper the policy preferences of blacks as a whole. Thus, while blacks still tended to hold more liberal policy preferences than their white (and white Democratic) counterparts, blacks became more conservative from the 1980s to the early 2000s (Tate 2010).

This does not negate the importance of racial identity to understanding black political beliefs and behavior. Dawson, for example, notes that in a 2005 survey, 73 percent of blacks reported believing in the idea of linked fate, or the idea that what happens to other blacks affects them (Dawson 2011, 3). Moreover, Shayla Nunnally found a strong correlation between race and racialized perceptions of the challenges President Obama faced. Using 2009 Pew research data, she found that black Democrats were more likely than white Democrats to believe that opposition to President Obama was racially motivated. Blacks who believed that President Obama shared their values were more likely to attribute opposition to him to racism (Nunnally 2012).

In addition, there is considerable evidence to validate black voters' perception that opposition to President Obama was racially motivated. A number of scholars and practitioners found that racial resentment was highly predictive of vote choice in 2008 and 2012 and portended attitudes toward certain policy initiatives. For instance, Michael Tesler and David Sears (2010) found that racial resentment was highly correlated with Barack Obama's performance in both the primary and general elections in 2008. To put it clearly, racially resentful white Democrats were less likely to support Obama in the primaries, and racially resentful whites overall were less likely to support Obama in the general election. This work corresponds with other studies which also found that Obama underperformed expectations in the 2008 primary and that racial resentment correlated with Republican vote choice in the general election (see Jackman and Vavreck 2010; Kinder and Dale-Riddle 2012; Belcher 2016, ch. 5) and sets up later work which continued to find a strong, negative relationship between racial resentment and support for President Obama's 2012 re-election bid (Tesler 2016, ch. 3).

Racial resentment retained its strong predictive power for political attitudes throughout the Obama Administration. Christopher Parker and Matt Barreto (2013) attributed the rise of the Tea Party, which emerged to oppose President Obama's economic stimulus and health care policies, to racial resentment, finding that Tea Party adherents were more likely to express racially resentful attitudes than those who did not support the Tea Party. Michael Tesler (2016) argued that racial resentment explained much of the opposition to President Obama's political agenda during his term in office. Tesler described a variety of survey experiments where respondents were asked to indicate their support for various public policies such as health care or gun control. In the treatment conditions, respondents were reminded that President Obama supported these policies. Respondents with high levels of racial resentment who were primed to associate President Obama with the proposed policies were significantly more likely to oppose health care and the stimulus package (though not gun control and increased taxes) (Tesler 2016, 104–112). Tesler found that racial resentment was so strongly correlated with attitudes toward Obama that it even correlated significantly with negative attitudes toward President Obama's dog, Bo (Tesler 2016, 90).

Hypothesis, data, and methods

There are two important things to glean from the extant literature. First, it is important to recognize the significance of public opinion scholars' findings that racial resentment correlated strongly and negatively with support for President Obama and some of his policies. Collectively, these findings confirm that President Obama operated in a racially charged environment.

Understanding that race played an important role in evaluations of President Obama and some of his policies provides an important foundation for studying blacks' attitudes toward President Obama. The literature provides conflicting evidence about the possibility that rank-and-file blacks may have different expectations for the Obama Administration than normative theorists such as Harris and Dawson. On the one hand, blacks' policy preferences may have grown less progressive over time. Thus, their expectations for the Obama Administration may be more muted than the expectations of Obama's critics in the academy. On the other hand, though, blacks still maintain discernible policy preferences from whites, and a majority of blacks believe that opposition to President Obama was racially motivated. Thus, I expect that the forthcoming data analysis will reveal support for the idea that blacks rallied around President Obama. Specifically, I predict a strong correlation between perceptions of racialized opposition to President Obama and 2012 vote choice and presidential job approval. Moreover, I hope to show that black voters had lower—perhaps more pragmatic— expectations for what they expected President Obama to achieve.

Results

Qualitative findings

I begin with qualitative findings from a series of interviews done with black voters, campaign workers, and businesspeople in the summer of 2014. For this chapter, I did two types of interviews. I conducted a focus group of three black voters and low-level campaign volunteers (i.e., canvassers and phone bankers) in Richmond, Virginia in August 2014. I then conducted three one-on-one interviews with businesspeople in metropolitan Washington, DC around Labor Day Weekend 2014. I supplemented this data with additional interview data conducted with a paid Obama field worker who worked in Ohio in 2012. I interviewed this subject in July 2014 for another research project and made sure to ask specific questions about the Obama campaign when I learned of his work experience.

These interview subjects constitute a convenience sample and should serve to help set up the subsequent quantitative analysis that I will present later in this chapter. That being said, I chose the types of respondents and their geographic location deliberately. I wanted to select respondents who lived in a battleground state[1] because voters in competitive states would have been exposed to more campaign information like television advertisements and had greater opportunities to participate in campaign activities like canvasses, rallies, and phone banks. I also deliberately chose a stratified sample of regular voters/campaign volunteers and Washington, DC-area businesspeople. In addition to the expected differences in socioeconomic status between the two groups (I predicted that the business owners would be better educated and have higher incomes), the businesspeople would bring a unique perspective because of their professional experience. They might be familiar with the implementation requirements of certain federal regulations, such as the employer mandates embedded in the Affordable Care Act. Moreover, my sample of businesspeople, by virtue of their geographic location, would be more likely to include professionals who were familiar with government contracting.

I identified my interview subjects through a combination of personal contacts and snowball sampling. To identify my Richmond interviewees, I contacted a family friend who I knew had volunteered on the Obama campaign. I asked her to recruit other campaign volunteers. She reached out to a local politician who sent an email solicitation to city workers. That yielded two respondents, in addition to my initial contact. I identified the businesspeople through a Washington political contact. That contact reached out to area businesspeople via an email solicitation, and then I arranged to meet the businesspeople at places of their convenience. Often, restaurants at mealtimes proved to be the ideal meeting setting. At these meetings, I paid for my respondents' meals. All respondents gave their informed consent before interviews began. The duration of the interviews varied. The focus group lasted approximately two hours, while the individual interviews lasted approximately 35–90 minutes.

By design, the respondents varied in age and life experience. The Richmond respondents, all black women, were in their fifties and sixties. They were all governmental employees. Two worked as administrative professionals, and one was a public school teacher. They varied in their level of education from some college to a master's degree. No one had a household income above $75,000 annually. The women were neither consistently liberal nor conservative, but two of the three identified as strong Democrats (the third declined to

---

1 Admittedly, selecting Virginia also worked well for me because I happen to have grown up there.

reveal a party identification), and all reported having voted enthusiastically for Barack Obama in 2008 and 2012. Two of the three Richmond respondents did volunteer election work (partisan and non-partisan), including canvassing, phone banking, and voter registration. I will supplement their perspectives with an interview conducted in New Jersey with Scott,[2] former Obama campaign worker who served in Ohio in 2012. He is a black male, and at the time of his interview, he was in his late twenties.

The businesspeople came from a different class stratum than the voters/campaign workers. This group included two men and one woman. They were in their forties and fifties, had bachelor's and master's degrees, and reported household incomes of at least $100,000 a year. Two of the three respondents identified themselves as Independents (one leaned Democratic and one leaned Republican) and identified ideologically as moderate to somewhat conservative. All were strong Obama supporters in 2008, and while all supported Obama in 2012, one reported supporting the president's re-election reluctantly. One businessperson did report attending fundraisers and doing some canvassing for Obama.

I began the interviews by asking respondents to tell me how they first heard about Barack Obama. In Richmond, respondents reported first learning about Obama from family members. One reported learning about Obama from a newspaper article. Another heard about him from her 18-year-old son, who became excited about the prospect of Obama becoming the first black president. Respondents in both Richmond and Metro Washington, DC both mentioned learning more about Obama through watching *Meet the Press*. Respondents generally reported a positive initial assessment of Obama, and thought that he was smart and handled himself well in interviews. When Obama announced his candidacy, they indicated that they were supportive, even if they initially thought he had no chance of winning. One of the DC area business people did note an initial concern with Obama's safety, reflecting long-held fears that a serious black candidate might face a heightened risk of assassination.

I asked respondents to discuss Obama in reference to his blackness. Did they feel that Obama as a candidate had made sufficient overtures to African Americans? Did they expect special treatment or special attention to "black" issues? Did he address racial issues to their satisfaction? Respondents indicated a pragmatic attitude about candidate Obama's stances toward race. John, one of the DC area businessmen, praised Obama for his "More Perfect Union" speech, in which he addressed concerns about his association with his

---

2 To protect the identities of my respondents, I use pseudonyms.

former pastor, Jeremiah Wright. When I asked John to consider the validity of the claims of critics that Obama scapegoated Wright, he dismissed the claim outright.

John's comments reflected a wider, general endorsement among respondents of Obama's deracialized campaign strategy. While respondents clearly took pride in an African American's ascension to the presidency and noted the novelty of electing the first black president, they also claimed that coethnicity was not the primary motivation for their support. As they talked, though, one detects the ways that racial solidarity and an awareness of the continued importance of race in political life informed their perceptions of Obama as a candidate. Take the comments of Ann, one of the Richmond respondents, as an example:

> It [race] really didn't matter. At least I really didn't think, "He's black, so I'm going to vote for him." That never crossed my mind. I know it was just a feeling of excitement. Just the thought of "Wow," just how intelligent this individual really was, and I kind of was like, "I hope he sticks it to the system." Because, considering our bigger demographic, the population, what are the odds of the average Caucasian voting for this man? And so, my think[ing] was that I hope and pray that what he does is flip the system and open up some eyes. It wasn't just "Oh, you're black, so I'm going to vote for you." It's more that I'm excited that you're African-American and that you are going to make a diffe-rence for those individuals that are coming up, like my grandchildren, their children. And the fact that my son brought it up to me, like wow.

Ann explicitly dismisses the idea that racial solidarity influenced her vote. As she continued talking, though, it was clear that she saw the election of Barack Obama as an act of self-determination for blacks. To Ann, an Obama's can-didacy would send an important signal about the status of blacks. And she implicitly expected Obama to use his candidacy (and by implication, his office, should he be elected president) to improve the lives of her children and grandchildren. I interpret her declaration that she hoped Obama would "flip the system" as evidence of her expectation that a black presidential candi-date would open the eyes of some resistant voters and show that blacks were equally capable of being full-fledged citizens and leaders.

Jane, another Richmond respondent, articulated symbolic expectations of President Obama. She said:

> I thought about him being a black president, especially for low income neighborhoods or neighborhoods where you have African American

young boys who don't have that role model to encourage them so they can do better than hang out on the street all the time … I hope they look at this like, "Wow, I can do this. I think there are some great opportunities for me. I can excel. If he can do it, I can do it …" I know right now we've got a lot of challenges, but I was hoping that that would encourage them.

Jane clearly recognizes that blacks, particularly young men like her son, are disadvantaged in American society. However, she did not seem to expect President Obama to enact policies to help address those disadvantages. Instead, she hoped that President Obama could serve as a role model for her son so that he can be his own change agent. Later in the conversation, I raised the issue of My Brother's Keeper, President Obama's initiative to reach out to disadvantaged black teenaged boys. Jane supported the program, as did other respondents in the Richmond group. I probed further to gauge their reaction to criticisms that My Brother's Keeper unnecessarily excluded girls. Jane listened respectfully, conceded that the critics had a point, and endorsed the idea of expanding the program to include girls. It seemed, though, that she had never considered standard progressive critiques of the Obama Administration.

Richmond respondents were not the only ones who had not considered standard progressive critiques of the Obama Administration. Mary, one of the businesspeople, and I discussed Barack Obama's 2008 Father's Day speech, in which he criticized black fathers for not being attentive enough to their children. Black progressives roundly criticized the speech as evidence of Obama's pandering to white television audiences (the actual audience of the speech was black) by demonstrating that he can publicly dress down blacks. When I explained the critique, Mary paused and said "Wow," as though she had never considered that critique but thought that it was somewhat off base. She explained that she did not hear pandering in Obama's critique at all. Instead, she saw Obama's comment as a positive exhortation for a group of people who might need the encouragement.

Overall, the respondents expressed satisfaction with Barack Obama's performance as president. Deborah, one of the Richmond respondents, noted that while she disagreed with President Obama's support of same-sex marriage, she continued to support the president. She explained that she did not vote based on social issues, and she noted that she initially supported Obama as opposed to Republicans because she associated the excesses and greed connected to the 2008 downturn in the American economy with Republicans. Essentially, Deborah supported the candidate who represented change.

For Ann, the passage of the Affordable Care Act (ACA) represented the ultimate achievement of the Obama Administration. Echoing the refrain of the Beverly Crawford gospel tune, she noted more than once that if Obama passed nothing other than the Affordable Care Act, "he's done enough." At the time of the focus group, she had a son under age 26 who had a disability or pre-existing medical condition. Because of the dependent and pre-existing condition provisions of the ACA, she had been able to keep him on her health insurance. For that, she was clearly grateful. When we discussed racial inequalities (i.e., disparities in unemployment rates, health disparities, etc.) that persisted into the Obama Administration, Ann continued to insist that Obama had done enough for her by getting Congress to pass the ACA.

The respondents were not blind to the reality that blacks' material situations had not improved over the course of the Obama presidency. However, they did not always blame the Obama Administration for these disparities. Mary, for instance, noted that the president is not well positioned to solve many of these problems. Rather, they saw these issues as the purview of individuals, the marketplace, or other governmental sectors.

And the respondents were not shy to criticize the president. The businesspeople were particularly vocal. Mary openly worried that the provisions of the ACA which mandated that businesses provide health insurance coverage for their employees would drive up business costs and raise unemployment levels. Thomas, another DC area businessman, complained that sequestration (which arguably implicates Congress) had created an adverse business climate.

Despite their complaints, the respondents still reported voting for Barack Obama's re-election. Mary was perhaps the most reluctant Obama supporter of the group. Given her criticisms of Obama, I was curious about why she continued to support him. She explained that even with her misgivings about President Obama, she thought that he was a better candidate than Mitt Romney in 2012.

Quantitative data

The qualitative data suggests that black voters viewed Barack Obama as an imperfect but good president. Will the quantitative data match the qualitative observations? To explore this question further, I look at two cross-sectional surveys: the 2014 Survey of Continuing Black Partisanship (Gillespie *et al.* 2014), a pilot, Internet-sample survey fielded by Knowledge Networks in April 2014 of African American registered voters with a large oversample of black Republicans. Because of the oversample of Republican voters (whose data will be presented in an upcoming, co-authored project) and because of my specific interest in understanding the attitudes of presumed Obama supporters in this survey, I am only using the unweighted Democratic subset of the sample, which comprised the majority of the sample's base. The truncated sample is small (N=187), which will limit my ability to detect small but significant correlations. Nevertheless, an analysis of this data will be helpful, as the survey included important questions about perceptions of Barack Obama.

To supplement the 2014 data, I also use an unweighted African American subsample from the 2016 James Weldon Johnson Institute (JWJI) Election Survey (Gillespie 2016). The JWJI Election Survey was fielded by Qualtrics on November 7–8, 2016. The larger survey included a national sample of registered voters of all races, and oversamples of minority Republicans, millennials of color, and white evangelicals. In all, this study will focus on the 380 subjects who identified as black or African American.

Table 6.1 presents a basic demographic overview of the samples I use in this analysis. Both samples skew heavily female. Given the higher levels of voter participation among black women compared to black men (and given the large numbers of black men who are unable to register to vote because of felon disenfranchisement), this is not surprising (see Smooth 2006, 405). The 2014 sample skews older. Because of the oversample of younger voters in the 2016 sample, there are (proportionally) twice as many respondents in the youngest age category in the 2016 survey.

There are a few more demographic characteristics to note. Levels of educational attainment varied across both samples. One-seventh of the 2014 sample did not complete high school, while nearly a quarter had at least a bachelor's degree. Just over 60 percent of the sample had at least some college education or an associate's degree. The 2016 sample had higher levels of education. Nearly 98 percent of the 2016 sample completed high school, and about 73 percent of the sample had at least attended college.

Southerners dominated both samples. About 52 percent of the 2014 respondents lived in the South, the traditional black belt of the United States, followed by Midwesterners (19 percent), Northeasterners (about 16 percent), and Westerners (about 13 percent). The 2016 sample also skewed heavily Southern (48 percent), with nearly equal numbers (19 percent each) of Northeastern and Midwestern respondents. About 15 percent of respondents were from the West.

There was also considerable economic diversity in both samples. Half of the respondents to the 2016 sample reported household incomes of less than $50,000. That is slightly less than the approximately 54 percent of respondents to the 2014 survey who reported annual incomes of less than $50,000. A substantial number of respondents in both samples also reported being evangelical Christians. About 49 percent of 2014 respondents reported being evangelical, compared to 56 percent of the 2016 respondents.

Table 6.1 Demographic breakdown of survey data

Variable	Percentage	
	2014 survey of continuing black partisanship (Democrats only)	2016 JWJI Election Survey
Male	39.0%	33.9%
Female	61.0%	65.8%
Age 18–29	9.1%	21.6%
Age 30–44	26.2%	29.2%
Age 45–59	32.1%	30.8%
Age 60 and older	32.6%	18.4%
Less than high school	15.0%	2.1%
High school	31.6%	14.5%
Some college/associate degree	30.5%	36.9%
Bachelor's degree or higher	23.0%	46.1%
Northeast (CT, DC, DE, MA, MD, ME, NH, NJ, NY, PA, RI, VT)	15.5%	17.4%
Midwest (IA, IL, IN, KS, MI, MO, MN, ND, NE, OH, OK, SD, WI)	19.3%	17.1%
South (AL, AR, GA, FL, KY, LA, MS, NC, SC, TN, TX, VA, WV)	52.4%	44.5%
West (AK, AZ, CA, CO, HI, ID, MT, NM, NV, OR, UT, WA, WY)	12.8%	13.4%
Under $50,000	53.5%	50.0%
$50,000 or more	46.6%	50.0%
Evangelical Christian	48.7%	56.1%
Democrats (including leaners)	100.0%	76.8%
Independents	N/A	10.5%
Republicans (including leaners)	N/A	12.6%
Conservative (including leaners)	44.9%	31.6%
Moderate	38.0%	32.1%
Liberal (including leaners)	17.2%	36.3%
N	187	380

Source: Survey of Continuing Black Partisanship (Gillespie *et al.* 2014); JWJI Election Survey (Gillespie 2016) Some categories will not add to 100% because of rounding error or omitted missing data.

Because I include all African American respondents from the 2016 survey, Table 6.1 shows the partisan and ideological distribution for that sample. About 13 percent of respondents to the 2016 sample reported being Republican (or Republican leaners); nearly 11 percent were pure independents; and 77 percent identified as Democrats (or Democratic leaners). Thirty-one percent of 2016 respondents identified as ideologically conservative, while 32 percent identified as moderates and 36 percent identified as liberals. In 2014, nearly 45 percent of respondents identified as conservative, with 38 percent identifying as moderate and 17 percent identifying as liberal.

Table 6.2 Descriptive statistics, respondent impressions of Obama

Variable (approximate question wording)		2014 percentage	2016 percentage
Obama favorability rating	Very favorable	71.1%	68.7%
	Somewhat favorable	19.3%	16.8%
Obama is honest and trustworthy	Describes Obama extremely well	50.3%	N/A
	Describes Obama pretty well	41.2%	N/A
Obama understands the problems Americans face in their daily lives	Describes Obama extremely well	50.8%	N/A
	Describes Obama pretty well	38.5%	N/A
Obama is a strong and decisive leader	Describes Obama extremely well	43.3%	N/A
	Describes Obama pretty well	40.6%	N/A
Obama shares your values	Describes Obama extremely well	39.0%	N/A
	Describes Obama pretty well	45.5%	N/A
	No opinion	3.7%	N/A
	Does not describe Obama too well	8.0%	N/A
	Does not describe Obama at all	2.7%	N/A
Obama has a clear plan for solving the country's problems	Describes Obama extremely well	31.6%	N/A
	Describes Obama pretty well	47.1%	N/A
What do you think of the job President Obama has done in helping to improve the lives of blacks?	More than I expected	11.8%	32.1%
	About what I expected	43.9%	38.2%
	Less than what I expected	19.3%	25.0%
Has the situation for Black people in this country improved in the last five years?	It is better	19.3%	N/A
	It is worse	18.7%	N/A
	It is about the same	59.9%	N/A
Is racism the primary reason Republicans oppose Obama?	Primary reason	58.8%	45.3%
	Secondary reason	8.0%	10.0%
	Tertiary reason	7.0%	25.8%
	Don't know/refused/missing*	26.2%	18.9%
Obama job approval	Strongly approve	48.7%	65.3%
	Somewhat approve	34.2%	17.9%
	Neutral/disapprove	16.6%	16.6%
2012 vote choice	Obama, enthusiastically	87.7%	N/A
	Obama, reluctantly	5.9%	N/A
	Someone else/did not vote	3.7%	N/A

Source: Survey of Continuing Black Partisanship (Gillespie *et al.* 2014); JWJI Election Survey (Gillespie 2016). Percentages in each category may not add to 100% because of omitted categories or rounding error.

Table 6.2 presents basic frequencies of the survey questions that gauged respondent attitudes toward President Obama. While the Democrats in the 2014 sample were clearly supportive of the president, there was some variation, depending on the question. About 90 percent of the respondents had some form of a positive perception of President Obama: 71 percent of respondents had a very favorable view of Obama, compared to 19 percent who only had a somewhat favorable view. The 2016 sample reported similar favorability ratings. There, about 69 percent of respondents reported having a favorable impression of Barack Obama, compared to 17 percent who had a somewhat favorable rating.

There was greater variation in job approval, though. Slightly less than 50 percent of the respondents in the 2014 sample strongly approved of the job President Obama was doing. Thirty-four percent somewhat approved, while 17 percent gave a neutral or negative response. Obama's job approval ratings were higher in the 2016 sample. There, 65 percent strongly approved of the job he was doing; 18 percent somewhat approved; and 17 percent gave him a neutral or negative job approval rating.

In the 2014 survey, respondents answered a short trait battery to gauge their perceptions of Obama's character and managerial skills. About 50 percent of respondents thought that "honest and trustworthy" described Obama extremely well, compared to 41 percent who thought that it only described him pretty well. A little more than half of the respondents thought that Obama understood the problems that regular people faced extremely well, and about 39 percent thought that the statement described Obama pretty well. Forty-three percent thought that "strong and decisive leader" described Obama extremely well, compared to 41 percent who thought it described him pretty well.

There was a little more variation on the other two trait dimensions. A majority of the respondents did not think that "has a plan for solving the country's problems" described Obama extremely well; 47 percent of respondents thought that "pretty well" was a more apt description. In addition, there was more variation on the "shares your values" dimension. Here, 39 percent of respondents thought it described Obama extremely well, compared to 46 percent who only thought it described Obama pretty well.

Here, unlike the other dimensions, there was a small cadre of respondents who did not think that their values were compatible with President Obama. About 11 percent of the sample indicated that they did not think that "shares your values" described President Obama well.

The 2016 survey did not include trait questions. However, both surveys did ask respondents to assess President Obama's performance on improving the lives of blacks. Did he meet, exceed, or underperform on this dimension? Respondents in both surveys tended to indicate that Obama had met or exceeded their expectations. The 2016 respondents were more sanguine in their assessment. In that year, a little more than a third of respondents said that Obama had exceeded their expectations, while 38 percent reported that he had met their expectations with regards to helping to improve black lives. In 2014, a plurality of black Democratic respondents (nearly 44 percent) reported that Obama had met their expectations, with an additional 12 percent saying that he had exceeded their expectations. Nineteen percent of 2014 respondents reported having been disappointed by Obama's efforts to improve the lives of blacks. In the 2016 sample, 25 percent of respondents expressed the same sentiment.

Both surveys also asked respondents to explain the source of friction between President Obama and the Republican-controlled Congress. Respondents had a choice to rank partisan differences, policy differences or racism in the order of their perceived influence on the tension.[3] As Table 6.2 shows, a plurality to majority of respondents ranked racism as the primary source of the conflict between the Executive and the Legislative Branches. Fifty-nine percent of black Democratic respondents in 2014 made this assertion, as did 45 percent of the respondents (who came from all partisan backgrounds) in the 2016 survey. Perhaps because the 2016 sample included independents and Republicans, the 2016 data includes more respondents who perceived racism to be a secondary or tertiary cause of the rift between Obama and Congress.

The descriptive statistics suggest that there may be interesting bivariate relationships between perceptions of how the Obama Administration confronted racial issues and evaluations of Obama. Table 6.3 presents responses to the 2014 questions about whether Obama had done enough about race, the status of race relations in the United States, and whether respondents perceived that Republican opposition to Obama was due to racism cross-tabulated by job approval ratings and 2012 vote choice. Overall, I found that President Obama's favorability ratings, perceptions of the job he did on improving the lives of blacks, and the status of race relations in the United States (whether generally or specifically related to how Obama was treated by Republicans) bore little relationship to vote choice. Despite any mild misgivings about race relations, President Obama, or lukewarm to negative assessments about the status of racial progress and President Obama's role in achieving that progress, black respondents overwhelmingly indicated having enthusiastically voted for Obama in 2012.

There is much more variation when we look at the cross-tabulation with job approval. Again, I look at the 2014 data. While most voters strongly

---

3 While the question wording was the same, the response choices were different in the 2016 survey than in 2014. In the 2014 survey, respondents could indicate that they did not know the answer to the question about what explained opposition to Obama.

Table 6.3 Cross-tabulations, job approval by respondent impressions of Obama, 2014

Variable (approximate question wording)		Obama job approval			2012 vote		
		Strongly approve	Somewhat approve	Neutral/ negative	Obama, w/ enthusiasm	Obama, reluctantly	Didn't vote
Obama favorability rating	Very favorable	86 (64.7%)	37 (27.8%)	10 (7.6%)	123 (92.5%)	3 (2.3%)	5 (3.8%)
	Somewhat favorable	1 (2.8%)	25 (69.4%)	10 (27.8%)	28 (77.8%)	6 (17.1%)	1 (2.8%)
What do you think of the job President Obama has done in helping to improve the lives of blacks?	More than I expected	19 (86.4%)	2 (9.1%)	1 (4.5%)	20 (90.9%)	0 (0%)	1 (4.5%)
	About what I expected	43 (52.4%)	31 (37.8%)	7 (8.5%)	78 (95.1%)	2 (2.4%)	1 (1.2%)
	Less than what I expected	10 (27.8%)	19 (52.8%)	7 (19.5%)	29 (80.6%)	6 (16.7%)	1 (2.8%)
Has the situation for black people in this country improved in the last five years?	It is better	22 (61.1%)	7 (19.4%)	6 (16.7%)	30 (83.3%)	2 (5.6%)	3 (8.3%)
	It is worse	18 (51.4%)	11 (31.4%)	6 (17.2%)	29 (82.9%)	4 (11.4%)	1 (2.9%)
	It is about the same	51 (45.5%)	44 (39.3%)	17 (15.2%)	102 (91.1%)	5 (4.5%)	3 (2.7%)
Is racism the primary reason Republicans oppose Obama?	Primary reason	64 (58.2%)	34 (30.9%)	12 (10.9%)	101 (91.8%)	6 (5.5%)	2 (1.8%)
	Secondary reason	2 (13.3%)	11 (73.3%)	2 (13.3%)	14 (93.3%)	1 (6.7%)	0 (0%)
	Tertiary reason	5 (38.5%)	6 (46.2%)	2 (15.4%)	10 (76.9%)	2 (15.4%)	1 (7.7%)
	Don't know/refused	20 (40.8%)	13 (26.5%)	15 (30.6%)	39 (79.6%)	2 (4.1%)	4 (8.2%)

Source: Survey of Continuing Black Partisanship (Gillespie et al. 2014). Row percentages omit refusals for the job approval and vote questions and may have rounding error.

Table 6.4 Cross-tabulations, job approval by impressions of the Obama Administration, 2016

Variable (approximate question wording)		Obama job approval		
		Strongly approve	Somewhat approve	Neutral/ negative
Obama favorability rating	Very favorable	231 (88.8%)	24 (9.2%)	5 (1.9%)
	Somewhat favorable	14 (21.9%)	36 (56.3%)	14 (21.9%)
	Somewhat/very unfavorable	1 (2.1%)	7 (14.9%)	39 (83.0%)
Black Lives Matter favorability rating	Very Favorable	148 (82.7%)	19 (10.6%)	12 (6.7%)
	Somewhat favorable	75 (64.1%)	29 (24.8%)	13 (11.1%)
	Very/somewhat unfavorable	18 (30.0%)	15 (25.0%)	27 (45.0%)
What do you think of the job President Obama has done in helping to improve the lives of blacks?	More than I expected	107 (88.4%)	10 (8.3%)	4 (3.3%)
	About what I expected	103 (71.0%)	27 (18.6%)	15 (10.3%)
	Less than what I expected	35 (36.8%)	25 (26.3%)	35 (36.8%)
Is racism the primary reason Republicans oppose Obama?	Primary reason	132 (76.7%)	25 (14.5%)	15 (8.7%)
	Secondary reason	19 (50%)	13 (34.2%)	6 (15.8%)
	Tertiary reason	50 (51.5%)	19 (19.6%)	28 (28.9%)
Party identification	Democratic (includes leaners)	220 (75.3%)	51 (17.5%)	21 (7.1%)
	Independent	16 (41.0%)	8 (20.5%)	15 (38.5%)
	Republican (includes leaners)	12 (25.0%)	9 (18.8%)	27 (56.3%)

Source: JWJI Election Survey (Gillespie 2016).

approved of the job President Obama did regardless of their perception of race relations, the status of blacks, or President Obama's role in improving the plight of blacks, respondents who had misgivings about some of these issues were less likely to give President Obama their highest stamp of approval. For instance, 53 percent of voters who said that Obama had not met their expectations in improving the lives of blacks only somewhat approved of the job he was doing as president. Voters who believed that racism was a secondary or tertiary explanation for Republican opposition to President Obama were also more likely to give him middling job approval ratings. And only a plurality of voters (46 percent) who thought that the status of blacks had not changed in the previous five years gave President Obama their highest approval. Cumulatively, this suggests that President Obama's overwhelming electoral support in the African American community obscured more nuanced (though still positive) assessments of him.

In Table 6.4, I look at those same bivariate relationships using the 2016 data, which includes independents and Republicans. Here, I find a positive correlation between Obama's favorability and job approval ratings. Nearly 90 percent of those who had a very favorable opinion of him strongly approved of the job he did as president. A majority of those who had a somewhat favorable impression of him also approved somewhat of his job performance. More than 80 percent of those who had an unfavorable impression of him gave him a neutral or negative job approval rating. (Respondents were nearly evenly split across the "neither approve nor disapprove," "somewhat disapprove," and "strongly disapprove" categories.) Party identification also appears to be positively correlated with job approval. Three-quarters of Democrats strongly approved of the job President Obama did, while 60 percent of Republicans gave him a neutral or negative job approval rating.

Because of the heightened political engagement around police shootings that has emerged since 2014, the 2016 survey asked respondents to rate the favorability of the Black Lives Matter movement. Clear majorities of respondents who had very or somewhat favorable impressions of Black Lives Matter strongly approved of the job President Obama did in office. While 30 percent of respondents with a negative impression of Black Lives Matter still strongly approved of President Obama's performance, 45 percent of those with negative impressions of Black Lives Matter also gave President Obama a neutral to negative job approval rating.

Similar to 2014, the 2016 survey asked respondents to rate President Obama's performance on improving the lives of blacks. I cross-tabulated these responses with job approval ratings. Just over 70 percent of respondents who believed that Obama had performed as expected and nearly 90 percent of those who believed that Obama had exceeded their expectations strongly approved of President Obama's job performance. Those who were disappointed in President Obama's performance on racial issues were more evenly split in their overall approval ratings of President Obama. Equal proportions of respondents who were underwhelmed strongly approved of President Obama's job performance or were neutral to negative (about 37 percent each), while about 26 percent of those who were disappointed with President Obama's efforts for blacks only somewhat approved of his job performance.

There does not appear to be a strong correlation between perceptions of the motivations of Republican opposition to President Obama and job approval ratings. While three-quarters of respondents who cited racism as the primary motivation behind Republican opposition to President Obama strongly approved of his job performance, more than half of those who thought racism was the second or third most important reason also strongly approved of President Obama's job performance.

In addition to asking a generic job approval question, the 2016 JWJI Election Survey also asked respondents to rate President Obama's job

Table 6.5 Obama job approval ratings by issue area, 2016

Issue area	Strongly approve	Somewhat approve	Neither approve nor disapprove	Strongly/ somewhat disapprove
The economy	144 (38.1%)	127 (33.6%)	61 (16.1%)	46 (12.2%)
Race relations	130 (34.3%)	103 (27.2%)	79 (20.8%)	67 (17.7%)
National defense	129 (34.3%)	127 (33.8%)	64 (17.0%)	56 (14.9%)
Foreign relations/diplomacy	122 (32.2%)	118 (31.1%)	77 (20.3%)	62 (16.4%)
The budget	127 (33.7%)	113 (30.0%)	82 (21.8%)	55 (14.6%)
Serving with integrity	222 (58.7%)	65 (17.2%)	57 (15.1%)	34 (9.0%)
Crime	111 (29.4%)	99 (26.2%)	88 (23.3%)	80 (21.2%)
Terrorism	123 (32.4%)	101 (26.6%)	68 (17.9%)	88 (23.2%)
Issues related to policing	109 (28.8%)	114 (30.1%)	91 (24.0%)	65 (17.2%)

Source: JWJI Election Survey (Gillespie 2016).
Percentages shown are valid percentages and may include rounding error.

performance on nine key issue areas: the economy, race relations, defense, foreign relations, budgeting, integrity, crime, terrorism, and policing. Those results are listed in Table 6.5. Overall, respondents tended to strongly or somewhat approve of President Obama's job performance in all of these areas. There seemed to be a consensus that President Obama had served with integrity; nearly 59 percent of respondents strongly approved of Obama's integrity, and another 17 percent somewhat approved. In the other areas, usually about a third of respondents would strongly approve, while a quarter to a third of respondents would somewhat approve. For instance, more than 70 percent of respondents strongly or somewhat approved of the job President Obama was doing on the economy, compared to 68 percent who strongly or somewhat approved of the job he did on national defense. Sixty-three percent of respondents strongly or somewhat approved of President Obama's performance on foreign relations, compared to nearly 64 percent who approved (strongly or somewhat) of how he handled the budget. President Obama earned slightly lower marks for his work on terrorism (59 percent strongly/somewhat approve). When asked specifically about crime, nearly 56 percent of respondents strongly or somewhat approved of his job performance, compared to 23 percent who gave him lukewarm ratings and 21 percent who gave him negative ratings.

On the two most explicitly racialized issues tested, President Obama earned mostly positive, but a fair number of lukewarm, approval ratings. Nearly 62 percent of respondents strongly or somewhat approved of the job President Obama did on race relations. Another fifth of respondents (21 percent) said that they neither approved nor disapproved of the job he did in this area, and 18 percent said that they strongly or somewhat disapproved of his job performance on race relations. And on policing issues, a bare plurality of respondents (30 percent) somewhat approved of the job President Obama did on this issue, compared to 29 percent who strongly approved, 24 percent who neither approved nor disapproved, and 17 percent who disapproved in some form.

The descriptive and bivariate analyses suggest that while some blacks were willing to criticize President Obama, most approved of his efforts and identified racism as an obstacle to his achieving more. To probe these relationships further, I created multivariate models to test the relationship between respondent assessments of Obama's traits, assessments of his work on behalf of blacks, and general perceptions of race relations with self-reported vote choice and job approval ratings. Because of the small sample size in the 2014 survey, I consolidate some of my response categories. Whereas I have previously presented my dependent variables (job approval and vote choice) as interval variables, I now operationalize these variables in binary terms. I code strong approval and enthusiastic vote choice as 1, and all other responses (including "somewhat approve" and "reluctantly" vote for Obama) as 0. For my independent variables, I code the trait battery questions on an interval from 0 to 1, with 0.5 being the "pretty well" category and 0 being the "not very well" and "not at all" categories.[4] I code the favorability question as a binary variable, giving very favorable responses a value of 1, and all other responses a value of 0. To include responses to the question about whether Obama met expectations in improving the lives of blacks, I created three dummy variables: one indicating the belief that Obama had exceeded expectations, one indicating that he had underperformed, and one expressing a belief that he had met the respondent's expectations. This allows me to collapse subjects who said that they did not know or that expectations did not matter into one comparison category. I coded beliefs about whether the status of blacks had improved in the last five years as an interval variable from -1 to 1, with -1 indicating a belief that blacks had fared poorly and 1 indicating a belief that the status of blacks had improved. To gauge the significance of the perception that racism hindered President Obama's relationship with Congress, I created a dummy variable for respondents who thought that racism was the primary motivation for Republican opposition. I also include standard control variables such as

---

4   The one exception will be the "shares my values." Because there were negative responses to that trait, those are coded on a 5- point scale of -1 to 1, with -1 meaning "does not describe Obama well at all" and 1 meaning "describes Obama extremely well."

Table 6.6 Logistic regression results, job approval and vote choice on traits and racial perceptions, 2014

Variable	DV: strongly approving of Obama's job as president		DV: enthusiastically voting for Obama in 2012	
	Coefficient	Odds ratio	Coefficient	Odds ratio
Constant	-9.225 (1.910)**		0.583 (1.780)	
Obama job approval (strongly)			-0.029 (1.026)	
Obama favorability (very)	3.362 (.916)**	28.856	1.494 (0.843)*	4.456
Obama is honest	3.577 (1.255)**	35.779	-1.562 (1.492)	
Obama understands regular people	0.930 (1.239)		0.129 (1.663)	
Obama is decisive	-0.334 (0.991)		0.522 (1.324)	
Obama shares my values	1.556 (1.134)		2.810 (1.455)*	16.618
Obama has a plan	0.742 (1.074)		-2.674 (1.542)*	0.069
Obama exceeds expectations on race	0.154 (1.032)		1.129 (1.358)	
Obama has performed as expected w/r to race	-0.645 (0.666)		0.935 (0.845)	
Obama has disappointed on race	-1.404 (0.810)*	0.246	-1.144 (0.803)	
Change in black condition in last five years	-0.108 (0.433)		-0.606 (0.486)	
Racism is primary reason for GOP opposition	0.066 (0.677)		0.575 (0.731)	
Evangelical Christian	-0.089 (0.530)		-0.780 (0.681)	
Age	0.993 (0.548)*	2.699	0.137 (0.349)	
Male	0.513 (0.315)		-0.458 (0.674)	
Education	0.565 (0.597)		0.353 (0.348)	
Income of less than $50,000	-0.398 (0.543)		-0.709 (0.765)	
Consumes news 5+ days a week	0.719 (0.539)		1.197 (0.694)*	3.309
South	0.554 (0.465)		0.369 (0.708)	
Cox and Snell Pseudo R-square	0.510		0.350	
N	173		171	

Source: Survey of Continuing Black Partisanship (Gillespie *et al.* 2014).
**p>0.05; * p>0.1.

gender (1=male), education (coded on a scale of 1 to 4, with 1=less than high school and 4=bachelor's degree or more), age (with 1=18–29 and 4=60 and older) and dummy variables for respondents who live in the South, make less than $50,000 annually, and consume news five or more days per week.

The 2014 regression results are listed in Table 6.6. Here, I include odds ratios for significant variables as well. The model on the left, which uses job approval as a dependent variable, indicates strong and significant correlations between perceptions that Obama is honest and trustworthy and strongly approving of the job the president was doing. Men also appear to be significantly more likely than women (at the p<0.1 level) to have strongly approved of the president's performance. Conversely, there was a significant (at the p<0.1 level) and negative correlation between perceptions that Obama had not done as much to help improve the position of blacks as was expected and strong job approval ratings of the president.

The model on the right hand side estimates the relationship between the independent variables and having voted enthusiastically for Barack Obama's re-election. Compared to the right-hand-side equation, this model has weaker goodness-of-fit measures. In addition, because respondents overwhelmingly supported Obama's re-election with enthusiasm (and because of the small sample size), it is very difficult to discern statistical relationships with the independent variables here. I find (at the p<0.1 level) that shared values was the strongest predictor of having enthusiastically voted for Obama in 2012. Voters were also more likely to report enthusiastically voting for Obama if they viewed him very favorably. And respondents who identified as heavy news consumers (five or more days per week) were also more likely to have been enthusiastic supporters of the president's re-election. Surprisingly, one's belief in whether "has a clear plan for solving the country's problems" described Obama well was negatively correlated with enthusiastic support for his re-election. The likely explanation for this is that there were many enthusiastic Obama voters who thought that this trait characteristic only described Obama pretty well.

I turn to a multivariate analysis of the 2016 data in Table 6.7. Here, Obama's general job approval rating serves as the dependent variable. I have coded the dependent variable on a -1 to 1 scale (where -1 connotes disapproval, 0 connotes neutrality, and 1 indicates approval, with -0.5 and 0.5 capturing those who were weaker in their approval/disapproval). Given the ordinal nature of the dependent variable, I use ordered logistic regression for this analysis.

My primary independent variables include favorability ratings, whether President Obama met the respondent's expectations with respect to improving black lives, and perceptions of why congressional Republicans opposed Obama. For the "meets expectations" questions, I code responses to the question as dummy variables, leaving the "did less than I expected" response (combined with the "don't know" and "doesn't matter" responses) as the comparison variable. I code the Obama and Black Lives Matter favorability ratings in the same way that I code the Obama favorability score, with 1 indicating strong favorability and -1 indicating strong unfavorability.

Table 6.7 Ordered logistic regression of Obama job approval on perceptions of racial issues and obstacles, 2016

Variable	Coefficient (SE)
Obama favorability	2.706 (0.362)**
Obama did more for blacks than I expected	1.728 (0.455)**
Obama did about what I expected for blacks	1.025 (0.378)**
Obama did about what I expected for blacks	0.587 (0.408)
Congressional GOP opposed Obama most because of racism	1.067 (0.390)**
Black Lives Matter favorability	0.589 (0.261)**
Republican	-0.071 (0.631)
Democrat	0.235 (0.511)
Conservative	0.541 (0.412)
Liberal	0.638 (0.374)*
Male	0.138 (0.328)
Age	0.280 (0.174)
Evangelical	0.197 (0.333)
Northeast	0.130 (0.507)
South	0.652 (0.418)
West	0.614 (0.581)
Less than a bachelor's degree	0.049 (0.328)
Under $30,000	-0.152 (0.472)
$30,000 to $49,999	0.129 (0.506)
$50,000 to $79,999	0.214 (0.443)
N	282
Pseudo R-Squared	0.3712

Source: James Weldon Johnson Institute 2016 Election Survey (Gillespie 2016).
**$p<0.05$; *$p<0.10$, two-tailed test.

For the question about why Obama clashed with Congress, I code individual responses as dummy variables and include in the model those who thought that Congress opposed Obama because of partisan differences and racial animus. In this case, the reference category is those who believed that policy differences explained congressional opposition. Those who did not answer the question were removed from this analysis.

I also include dummy variables for control variables such as party (independents are the reference category), ideology (moderates are the reference category), gender (male=1), region (Midwest is the reference category), and whether respondents identify as evangelical Christians. I code age as an interval variable with millennials (age 18–34) equaling 1 and those aged 65 and older equaling 4; I also include dummy variables for whether respondents do not have a bachelor's degree and for income, with those making $80,000 or above as the reference category.

I present the models in Table 6.7. I find that a respondent's favorability rating of Obama is the strongest predictor of whether or not she approved of the job he did as president. Respondents with stronger favorability ratings gave Obama higher approval ratings. Next in importance was whether respondents thought that Obama had met their expectations with respect to improving the lives of blacks. Those who thought that Obama met or exceeded their expectations were significantly more likely to give him a higher approval rating than those who reported that Obama had done less than they expected for blacks, who did not know or who thought that this question did not matter to them. As is perhaps not surprising, respondents who thought that Obama had exceeded their expectations were particularly inclined to approve of President Obama's job performance. Having a favorable view of Black Lives Matter was also positively correlated with giving President Obama a positive job approval rating.

In addition, there is evidence of a significant racial rally. Respondents who thought that congressional Republicans opposed Obama because of racism were more likely to give him high job approval ratings compared to those who thought that Congress opposed the president because of policy differences.

As is perhaps not surprising, responses to the specific job approval questions (i.e., whether respondents approve of the job President Obama did on the economy, crime, terrorism, diplomacy, etc.) were highly correlated with one another. As such, I excluded them from this model. I did run separate models including one of these job approval metrics at a time. Again, it should not be surprising that, with the exception of one variable (diplomacy), each of these job approval ratings was significantly and positively correlated with Obama's general job approval rating (serving with integrity and race relations were significant at the $p<0.1$ level). The only other difference across models was that in some regressions, being liberal was not significantly correlated with approving of the job President Obama did (at the $p<0.1$ level), as it is in the model presented here.

Analysis and conclusion

Collectively, the data sources reviewed in this chapter reveal that the predictors of support for President Obama were multifaceted. Obama's high approval ratings among blacks, driven partially by high favorability ratings, clearly illustrate his symbolic importance in black communities. However, favorability alone does not explain why blacks gave him such high job approval ratings. For instance, there is evidence that respondents approved of the job Obama did managing the budget, and this correlated with positive approval ratings.

There is also evidence that black voters viewed the Obama presidency through the prism of race. Though the 2014 dataset was too small to detect a relationship between perceptions of racialized gridlock and Obama's job approval, the 2016 data does show that those who perceived a racial undercurrent to Obama's tense relationship with congressional Republicans were more likely to approve of the job that he was doing. Moreover, 2016 respondents who indicated that Obama had met or exceeded their expectations for helping to improve black lives were also more inclined to give him high marks.

That I was able to detect nuances in levels of support for Barack Obama using surveys of small sample size suggests the need for more detailed analysis in the years ahead. Future surveys should ask similar questions to the ones included in this survey, using much larger sample sizes. Given the significant findings presented in this chapter, I suspect that larger sample surveys will likely find greater complexity in the relationships between black voters' perceptions of the state of race and their assessments of President Obama.

The findings in this chapter confirm a long-held axiom in the study of African American politics. The structural limitations of American politics which privilege two party politics limit political options for blacks, whose policy preferences are often not completely in sync with the Democratic Party (see Frymer 1999). As a result, the near unanimous Democratic voting behavior in black communities masks important complexity in black political attitudes and behavior. The data in this chapter show that blacks were certainly supportive of the president, but that they harbored a little skepticism. When they perceived that President Obama's leadership was lacking or that he had not done enough to help blacks, their support was less enthusiastic. This suggests that the continued support of the president that we witnessed in the Obama years was not evidence of blind loyalty. Rather, it reflected blacks' belief that Obama was the best imperfect option they had.

Conclusion: Was it worth it?

This book seeks to build upon existing scholarly work to further understand the complicated relationship between African American pride in the election of a black president and the problem of persistent racial inequality. Political scientists such as Dawson and Harris—along with other public intellectuals such as Tavis Smiley and Cornel West (see "Tavis Smiley, Cornel West on the 2012 Election…" 2012)—point out the structural stability of persistent inequality and criticize the president for not having done enough to narrow the gaps. At the same time, they argue that black voters seem to have been comfortable with the president's performance. Were they, as Harris contended, content with the "symbolism of a black president and a black family in the White House," regardless of whether the overall plight of blacks improved (Harris 2012, 185)?

The data in this volume urge the critics to consider more evidence. Contrary to some claims that President Obama catered to other identity groups to the exclusion of his most loyal constituency, his administration did provide evidence that they at least tried to address issues of concern to black communities, both substantively and symbolically and sometimes with greater frequency than did his two immediate predecessors. And when we consider a wider universe of actions that the administration took—not just the high profile efforts—it is harder to make the argument that the Obama Administration ignored the interests of blacks to boost the causes of other groups.

The purpose of this volume is to consider the volume of racial activity in presidential administrations. In that respect, the Obama Administration did demonstrate greater activity on racial issues—affecting blacks and other minorities—on some dimensions. One can observe this activity in President Obama's symbolic and substantive efforts. The larger question is whether those overtures were adequate. Future work should probe this question in greater detail, but the findings here suggest that there is evidence to support praising and critiquing President Obama. For instance, supporters of

President Obama could point to the Department of Education's aggressive advocacy of racial groups and issues in its press releases; or the Labor Department's championing of "vulnerable" populations; or the fact that the Civil Rights Division of the Justice Department was more likely to publicize activities it took on behalf of blacks than any other group. President Obama also deserves credit for issuing more executive orders that addressed race and for appointing more blacks to appointed positions within his administration.

This praise, though, can reasonably come with criticism. The general state of inequality between blacks and whites across numerous dimensions (health, educational, and economic) persisted over President Obama's tenure in office. One can interpret this two ways. First, it raises general questions about whether or not the Obama Administration was aggressive enough in addressing racial inequality. Take Obamacare, for example. The Obama Administration really did not frame the policy in racialized terms. And though the percentage of blacks who did not have insurance decreased after the law went into effect, a higher percentage of blacks relative to whites still lacked insurance. Would outcomes have been better (i.e., would there have been a smaller ratio of black–white uninsurance rates) if the policy had been more explicitly framed to target groups (i.e., blacks and Latinos/as) who were more likely to not have insurance?

This line of questioning highlights concerns about strategy and whether President Obama's tendency to play down racial activities or frame them in transcendent terms actually hampered his ability to address obvious forms of inequality. This is a variation on the common critique of deracialized campaign strategies. While there has been considerable scholarly focus on whether deracialized politicians can maintain multiracial electoral coalitions after employing such a strategy (see McCormick and Jones 1993; Gillespie 2010a; 2012), scholars also consider whether one can actually address problems which disproportionately affect some communities with transcendently framed programs. Targeted problems warrant intentionally targeted solutions, or so the logic goes.

We know from previous experimental studies that highly racialized policies like welfare generate greater public support among whites when respondents are primed to think about white as opposed to black beneficiaries (see Valentino et al. 2002). Furthermore, other findings suggest that when survey respondents were primed to associate policy initiatives with President Obama, they were more likely to oppose his proposals (see Tesler 2016). Findings like these help to provide a contextual justification for Obama's reticence to act as aggressively as some would have hoped on reducing racial inequalities.

This raises an even bigger question—one that unfortunately goes beyond the scope of this work but will be debated for years to come. There will likely be considerable debate about whether Obama actually wanted to reduce inequality. Assuming that he did, whose fault is it that President Obama may not have actually been able to act aggressively on behalf of blacks? Scholars, analysts, and citizens must consider the balance between three players: an uncooperative Congress; citizens who resisted attempts to change the status quo or were content to be satisfied with incremental change; and a presidential administration which may have been too cautious.

Resolving this debate requires the following considerations. First, divided government control and partisan polarization have to be considered as legitimate structural barriers to reducing inequality. Sarah Binder (2014) finds increasing legislative gridlock in Congress over time. While gridlock lessens during periods of unified partisan control (of Congress and the presidency), divided government alone cannot explain the current legislative stalemate. Binder contends that it is important to consider intra-legislative institutional barriers, increased electoral competition, and ideological polarization as well. That the rules governing bill passage differ across chambers, increasing electoral competitiveness (as measured by the Electoral College vote margin in presidential elections and the partisan balance of seats in congressional and Senate elections), and increasing ideological polarity among members of Congress also help to explain Congress' inability to pass legislation. These factors can all be deployed to explain President Obama's difficulty—especially after the Democrats lost partisan control of the legislature—in getting bills through Congress.

Second, it would be unwise to ignore the impact of public sentiment in reining in any potential ambition to advance radically redistributive policies intended to reduce inequality along racial lines. Congressional elites are not the only group of people who are increasingly polarized; there is also evidence that the American electorate in general is increasingly polarized ideologically as well (see Abramowitz and Saunders 2008). And while scholars held out hope nearly a decade ago of there being a gradual convergence (at least among black and white Democrats) in policy preferences (see Tate 2010), other scholarship points to the persistent, predictive power of racially resentful attitudes toward blacks and support for racially conservative policy positions. Scholars making these findings see a direct connection between these attitudes and the emergence of the Tea Party and connections between perceptions of strong white identity and support for Republican presidential candidates (see Parker and Barreto 2013; Jardina 2014; Tesler 2016).

Perhaps because of these challenges, many rank-and-file African Americans tempered their expectations about what to expect from the Obama Administration. As the public opinion data in Chapter 6 show, a majority of black Democrats—Obama's base—thought that Obama had at least met their expectations for addressing racial issues. So, while the debate about whether black expectations were too small will likely continue for some time, we have to acknowledge the ways that black voters articulated their satisfaction with his performance overall and the ways that by the end of his term, they blamed the perceived racism of congressional Republicans for President Obama's inability to pass parts of his legislative agenda.

A new strategy for black politics? A diffused approach to the inside-outside strategy

These factors help to explain, at least in part, the factors which constrained President Obama from being successful in reducing inequality. They also may hold the keys to crafting a new black political strategy going forward. Now that America has elected a black president, we know that one president or two presidential terms cannot be a panacea for centuries of discrimination and inequality.

Years ago, in a warning to black communities to not put all of their hopes on elected leadership to fulfill the promises of the civil rights movement, Ronald Walters urged black political actors to maintain a diversified portfolio of political strategies to achieve their policy goals. Blacks should pursue formal elective offices, but they should also maintain robust protest organizations that can serve as gadflies to spur the elected officials to add black issues to their legislative and policy agendas (Walters and Smith 1999, ch. 9).

Though not specified, scholars have often spoken of this "insider-outsider" strategy in the context of national politics (Walters and Smith 1999, ch. 9). Indeed, when Harris (2012) spoke about the need for the emergence of a robust social movement to occur to keep President Obama accountable, it was reminiscent of Walters' initial call. The events of the Obama Administration point to the strategy's efficacy and exigence at the state and local level as well. Blacks have historically appealed to the federal government for redress because state and local governments were often unresponsive or hostile to civil rights concerns (see McClain and Stewart 1995, 105–106). The issues of policing, while having some federal oversight, are largely the jurisdiction of state and local government. These issues exemplify the limits of President Obama's capacity. Even if the Justice Department had indicted and secured convictions of police officers, certain policy deliberations still would have to take place at the state and local levels. Perhaps Obama's successes and failures highlight the ways that we as citizens should not look to one elected official or one branch or level of government to quickly resolve an entrenched problem that is centuries old.

In many ways, thinking about the insider-outsider strategy comes back full circle to Dawson's (2011) critique as well. In chapter 4 of his book, he observes that Obama's election did not initially coincide with a resurgence in local black political organizing. It was as though all of the attention focused on the federal Executive Branch, and then the events of 2014 and its aftermath reminded black communities that state and local authorities were significant actors in racial flashpoint issues as well. Perhaps one of the more important takeaways of the Obama Administration is the recognition that diffused governmental power requires diffused social movement action and the targeting (and holding accountable) of multiple layers and branches of elected officials.

Is deracialization dead in the age of Black Lives Matter?

At this point, it would be remiss to ignore the implications of the emergence of Black Lives Matter for understanding and evaluating President Obama's overall legacy. After the mainstream media declared America "post-racial" in the wake of Barack Obama's election in 2008, few would have predicted that five to six years later, the high-profile murders of unarmed blacks—often but not always at the hands of police officers—would birth a social movement dedicated to completing the unfinished business of the twentieth-century civil rights movement.

Or perhaps we should have seen it coming. The post-racial proclamation of 2008 simultaneously embodied the racial hopes and anxieties of a wide spectrum of the American population. African Americans and their allies could take pride in America having broken the racial glass ceiling in electing the first black president. Those predisposed to colorblind philosophies hoped that the election of a black president signaled the culmination of having to actively and aggressively enforce civil rights legislation. Under this point of view, Obama's breakthrough denoted the success and obsolescence of civil rights enforcement. Finally, racial conservatives looked at the election of Barack Obama and the ability of a black person to supplant the racial caste system as the manifestation of a nightmare which would need to be resisted.

Conflict was inevitable. In the Epilogue, I will discuss the racial backlash that resulted from Obama's election. For now, it is helpful to focus on the implications of black pride in the election of Barack Obama. As blacks began to be elected to lower level offices en masse in the 1960s–1980s, scholars began to reflect on the impact of black officeholding on black political engagement. They noted that the emergence of successful black political candidates coincided with increased efficacy, empowerment, and black voter turnout, especially in those contests which elected the historic first black candidate (see Bobo and Gilliam 1990; Gay 2001).

The increased empowerment that likely emerged as a result of Barack Obama's election could have indirectly contributed to the emergence of Black Lives Matter. In his classic exposition of the emergence of the twentieth-century civil rights movement, Doug McAdam (1982) argues that it emerged mid-century because of a confluence of favorable social, economic, and political changes, plus a sense of cognitive liberation, or recognition that those changes increased the likelihood of movement success.

In many ways, the election of Barack Obama could count as the type of major political shift that could empower a new generation of blacks to believe in the efficacy of their movement efforts. If a black man can be elected president, then surely America can address the injustice of recurring, seemingly unjustified, police murders of unarmed blacks. In short, perhaps Black Lives Matter activists felt emboldened to mobilize because the election of Barack Obama—whether or not they agreed with his policies or thought that he had done enough for blacks—signaled that they themselves had powerful voices and could effect change.

We also have to consider the ways that the emergence of Black Lives Matter will have a reciprocal, long-term impact on the legacy of Barack Obama. It is difficult in the aggregate to detect the impact in President Obama's behavior. When I look at the Justice Department's reports of its own activity, I find that the Civil Rights Division actively investigated police misconduct cases throughout President Obama's tenure. I also do not find a sustained increase in the proportion of press releases issued after the deaths of people like Michael Brown and Eric Garner. In addition, while the Justice Department did use the investigative and consent decree process to identify systemic, discriminatory practices in police departments around the country—particularly after high-profile police killings—they also came to the conclusion that they did not have the evidence to proceed with criminal prosecutions against the officers implicated in some of the most high-profile cases. While these decisions might have been procedurally necessary, they came with a political cost that must be acknowledged.

In the immediate short-term, politicians seeking to don Barack Obama's mantle will likely shoulder the political costs. The increasing racial and political polarization of the current political moment creates push-and-pull forces for ambitious black politicians who aspire to statewide and national office. Barack Obama's election and re-election confirms the efficacy of using deracialized campaign strategies to win office (see Canon *et al.* 1996). It is still hard to imagine a truly viable black candidate for statewide or national office who would not have to frame a significant part of his or her platform in racially transcendent terms. Despite the growth in the nonwhite, largely Democratic voting population, Democratic candidates still need some white votes to win. Even Barack Obama's electoral coalition (in 2008 at least) included some racially resentful whites (see Hutchings 2009).

What is less likely in the short and near term is the emergence of deracialized black politicians adopting an optimistic (or even Pollyannish) deracialized posture. The next black candidates for president (and at the time of this writing, political analysts have identified Senators Cory Booker (D-NJ), Kamala Harris (D-CA), and former Governor Deval Patrick (D-MA)—all of whom have employed deracialized tactics at various points in their career, as potential candidates for president in 2020) (see Zengerle 2017), will likely engage in a form of quasi-deracialization. In his piece analyzing the deracialization tactics of Rep. Harold Ford Jr.'s 2006 Senate campaign, Sekou Franklin (2010, 215) observed that Ford engaged in "situational deracialization." Ford carefully cultivated a racially transcendent image for white audiences in majority white parts of Tennessee, but behind closed doors, he did engage black stakeholders on racial issues. Quasi-deracialization is similar, but the racialized postures that are hidden in situational deracialization would have to be visible. In short, deracialized politicians post-Obama cannot be satisfied with talking about race with black constituents behind closed doors or in unavoidable situations (like when President Obama was forced to deliver his "A More Perfect Union" speech in the wake of the Jeremiah Wright scandal). They are going to have to be proactive in openly initiating key discussions about their racial agenda while couching those issues within a larger, inclusive, racially transcendent agenda that demonstrates their agility in appealing to as wide a cross-section of the American electorate as possible.

A contemporary example may be useful here. In the 2016–2017 season of the National Football League, San Francisco 49ers quarterback Colin Kaepernick chose to kneel during the playing of the US National Anthem to protest racial injustice, particularly the police killings of unarmed blacks. At the start of the protest, a citizen asked President Obama for his reaction to Kaepernick's actions in a CNN town hall meeting. Obama responded with a characteristically nuanced response that explained the motivations of Kaepernick and his allies while acknowledging the concerns of critics: "I want (the protesters) to listen to the pain that that may cause somebody who, for example, had a spouse or a child who was killed in combat and why it hurts them to see somebody not standing ... But I also want people to think about the pain he may be expressing about somebody who's lost a loved one that they think was unfairly shot" (Obama, quoted in Diaz 2016). At the time, Senator Cory Booker also tried to parse the issue. He gave a full-throated defense of the issues which motivated Kaepernick's protest, noting that "People seem to be more outraged over taking a knee than the killing of an unarmed black man" and calling for extensive public dialogue on the subject off of the football field (SI Wire 2016). In the same interview, however, he also said that he disagreed with Kaepernick's chosen method of protest (SI Wire 2016). A year later, after President Donald Trump issued tweets and public statements criticizing protesting players[1] and calling for NFL owners to discipline them, Booker offered a more full-throated defense of the football players who chose to protest. In an interview on MSNBC, Booker contended that "protest is patriotism," that the kneeling football players were "doing this because of real issues in this country," and that anyone who claimed to be more patriotic than those who protested demonstrated "a shallow patriotism that seeks more to divide, demean, degrade others and lift themselves up" (Booker, quoted in Brown 2017). Booker's quotes stoked the ire of in conservative media (see Brown 2017), but the Congressional Black Caucus also featured the comments on its website, which were made in the same week as the convening of the caucus' Annual Legislative Conference ("Senator Cory Booker on NFL Anthem Protests" 2017).

Booker, like Obama, has a long-standing personal and philosophical commitment to deracialized or racially transcendent politics (see Gillespie 2012). However, the current racially charged political environment—which is animated by a range of issues, from policing to the current president's divisive rhetoric—makes it difficult for black politicians to be totally transcendent. The NFL protests are a particularly divisive issue. CNN reported that Americans were nearly equally split in their reaction to the NFL protests: 49 percent opposed the protest, while 43 percent supported it. There was notable racial polarization on this issue: 59 percent of whites polled said the protest was wrong, while 82 percent of blacks supported it (Agiesta 2017). Classic deracialization theory suggests that this would be the type of issue that racially transcendent politicians would try to avoid at all costs. That Booker could not escape this issue and that he strengthened and reaffirmed his support for African Americans in the face of white opposition on a divisive

---

[1] Kaepernick did not play football during the 2017–2018 NFL season. Other players around the league continued protesting in Kaepernick's absence.

issue demonstrates that even the most deracialized black politicians have had to recalibrate their political style in light of the current, racially charged political moment.

Future directions

It is impossible to write a truly comprehensive review of the Obama Administration in any one volume, much less a small book that was completed in the 18 months after President Obama left office. This is not the last word on the Obama Administration—by me or anyone else. We will spend the next 20 years (and more) deconstructing the Obama Administration and its long-term impact on black political, social, and economic well-being. I hope that I have been able to contribute a small but important piece to this debate. My work continues, though. Time and space considerations prevented me from addressing a number of issues that I would have loved to have addressed in this book. For instance, as I mentioned in the introduction, I did not focus on foreign policy at all. I also do not examine President Obama's record on civil liberties—a place where he encountered strong criticism from the ideological left. While I do conduct a preliminary analysis of four Cabinet-level departments, there are still other departments to examine and more issues to probe, even within the departments I do study. And there are other aspects of Executive Branch politics to study. For instance, given the Trump Administration's predilection for dismantling the regulatory state, future scholars—particularly those studying racial and ethnic politics—need to devote time to comparing the regulatory regimes of President Obama, his predecessors, and his successors. And now that there is a critical mass of current and former Cabinet secretaries of color, particularly in key departments such as Justice and State, we are now able to conduct case studies examining the ways that minority Cabinet officials may subtly or not-so-subtly add racial issues to the agenda through departmental initiatives, rhetoric, congressional testimony, etc.

In addition, the role of First Lady Michelle Obama in representing racialized interests in the Obama Administration is a fruitful topic. I only scratched the surface of this topic in the symbolic politics chapter. I hope to finish a book-length examination of Mrs. Obama soon.

These studies have become even more necessary in the wake of the election of Donald Trump to succeed Barack Obama. Scholars were already producing work examining the continued significance of racial resentment to understanding the growth of oppositional political movements and to understanding policy preferences and voting behavior (see Parker and

Barreto 2013; Jardina 2014; Anderson 2016; Tesler 2016). In the wake of the 2016 election outcome, there is now greater interest in trying to understand the election results and to determine the correlation between President Trump's explicit racial appeals and his electoral performance. The initial wave of scholarship will no doubt focus on the 2016 election, but subsequent studies must not neglect considering the role President Obama's success played in activating the latent worldviews of President Trump's supporters and in motivating national Republican efforts to align with President Trump. Future studies must also determine if any effort of President Trump to reverse Obama-era policies will have a disproportionate impact on black and other minority communities.

Epilogue: Considering the Obama legacy in the age of Trump

I, like many people, assumed that Hillary Clinton would win the 2016 election. She was a flawed candidate, for sure, but she led most of the national polls, and the statisticians who examined statewide trends predicted a solid Electoral College lead for her ("General Election: Trump vs. Clinton" n.d.; Linzer 2016; Wang 2016; "Who Will Win the Presidency?" 2016). Beyond that, it seemed inconceivable that America would actually go through with electing a candidate who started his campaigning maligning Mexicans, insulted a Muslim family who had lost a child in combat, and was accused of sexual harassment by more than a dozen women (See BBC News 2016). After all, there was scholarly evidence to suggest that overt political displays of racism turned off voters and were less effective than more subtle racial appeals. In her classic work, *The Race Card*, Tali Mendelberg (2001) argued that the norm of equality so dominated American culture that modern politicians made overt racial appeals at their peril. And when audio evidence of Donald Trump bragging about grabbing women by the genitals emerged, many assumed that Trump's apparent racism and misogyny would deliver the one-two punch that would doom his candidacy.

We were wrong. And we probably should have seen this coming. On Election Night 2016, CNN commentator Van Jones described the results as "a whitelash against a changing country. It was whitelash against a black president in part. And that's the part where the pain comes" (Jones, quoted in Ryan 2016). Jones' phrasing was a cogent way of describing what scholars have long observed about the civil rights struggle. President Obama often quoted Martin Luther King's sentiment that "the arc of the moral universe is long, but it bends toward justice." Many scholars—from political scientists Rogers Smith and Phillip Klinkner to historians William Jelani Cobb and Carol Anderson—would argue that the arc is also jagged and will sometimes regress before it progresses. As they note, major civil rights progress in America—say, emancipation and Reconstruction or the passage of civil rights legislation in the 1960s—has usually been met with some type of backlash. Reconstruction was followed by Redemption, or the violent emergence of the Jim Crow regime in the South. The Civil Rights Act and the Voting Rights Act were followed by the Republican Party's efforts (called the Southern Strategy) to woo voters who opposed the societal changes ushered in by the civil rights movement (see Klinkner and Smith 1999; Cobb 2010; Anderson 2016).

In the months since Donald Trump won his election and ascended to the presidency, citizens and scholars have been trying to gauge the effects. The data-gathering is a work in progress, and people will spend many years and a lot of ink (both literal and digital) trying to understand the impact of the election of Donald Trump. One thing is clear: Donald Trump represents a clear departure from the Obama era. Based on how President Trump has governed so far, a lot of the early analysis will focus on the long-term difference he will play in promoting positive race relations, in using executive power to protect the civil rights of minorities, and in reducing inequality. Indeed, the contrasts between the Trump and Obama presidencies may prompt people to think differently about how they judge President Obama's substantive and symbolic race politics.

The contrasts begin in their formative years. One only has to look at their reflections on their schooling to see the stark differences. In letters to his college girlfriend from the early 1980s, Barack Obama spoke eagerly about his studies. These letters, now archived at Emory University, were written from 1982 to 1984. Obama had transferred to Columbia University, leaving his then-girlfriend, Alexandra McNeal, back at Occidental College, where they first met. Obama is getting ready to delve into the courses he will need to complete his major. In the first letter, he mourns the fact that he is going to have to take more major-specific than general education classes. His lament reflects the sober realization that he cannot master all of the liberal arts. He says, "I can do anything, but not everything" (Obama 1982).

Later in the letter, he talks about being excited to take a physics class. He describes it as a break from his political science classes; however, he also notes how nuclear policy links politics to physics:

> My favorite [class] so far is a physics course for non-mathematicians that I'm taking to fulfill the science requirement. We study electrons, neutrons, quarks, electromagnetic fields and other tantalizing phenomenon ... thinking in purely scientific terms, and dealing with scales far removed from the human world gives me a release and creative

escape from the frustrations of studying men and their frequently dingy institutions. Of course, the fact that the knowledge I absorb in the class facilitates nuclear war prevents a real clean break. (Obama 1982)

In this letter and others, Obama's casual references evince his voracious reading appetite. He quotes William Yeats, T.S. Eliot, and Friedrich Nietzsche. He sends his girlfriend a book review of a work by a feminist literary critic because they have apparently been talking about how gender norms place expectations on women's life trajectories generally and on her path in particular.[1] In total, young Obama's letters betray an intellectual agility and curiosity that would presage the person who would be called the "professor-in-chief" (Obama 1982; 1983; Kantor 2008).

In contrast, Donald Trump describes his intellectual pursuits as instrumental and motivated by a drive to compete. In his book, *The Art of the Deal,* Trump explains his decision to transfer from Fordham University to the Wharton School of Business at the University of Pennsylvania. In his words, "as long as I had to be in college, I might as well test myself against the best" (Trump 1987, 77).[2] Once enrolled, Trump said, "It didn't take me long to realize that there was nothing particularly awesome or exceptional about my classmates … The other important thing I got from Wharton was a Wharton degree. In my opinion, that degree doesn't prove very much, but a lot of people I do business with take it very seriously, and it's considered very prestigious" (Trump 1987, 77). Trump's comments suggest that he pursued an elite education because it opened professional doors, not because he cared about learning.

The contrasts continue in terms of policy agenda. Given President Trump's affiliation with the Republican Party, it is not surprising that his policy agenda looks different from President Obama's agenda. Initial observers have raised the question of whether Trump will try to singlehandedly dismantle Obama's policies through legislative initiative and regulatory reform. As Peter Baker writes, "Whether out of personal animus, political calculation, philosophical disagreement or a conviction that the last president damaged the country, Mr. Trump has made clear that if it has Mr. Obama's name on it, he would just as soon erase it from the national hard drive" (Baker 2017). One of the key places that this could happen silently is in the realm of regulation. On January

---

1   The work in question is Rachel Brownstein's *Becoming a Heroine,* a literary analysis of nineteenth-century British novels with female protagonists written by female authors such as Charlotte Brontë, George Eliot, and Jane Austen (Broyard 1982).

2   To be fair, Trump also said that he chose Wharton over Harvard because Wharton produced entrepreneurs he admired (Trump 1987). However, keep in mind that while Harvard has a famed graduate business school, it does not have an undergraduate business program (See Harvard University n.d.).

30, 2017, President Trump issued Executive Order 13771, which calls for the elimination of at least two regulations for every new rule proposed (Trump 2017). Going forward, scholars should monitor regulatory changes to gauge the implications of these changes on racial politics. Do these rule changes make it easier or harder to reduce inequality?

Beyond rule changes, the ascension of President Trump brought in a new crop of political appointees, some of whom have a checkered record on civil rights. For instance, President Trump nominated Sen. Jeff Sessions of Alabama to serve as his attorney general. The Senate refused to confirm Sessions for a federal judgeship in 1986 after critics accused Sessions of making racially insensitive comments. The Leadership Conference on Civil Rights assessed Sen. Sessions' support for civil rights legislation in 2010 and gave him a grade of zero out of 100. Since taking the helm at the Department of Justice, Sessions has signaled sympathy for white and Asian American college applicants who believe that they have been disadvantaged by affirmative action policies in college admissions. And he has ordered prosecutors in his office to pursue maximum sentences for drug crimes, including low-level offenses (Leadership Conference on Civil Rights 2010; Ford 2017; LaFraniere and Apuzzo 2017; Savage 2017).

Then there is the symbolic politics. If we have learned anything over the course of the last two years, it is that optics matter, if only because they are often intimately tied to substance. Whereas Barack Obama invited Lin-Manuel Miranda to the White House to workshop the music for what would become the Broadway hit *Hamilton*, Donald Trump puzzled audiences with his present-tense praise for Frederick Douglass, who died in 1895 (many observers believed that Trump thought Douglass was still alive). And where Obama comforted mourners at the funeral of Rev. Clementa Pinckney, the pastor of Emanuel AME Church who was killed by a white supremacist—even breaking into singing *Amazing Grace*—Trump alienated many when he defended white supremacists marching to maintain Confederate monuments in Charlottesville, Virginia—even after one of them killed a woman by running her over with his car—by saying that "both sides" were to blame for the violence that ensued in the demonstrations and that not all of the pro-Confederate protesters were white supremacists (Obama 2015e; "'Hamilton' at the White House Then and Now" 2016; Shear and Haberman 2017; Wootson 2017).

To be sure, substantive politics are still more important than symbolic gestures. However, even if President Trump quietly pursued policies to help blacks, critics would still have much to critique in his race-baiting and general insensitivity because the incendiary rhetoric would negate at least some of the positive impact of the policies. At its core, then, the Trump presidency demonstrates the strong linkages between symbols and substance.

The symbolic politics are a signal about what types of substantive policies to anticipate.

In retrospect, then, Barack Obama's symbolic achievements should not be underestimated. Yes, there are legitimate reasons to be dissatisfied with the glacial pace of reducing racial inequality in this country. And no, politicians should not be able to rest on the laurels of symbolic gestures to black voters. In the future, though, perhaps we should consider the ways that symbols are signals of a president's desired agenda. And beyond that, we should look for the ways that presidents try to enact that agenda in heralded and unheralded, successful and unsuccessful ways.

Thinking about the Obama presidency as a relay leg

In a March 2016 press conference, a reporter asked President Obama to reflect on his legacy. In crafting his answer, Obama used the analogy of a relay runner to describe how he perceived his role and how he wanted to be judged:

> Now, one of the things I learned after 7½ years in office is that … we're like a relay runner. We take the baton. And sometimes, when we take the baton, we're behind in the race. And we don't always choose the circumstances when we get the baton. The question is, for our leg of the race, did we advance the causes we care about? Did our team gain ground against the challenges that we care about? And on that front, I believe we have achieved that. (Obama 2016c)

The impatient will likely be dissatisfied by that answer. It connotes a certain type of incrementalism that seems antiquated. And for those who come from groups that have experienced generations of disadvantage and discrimination, being asked to wait further may seem unreasonable or unbearable.

A person's perspective on the Obama Administration is likely contingent on their level of patience and the expectations they had of him when he was first elected president. Those who thought Obama's election represented a sea change in American politics expected that the electoral victory would be matched by a sea change in policy. While Obama could have done more from a policy standpoint, it was unrealistic to expect him, as the head of one-third of the American national government, to make all the changes and to succeed in every initiative he undertook. As a result, the more patient (or perhaps the more privileged who can afford to wait longer) will probably have a more positive view of the president's record on racial issues. For those whose needs are more urgent or whose patience has worn thin, they have reason to be more critical.

Only time will tell what President Obama's legacy will be. If I had to guess his overall ranking in the pantheon of American presidents, I would guess that he will land between the 15th and 50th percentile—not Washington, but not Harding or Buchanan, either.[3] A number of factors will inform how historians will rank Obama. His role as the first black president will help him stand out. His support of civil rights issues may serve him well with modern rankers who tend to weigh civil rights advocacy favorably (see Nichols 2012). It will be years before we have a full picture of the long-term policy impact of some of Obama's initiatives, though.

The question remains about whether Obama will be perceived as a transformative president. Stephen Skowronek defined a transformative president as one who reshaped the office and created policies whose impact would last far beyond his presidency (as an analog, Franklin Roosevelt would be considered transformative because his New Deal program impacted the American economy for decades after his death). Presidents who succeed troubled predecessors also tend to be viewed more favorably (Skowronek 2008; Skowronek 1997). Going into the presidency, Obama had the advantage of following an unpopular president. The dissatisfaction with the Bush Administration did create opportunities for Obama to present a vision of change. While this certainly helped him get elected (see McIlwain 2010), he later encountered structural and political obstacles to enacting that change—namely, having to navigate divided party control with an uncooperative opposition party for the last three-quarters of his time in office.

In many ways, whether Barack Obama will be perceived as a transformative president is contingent on the future trajectory of American presidential leadership. In many ways, Obama's legacy is inversely tethered to the legacy of Donald Trump. Beyond Trump's apparent desire to dismantle Obama's policy program, if Trump's policy agenda—arguably the antithesis of Obama's agenda—succeeds in producing better outcomes for Americans, including blacks, it is likely that Obama will not be viewed as transformative. In that case, Trump's agenda and vision would shape America's future trajectory. If Trump fails miserably, Obama could be vindicated; his policy agenda could be rebuilt; and in comparison, his legacy will appear stronger (though he would have to share his legacy with the president who rebuilt that agenda).

To be sure, though, a future resurrection of Obama's legacy is likely contingent on America's overall civic health. We do not know yet the extent to which President Trump, through his bravado and seeming disregard for norms, will indelibly reshape American political institutions. If he succeeds in permanently transforming American government—and especially if this success marginalizes blacks—then Obama's legacy will be moot.

3 As an example, Rottinghaus and Vaughn's 2018 President's and Executive Politics Presidential Greatness Survey ranks Lincoln and Washington at the top of the list and Obama as 8th overall. More rankings will follow in the years to come (See Dunn 2018).

Appendix

Black issue themed promises made by Barack Obama, by promise status

Status of the promise

Kept	Broken	Compromised
1. Recruit math and science graduates to the teaching profession.	1. Sign the Deceptive Practices and Voter Intimidation Prevention Act into law.	1. Improve high school graduation rates.
2. Push for the enactment of the Matthew Shepard-James Byrd Hate Crimes Prevention Act.	2. Allow bankruptcy judges to modify terms of a home mortgage.	2. Eliminate disparity in sentencing for crack and powder cocaine.
3. Vigorously pursue hate crimes and civil rights abuses.	3. Fully fund the COPS program.	3. Ban racial profiling in federal law enforcement agencies.
4. Reform mandatory minimum sentences.	4. Encourage diversity in media ownership.	4. Increase the supply of affordable housing throughout metropolitan regions.
5. Create a White House Office on Urban Policy.	5. Double federal program to help reverse commuters who go from city to suburbs.	5. Sign the Responsible Fatherhood and Healthy Families Act.
6. Fully fund the Community Development Block Grant.		6. Strengthen the levees in New Orleans.
7. Create a Homeowner Obligation Made Explicitly (HOME) score for mortgage comparisons.		7. Strengthen the African Growth and Opportunity Act.
8. Establish Promise Neighborhoods in areas of concentrated poverty.		8. Pressure Sudan to end violence in Darfur.
9. Cap interest rates on payday loans and improve disclosure requirements.		9. Fix problems of voter access such as long lines on Election Day and early voting days.

Status of the promise

Kept	Broken	Compromised
10. Establish school programs to highlight space and science achievements.		
11. Establish special crime programs for the New Orleans area.		
12. Attract more students to science and math.		
13. Attract more doctors to rural areas.		
14. Send first-time non-violent drug offenders to rehab if appropriate.		
15. Create youth service corps.		
16. Create job training programs for clean technologies.		
17. Help restore Gulf Coast wetlands that protect against hurricanes.		
18. Increase minority access to capital		

Source: Author's compilation using Politifact's "Obameter" (Politifact n.d.) Promises were coded using the descriptions of the promises included on the website.

Bibliography

Abramowitz, Alan and Kyle Saunders. 2008. "Is Polarization a Myth?" *The Journal of Politics.* 70(2): 542–555.

ACT, Inc. n.d. "The ACT Profile Report—National. Graduating Class 2015." Retrieved from www.act.org/content/dam/act/unsecured/documents/ACT-National-Profile-Report-2015.pdf, September 10, 2017.

Adair, Bill and Angie Drobnic Holan. 2013. "The Principles of Poltifact, Punditfact and the Truth-O-Meter." *Politifact.com.* November 1, 2013. Retrieved from www.politifact.com/truth-o-meter/article/2013/nov/01/principles-politifact-punditfact-and-truth-o-meter/#, September 30, 2016.

Agiesta, Jennifer. 2017. "CNN Poll: Americans Split on Anthem Protests." *CNN.com.* September 30. Retrieved from www.cnn.com/2017/09/29/politics/national-anthem-nfl-cnn-poll/index.html, October 20, 2017.

Aisch, Gregor and Alicia Parlapiano. 2017. "'What Do You Think Is the Most Important Problem Facing This Country Today?'" *New York Times.* February 27. Retrieved from www.nytimes.com/interactive/2017/02/27/us/politics/most-important-problem-gallup-polling-question.html?mcubz=3, September 7, 2017.

Albritton, Robert, George Amedee, Keenan Grenell, and Don-Terry Veal. 1996. "Deracialization and the New Black Politics." In *Race, Politics and Governance in the United States.* Huey L. Perry (Ed.). Gainesville: University of Florida Press. 173–192.

Alexander, Michelle. 2010. *The New Jim Crow.* New York: New Press.

Allen, Ron. 2016. "College Freshman Recounts Impact of Obama's My Brother's Keeper Program." *NBCBLK.com.* December 14. Retrieved from www.nbcnews.com/news/nbcblk/college-freshman-recounts-impact-obama-s-my-brother-s-keeper-n696196, November 10, 2017.

Anderson, Carol. 2016. *White Rage.* New York: Bloomsbury Press.

Anderson, Nick. 2013. "Tighter Federal Lending Standards Yield Turmoil for Historically Black Colleges." *Washington Post.* June 22. Retrieved from www.washingtonpost.com/local/education/tighter-federal-lending-standards-yield-turmoil-for-historically-black-colleges/2013/06/22/6ade4acc-d9a5-11e2-a9f2-42ee3912ae0e_story.html, July 20, 2015.

Associated Press. 1987. "Nancy Gives Keynote Address." *Houston Chronicle.* May 26. 5.

Associated Press. 2012. "The Associated Press Racial Attitudes Survey." October 26.

Baker, Peter. 2010. "Obama Signs Law Narrowing Cocaine Sentencing Disparities." *New York Times.* August 3. Retrieved from https://thecaucus.blogs.nytimes.com/2010/08/03/obama-signs-law-narrowing-cocaine-sentencing-disparities/, October 18, 2017.

Baker, Peter. 2017. "The Anti-Legacy." *New York Times.* June 25. SR1.

Barker, Lucius J. and Mack H. Jones. 1994. *African Americans and the American Political System.* Englewood Cliffs: Prentice Hall.

Barnett, Jessica C. and Edward R. Berchick. 2017. *Health Insurance Coverage in the United States: 2016.* United States Census Bureau. Retrieved from www.census.gov/library/publications/2017/demo/p60-260.html, September 10, 2017.

BBC News. 2016. "US Election: What Are the Sexual Allegations against Donald Trump?" *BBCNews.com.* 23 October. Retrieved from https://www.bbc.com/news/election-us-2016-37641814, 9 July 2018.

Bean, Annemarie, James V. Hatch, and Brooks McNamara. 1996. "Editor's Preface." In *Inside the Minstrel Mask: Readings in Nineteenth-Century Blackface Minstrelsy.* Annemarie Bean, James V. Hatch and Brooks McNamara (Eds). Middletown: Wesleyan University Press. xi–xiv.

Belcher, Cornell. 2016. *A Black Man in the White House: Barack Obama and the Triggering of America's Racial Aversion Crisis.* Healdsburg, CA: Uptown Professional Press.

Berman, Russell. 2014. "The House Republicans Finally Sued Obama." *The Atlantic.* November 21. Retrieved from www.theatlantic.com/politics/archive/2014/11/house-republicans-finally-sue-obama-over-affordable-care-act-speaker-john-boehner/383047/, November 11, 2017.

Best, James J. 1981. "Presidential Cabinet Appointments, 1953–1976." *Presidential Studies Quarterly.* 11(1): 62–66.

Bialik, Carl. 2016. "Sitting Presidents Give Way More Commencement Speeches Than They Used To." *FiveThirtyEight.com.* May 11. Retrieved from https://fivethirtyeight.com/features/sitting-presidents-give-way-more-commencement-speeches-than-they-used-to/, November 1, 2017.

Binder, Sarah. 2014. "Polarized We Govern?" Center for Effective Public Management. Brookings Institution. Retrieved from www.brookings.edu/wp-content/uploads/2016/06/BrookingsCEPM_Polarized_figReplacedTextRevTableRev.pdf, November 7, 2017.

Blair, Diane M. 2005. "We Go Ahead Together or We Go Down Together: The Civil Rights Rhetoric of Eleanor Roosevelt." In *Civil Rights Rhetoric and the American Presidency*. James Arnt Aune and Enrique D. Rigsby (Eds). College Station: Texas A&M University Press. 62–82.

Bobo, Lawrence and Frank Gilliam. 1990. "Race, Sociopolitical Participation and Black Empowerment." *American Political Science Review*. 84: 377–393.

Borrelli, MaryAnne. 1997. "Gender, Credibility and Politics: The Senate Nomination Hearings of Cabinet Secretaries-Designate, 1975–1993." *Political Research Quarterly*. 50(1): 171–197.

Borrelli, MaryAnne. 2010. "The Contemporary Presidency: Gender Desegregation and Gender Integration in the President's Cabinet, 1933–2010." *Presidential Studies Quarterly*. 40(4): 734–749.

Bositis, David A. 2002. *2002 National Opinion Poll: Politics*. Washington, DC: Joint Center for Political and Economic Studies.

Bositis, David A. 2008. *2008 National Opinion Poll: Politics*. Washington, DC: Joint Center for Political and Economic Studies.

Breitzer, Susan Roth. 2003. "Eleanor Roosevelt: An Unlikely Path to Political Activist." In *The Presidential Companion: Readings on the First Ladies*. Robert Watson and Anthony Eksterowicz (Eds). Columbia: University of South Carolina Press. 150–168.

Brown, Lauretta. 2017. "Sen. Cory Booker on NFL Anthem Protests: 'Protest is Patriotism.'" *Townhall.com*. September 27. Retrieved from https://townhall.com/tipsheet/laurettabrown/2017/09/27/sen-cory-booker-on-nfl-anthem-protests-protest-is-patriotism-n2387285, October 20, 2017.

Browning, Rufus, Dale Rogers Marshall, and David Tabb. 1984. *Protest Is Not Enough*. Berkeley: University of California Press.

Broyard, Anatole. 1982. "Books of the Times; Revising the Heroine." *New York Times*. September 11. Retrieved from www.nytimes.com/1982/09/11/books/books-of-the-times-revising-the-heroine.html, October 25, 2017.

Bureau of Labor Statistics. n.d. "Data Retrieval: Labor Force Statistics (CPS)." Retrieved from www.bls.gov/webapps/legacy/cpsatab2.htm, September 9, 2017.

Bureau of Labor Statistics. 2017. "Labor Force Statistics from the Current Population Survey. Table 18: Employed Persons by Detailed Industry, Sex, Race, and Hispanic or Latino Ethnicity." February 8. Retrieved from www.bls.gov/cps/cpsaat18.htm, October 17, 2017.

Bush, George H.W. 1989a. "The President's News Conference." January 27. Online by Gerhard Peters and John T. Woolley, *The American Presidency Project*. Retrieved from www.presidency.ucsb.edu/ws/?pid=16629, September 30, 2016.

Bush, George H.W. 1989b. "The President's News Conference in Helena, Montana." September 18. Online by Gerhard Peters and John T. Woolley, *The American Presidency Project*. Retrieved from www.presidency.ucsb.edu/ws/?pid=17538, September 30, 2016.

Bush, George H.W. 1990a. "The President's News Conference With Regional Reporters." December 18. Online by Gerhard Peters and John T. Woolley, *The American Presidency Project*. Retrieved from www.presidency.ucsb.edu/ws/ ?pid=19166, September 30, 2016.

Bush, George H.W. 1990b. "The President's News Conference Following Discussions With Prime Minister Toshiki Kaifu of Japan in Palm Springs, California." March 3. Online by Gerhard Peters and John T. Woolley, *The American Presidency Project*. Retrieved from www.presidency.ucsb.edu/ws/ ?pid=18215, September 30, 2016.

Bush, George H.W. 1991a. "The President's News Conference." October 25. Online by Gerhard Peters and John T. Woolley, *The American Presidency Project*. Retrieved from www.presidency.ucsb.edu/ws/?pid=20139, September 30, 2016.

Bush, George H.W. 1991b. "The President's News Conference in Kennebunkport, Maine." July 1. Online by Gerhard Peters and John T. Woolley, *The American Presidency Project*. Retrieved from www.presidency.ucsb.edu/ws/?pid=29651, September 30, 2016.

Bush, George H.W. 1992. "The President's News Conference With President Leonid Kravchuk of Ukraine." May 6. Online by Gerhard Peters and John T. Woolley, *The American Presidency Project*. Retrieved from www.presidency. ucsb.edu/ws/?pid=20919, September 30, 2016.

Bush, George W. 2005a. "The President's News Conference." January 26. Online by Gerhard Peters and John T. Woolley, *The American Presidency Project*. Retrieved from www.presidency.ucsb.edu/ws/?pid=64292, September 30, 2016.

Bush, George W. 2005b. "The President's News Conference." October 4. Online by Gerhard Peters and John T. Woolley, *The American Presidency Project*. Retrieved from www.presidency.ucsb.edu/ws/?pid=73824, September 30, 2016.

Bush, George W. 2007. "The President's News Conference." September 20. Online by Gerhard Peters and John T. Woolley, *The American Presidency Project*. Retrieved from www.presidency.ucsb.edu/ws/?pid=75807, September 30, 2016.

Bush, Laura. 2006. "Text of First Lady Laura Bush's Senior Class Day Address." *Vanderbilt News*. 11 May. Retrieved from https://news.van-derbilt.edu/2006/05/11/text-of-first-lady-laura-bushs-senior-class-day-address-56710/, August 5, 2018.

Caliendo, Stephen M. 2014. *Inequality in America: Race, Poverty and Fulfilling Democracy's Promise*. Boulder: Westview Press.

Camera, Lauren. 2016. "Pell Grant Changes Aimed at Allowing Poor Students to Graduate Faster." *USNews.com*. January 19. Retrieved from www.usnews. com/news/articles/2016-01-19/obama-administration-proposes-changes-to-pell-grant-program, November 11, 2017.

Cameron, Charles, David Epstein, and Sharyn O'Halloran. 1996. "Do Majority Minority Districts Maximize Substantive Black Representation in Congress?" *American Political Science Review*. 794–812.

Campbell, Colton and Sean McCluskie. 2003. "Policy Experts: Congressional Testimony and Influence of First Ladies." In *The Presidential Companion: Readings on the First Ladies*. Robert Watson and Anthony Eksterowicz (Eds). Columbia: University of South Carolina Press. 169–191.

Canon, Matthew, Matthew Schousen, and Patrick Sellers. 1996. "The Supply-Side of Congressional Redistricting: Race and Strategic Politicians, 1972–1992." *Journal of Politics*. 58(3): 837–853.

Carlin, Diana B. 2004. "Lady Bird Johnson: The Making of a Public First Lady With Private Influence." In *Inventing a Voice: The Rhetoric of American First Ladies of the Twentieth Century*. Molly Meijer Wertheimer (Ed.). New York: Rowman & Littlefield. 273–296.

Caroli, Betty Boyd. 2010. *First Ladies: From Martha Washington to Michelle Obama*. New York: Oxford University Press.

Carroll, Susan J. 1986. "Women Appointed to the Carter Administration: More or Less Qualified?" *Polity*. 18(4): 696–706.

Carter, Jarret L. 2013. "Barack Obama and the $300 Million War on HBCUs." *Huffington Post*. July 10. Retrieved from www.huffingtonpost.com/jarrett-l-carter/barack-obama-and-the-300-_b_3563173.html, July 20, 2015.

Caswell, Bruce. 2012. "Obama by the Numbers: A Comparison with Previous Presidencies." In *The Obama Presidency: Promise and Performance*. William Crotty (Ed.). Lanham: Lexington Books. 45–70.

City of Richmond v. *J.A. Croson* (488 U.S. 469 (1989)). United States Supreme Court.

Clark, Charles S. 1996. "Child Labor and Sweatshops: Do US Consumers Abet Worker Exploitation?" *CQ Researcher*. August 19. 6(31): 721–744. Retrieved from http://library.cqpress.com/cqresearcher/document.php?id=cqresrre1996081600, October 17, 2017.

Clinton, William J. 1993a. "The President's News Conference." May 14. Online by Gerhard Peters and John T. Woolley, *The American Presidency Project*. Retrieved from www.presidency.ucsb.edu/ws/?pid=46561, September 30, 2016.

Clinton, William J. 1993b. "The President's News Conference." June 15. Online by Gerhard Peters and John T. Woolley, *The American Presidency Project*. Retrieved from www.presidency.ucsb.edu/ws/?pid=46689, September 30, 2016.

Clinton, William J. 1993c. "The President's News Conference." June 17. Online by Gerhard Peters and John T. Woolley, *The American Presidency Project*. Retrieved from www.presidency.ucsb.edu/ws/?pid=46708, September 30, 2016.

Clinton, William J. 1993d. "The President's News Conference." November 10. Online by Gerhard Peters and John T. Woolley, *The American Presidency Project*. Retrieved from www.presidency.ucsb.edu/ws/?pid=46092, September 30, 2016.

Clinton, William J. 1994. "The President's News Conference." October 21. Online by Gerhard Peters and John T. Woolley, *The American Presidency*

Project. Retrieved from www.presidency.ucsb.edu/ws/?pid=49341, September 30, 2016.

Clinton, William J. 1995. "The President's News Conference." March 3. Online by Gerhard Peters and John T. Woolley, *The American Presidency Project*. Retreived from www.presidency.ucsb.edu/ws/?pid=51053, September 30, 2016.

Clinton, William J. 2000. "The President's News Conference." March 29. Online by Gerhard Peters and John T. Woolley, *The American Presidency Project*. Retrieved from www.presidency.ucsb.edu/ws/?pid=58305, September 30, 2016.

Clymer, Adam, Robert Pear, and Robin Toner. 1994. "The Health Care Debate: What Went Wrong? How the Health Care Campaign Collapsed – A Special Report; For Health Care, Times Was A Killer." *New York Times*. August 29. Retrieved from www.nytimes.com/1994/08/29/us/health-care-debate-what-went-wrong-health-care-campaign-collapsed-special-report.html?pagewanted=all, November 10, 2017.

CNN Wire Staff. 2010. "Obama Signs Bill Reducing Cocaine Sentencing Gap." *CNN.com*. August 3. Retrieved from www.cnn.com/2010/POLITICS/08/03/fair.sentencing/index.html, October 18, 2017.

Coates, Ta-Nehisi Paul. 2007. "Is Obama Black Enough?" *Time.com*. Retrieved from www.time.com/printout/0,8816,1584736,00.html, March 16, 2010.

Coates, Ta-Nehisi. 2013. "How the Obama Administration Talks to Black America." *The Atlantic*. May 20. Retrieved from www.theatlantic.com/politics/archive/2013/05/how-the-obama-administration-talks-to-black-america/276015/, November 10, 2017.

Coates, Ta-Nehisi. 2017. "My President Was Black." *The Atlantic*. January/February. 47–66.

Cobb, William Jelani. 2010. *The Substance of Hope: Barack Obama and the Paradox of Progress*. New York: Bloomsbury Press.

Cohen, Robin A. and Michael E. Martinez. 2014. "Health Insurance Coverage: Early Release of Estimates from the National Health Interview Survey, January-March 2014." Washington, DC: Department of Health and Human Services. Retrieved from www.cdc.gov/nchs/data/nhis/earlyrelease/insur201409.pdf, September 30, 2016.

Conley, Dalton. 1999. *Being Black, Living in the Red: Race, Wealth and Social Policy in America*. Berkeley and Los Angeles: University of California Press.

Cooper, Helene. 2010. "The Label Factor: Is Obama a Wimp or a Warrior?" *New York Times*. January 10. Retrieved from www.nytimes.com/2010/01/10/weekinreview/10cooper.html?_r=0, September 30, 2016.

Costain, Anne N. 1991. "After Reagan: New Party Attitudes toward Gender." *Annals of the American Academy of Political and Social Science*. 515: 114–125.

Crenshaw, Kimberle Williams. 2014. "The Girls Obama Forgot." *New York Times*. July 29. Retrieved from www.nytimes.com/2014/07/30/opinion/Kimberl-Williams-Crenshaw-My-Brothers-Keeper-Ignores-Young-Black-Women.html, September 30, 2016.

Crotty, William (Ed.). 2012a. *The Obama Presidency: Promise and Performance*. Lanham: Lexington Books.

Crotty, William. 2012b. "Representation and Counter-Representation in the Obama Presidency." In *The Obama Presidency: Promise and Performance*. William Crotty (Ed.). Lanham: Lexington Books. 1–44.

Dawes, Daniel. 2016. *150 Years of Obamacare*. Baltimore: Johns Hopkins University Press.

Dawson, Michael. 1994. *Behind the Mule*. Princeton: Princeton University Press.

Dawson, Michael. 2011. *Not in Our Lifetimes: The Future of Black Politics*. Chicago: University of Chicago Press.

De Luca, Vanessa. 2016. "The Obama Legacy." *Essence*. October. 100–105.

Diaz, Daniella. 2016. "Obama Defends Kaepernick's Anthem Protest." *CNN.com*. Retrieved from www.cnn.com/2016/09/28/politics/obama-colin-kaepernick-nfl-national-anthem-presidential-town-hall-cnn/index.html, October 20, 2017.

Dickinson, Matthew J. 2009. "We All Want a Revolution: Neustadt, New Institutionalism and the Future of Presidency Research." *Presidential Studies Quarterly*. 39(4): 736–770.

Dickinson, Tim. 2017. "Introduction." *Rolling Stone* [Special Collector's Edition, *The Obama Years: Inside a Historic Presidency*]. 6–7.

Dillon, Sam. 2017. "Study Sees an Obama Effect As Lifting Black Test-Takers." *The New York Times*. 22 January. A15.

Dionne, Evette. n.d. "Obama's Morehouse Commencement Speech Causes Controversy." *Clutch Magazine*. Retrieved from http://clutchmagonline.com/2013/05/obamas-morehouse-commencement-speech-causes-controversy/, November 10, 2017.

Dodds, Graham. 2012. "Unilateral Directives." In *The Obama Presidency: A Preliminary Assessment*. Robert P. Watson, Jack Covarrubias, Tom Lansford, and Douglas M. Brattebo (Eds). Albany: SUNY Press. 343–362.

Dolan, Julie. 2001. "Political Appointees in the United States: Does Gender Make a Difference?" *PS: Political Science and Politics*. 34(2): 213–216.

Dowdle, Andrew J., Dirk C. Van Raemdonck, and Robert Maranto (Eds). 2012. *The Obama Presidency: Change and Continuity*. New York: Routledge.

DuBois, W.E.B. 1996. *The Souls of Black Folk*. Electronic Version. Retrieved from http://web.archive.org/web/20110116163634/http://etext.lib.virginia.edu/etcbin/toccer-new2?id=DubSoul.sgm&images=images/modeng&data=/texts/english/modeng/parsed&tag=public&part=teiHeader, July 24, 2014.

Dunn, Andrew. 2018. "Political Scientists Rank Trump Last, Lincoln First in Presidential Greatness Survey." *CNN.com*. Retrieved from https://www.google.com/amp/s/amp.cnn.com/cnn/2018/02/19/politics/trump-lincoln-presidential-greatness-survey/index.html, 14 July 2018

Dye, Thomas R., George C. Edwards III, Morris P. Fiorina, Edward S. Greenberg, Paul C. Light, David B. Magleby, and Martin P. Wattenberg. 2010. *Obama: Year One*. New York: Longman.

Dyson, Michael Eric. 2016a. "The President of Black America?" *New York Times*. June 26. Sunday Review Section: 1, 7.

Dyson, Michael Eric. 2016b. *The Black Presidency: Barack Obama and the Politics of Race in America*. Boston and New York: Houghton Mifflin Harcourt.

Edwards, George C. III. 2009. *The Strategic President: Persuasion and Opportunity in Presidential Leadership*. Princeton: Princeton University Press.

"Election 2016 Election Polls." 2016. *RealClearPolitics.com*. Retrieved from www.realclearpolitics.com/epolls/latest_polls/president/, October 25, 2017.

Esposito, Luigi and Laura L. Finley (Eds). 2012. *Grading the 44th President: A Report Card on Barack Obama's First Term as a Progressive Leader*. Santa Barbara: Praeger.

Fabry, Merrill. 2016. "The Long History behind Your Favorite Celebrity Commencement Speech." *Time*. May 13. Retrieved from http://time.com/4327774/history-commencement-speech/, November 1, 2017.

Fairey, Shepard. 2008. "Hope." Artwork. Self-made, Fair use. Retrieved from https://en.wikipedia.org/w/index.php?curid=32592376. September 10, 2015.

Fantz, Ashely and Emanuella Grinberg. 2016. "Former New Orleans Officers Plead Guilty in Danziger Bridge Shootings." *CNN.com*. April 21. Retrieved from www.cnn.com/2016/04/20/us/new-orleans-danziger-bridge-plea-deal/index.html, October 18, 2017.

Federal Bureau of Investigations. 1995–2015. "Uniform Crime Reports: Hate Crime." Retrieved from https://ucr.fbi.gov/hate-crime, September 10, 2017.

Federal Reserve Board of Governors. 2017. "Survey of Consumer Finances. Historic Table 4: Family Net Worth, By Selected Characteristics of Families, 1989–2016 Surveys." Retrieved from www.federalreserve.gov/econres/scfindex.htm, October 14, 2017.

Fett, Patrick J. 1992. "Truth in Advertising: The Revelation of Presidential Legislative Priorities." *The Western Political Quarterly*. 45(4): 895–920.

Ford, Matt. 2017. "Jeff Sessions Reinvigorates the Drug War." May 12. *The Atlantic*. Retrieved from www.theatlantic.com/politics/archive/2017/05/sessions-sentencing-memo/526029/, October 25, 2017.

Franklin, Sekou. 2010. "Situational Deracialization, Harold Ford, and the 2006 Senate Race in Tennessee." In *Whose Black Politics? Cases in Post-Racial Black Leadership*. Andra Gillespie (Ed.). New York: Routledge. 214–240.

Frasure, Lorrie. 2010. "The Burden of Jekyll and Hyde: Barack Obama, Racial Identity and Black Political Behavior." In *Whose Black Politics? Cases in Post-Racial Black Leadership*. Andra Gillespie (Ed.). New York: Routledge. 133–154.

Fritsch, Jane. 2000. "4 Officers in Diallo Shooting Are Acquitted of All Charges." *The New York Times*. 26 February. A1.

Frymer, Paul. 1999. *Uneasy Alliances: Race and Party Competition in America*. Princeton: Princeton University Press.

Fuller, Jaime. 2014. "How Has Voting Changed Since Shelby County v. Holder?" *Washington Post*. July 7. Retrieved from www.washingtonpost.com/news/the-fix/wp/2014/07/07/how-has-voting-changed-since-shelby-county-v-holder/, August 25, 2016.

Gallup. n.d.a. "Most Important Problem." *Gallup.com*. Retrieved from www.gallup.com/poll/1675/most-important-problem.aspx. August 1, 2014.

Gallup. n.d.b. "Presidential Job Approval Center." *Gallup.com*. Retrieved from www.gallup.com/poll/124922/Presidential-Job-Approval-Center.aspx?g_source=POLITICS&g_medium=topic&g_campaign=tiles, August 25, 2016.

Gay, Claudine. 2001. "The Effect of Black Congressional Representation on Political Participation." *American Political Science Review*. 95(3): 589–602.

"General Election: Trump vs. Clinton." n.d. *RealClearPolitics.com*. Retrieved from www.realclearpolitics.com/epolls/2016/president/us/general_election_trump_vs_clinton-5491.html, November 7, 2017.

Genius.com. n.d. Annotated Lyrics to "My President" with commentary from Jeezy. *Genius.com*. Retrieved from https://genius.com/Jeezy-my-president-lyrics, November 7, 2017.

Gilens, Martin. 1999. *Why Americans Hate Welfare*. Chicago: University of Chicago Press.

Gillespie, Andra. 2009. "The Third Wave: A Theoretical Introduction To The Post-Civil Rights Cohort of Black Elected Leadership." *National Political Science Review*. February. 12(1): 139–161.

Gillespie, Andra. 2010a. "Meet the New Class: Theorizing Young Black Leadership in a 'Post-Racial' Era." In *Whose Black Politics? Cases in Post-Racial Black Leadership*. Andra Gillespie (Ed.). New York: Routledge Press. 9–42.

Gillespie, Andra. 2010b. "Judged by His Actions: How President Obama Addressed Race in the First Six Months of His Campaign." *Journal of Race and Policy*. 6(1): 8–22.

Gillespie, Andra. 2012. *The New Black Politician: Cory Booker, Newark and Post-Racial America*. New York: New York University Press.

Gillespie, Andra. 2013. "Red, White and Black: Three Generations of African American Politicians." *Washington Monthly*. January/February. 64–66.

Gillespie, Andra. 2016. JWJI Election 2016 National Survey.

Gillespie, Andra. n.d. "Race, Real Estate, and Responsiveness: A Review of Housing Policy and Outcomes in the Obama Administration." In *After Obama: African American Politics in the Post-Obama Era*. Todd Shaw, Robert Brown and Joseph McCormick II (Eds.). Unpublished Manuscript.

Gillespie, Andra and Menna Demessie. 2013. "From Fenty to Gray: The Salience of Urban Gentrification, Black Politics, and Substantive Representation in Washington D.C.'s 2010 Mayoral Elections." In *21st Century Urban Race Politics: Representing Minorities as Universal Interests*. Ravi Perry (Ed.). Bingley: Emerald Publishing Group. 275–300.

Gillespie, Andra, Niambi Carter, Shayla Nunnally, and Tyson King-Meadows. 2014. Survey of Continuing Black Partisanship. [Survey Instrument].

Gillion, Daniel Q. 2016. *Governing with Words*. New York: Cambridge University Press.

Glaude, Eddie Jr. 2016. *Democracy in Black: How Race Still Enslaves the American Soul*. New York: Crown Books.

Good, Chris. 2011. "Obama Says it Plainly: He Was Nervous About Bin Laden Raid." *The Atlantic*. May 9. Retrieved from www.theatlantic.com/politics/archive/2011/05/obama-says-it-plainly-he-was-nervous-about-bin-laden-raid/238611/, October 15, 2017.

Gray, Freddy. 2012. "The Professorial President: Is Obama Super-Smart or Just Academic?" *The Spectator*. October 6. Retrieved from www.spectator.co.uk/2012/10/the-professorial-president/, October 24, 2017.

Grose, Christian. 2011. *Congress in Black and White: Race and Representation in Washington and at Home*. New York: Cambridge University Press.

Hajnal, Zoltan. 2007. *Changing White Attitudes toward Black Political Leadership*. New York: Cambridge University Press.

Hall, Matthew, Kyle Crowder, and Amy Spring. 2015. "Variations in Housing Foreclosures by Race and Place, 2005–2012." *Annals of the American Association of Political and Social Science*. 660(July): 217–237.

"'Hamilton' at the White House Then and Now." 2016. *Los Angeles Times*. June 13. Retrieved from www.latimes.com/entertainment/la-et-cm-tony-awards-live-updates-hamilton-at-the-white-house-then-and-1465612652-htmlstory.html, October 25, 2017.

Hamilton, Charles. 1977. "Deracialization: Examination of a Political Strategy." *First World*. March–April. 3–5.

Hancock, Ange-Marie. 2004. *The Politics of Disgust*. New York: New York University Press.

Harris, Frederick. 2012. *The Price of the Ticket: Barack Obama and the Rise and Decline of Black Politics*. New York: Oxford University Press.

Harris-Lacewell, Melissa V. 2004. *Barbershops, Bibles, and BET: Everyday Talk and Black Political Thought*. Princeton: Princeton University Press.

Harvard University. n.d. "Harvard College: Concentrations." Retrieved from *https://college.harvard.edu/academics/fields-study/concentrations*, 10 July 2018.

Heilemann, John and Mark Halperin. 2010. *Game Change: Obama and the Clintons, McCain and Palin and the Race of a Lifetime*. New York: Harper.

Hennessy-Fiske, Molly, Michael Muskal, and Timothy M. Phelps. 2015. "Justice Department Won't Charge Officer, Calls for Ferguson Police Reform." *Los Angeles Times*. March 4. Retrieved from www.latimes.com/nation/la-na-ferguson-police-racist-bias-justice-report-20150304-story.html, October 18, 2017.

Hochschild, Jennifer, Vesla Weaver, and Traci Burch. 2012. *Creating a New Racial Order*. Princeton: Princeton University Press.

Hodson, Randy. 1999. *Analyzing Documentary Accounts*. Iowa City: Sage Publications.

Holan, Angie Drobnic. 2011. "Who is Politifact? Who Pays for Politifact?" *Politifact.com*. October 6. Retrieved from www.politifact.com/truth-o-meter/blog/2011/oct/06/who-pays-for-politifact/, September 30, 2016.

Hollis, Meldon. 2017. "The Real Story of Obama's White House Initiative on HBCUs—Part I." *HBCUDigest.com*. Retrieved from https://hbcudigest.com/the-real-story-of-obamas-white-house-initiative-on-hbcus-part-i/, October 10, 2017.

Holmes, Robert A. 2011. *Maynard Jackson*. Miami: Barnhardt and Ashe Publishing, Inc.

Howell, William G. and David E. Lewis. 2002. "Agencies by Presidential Design." *The Journal of Politics*. 64(4): 1095–1114.

Hutchings, Vincent L. 2009. "Change or More of the Same? Evaluating Racial Attitudes in the Obama Era." *Public Opinion Quarterly*. 73(5): 917–942.

Ifill, Gwen. 2009. *The Breakthrough: Politics and Race in the Age of Obama*. New York: Random House.

In re Black Farmers Discrimination Litigation (856 F.Supp.2d 82 (2013)). United States Court of Appeals for the District of Columbia Circuit.

"Jackie Kennedy Returns to Complete Year: Talks About Politics." 1963. *Vassar Miscellany Muse*. April 3. Retrieved from http://newspaperarchives.vassar.edu/cgi-bin/vassar?a=d&d=miscellany19630403-01.2.5, November 1, 2017.

Jackman, Simon and Lynn Vavreck. 2010. "Primary Politics: Race, Gender, and Age in the 2008 Democratic Primary." *Journal of Elections, Public Opinion and Parties*. 20(2): 153–186.

Jackson, David. 2015. "Obama Stands by the Term 'Thugs,' White House Says." *USA Today*. April 29. Retrieved from www.usatoday.com/story/theoval/2015/04/29/obama-white-house-baltimore-stephanie-rawlings-blake/26585143/, October 24, 2017.

Jacobs, Lawrence and Theda Skocpol. 2010. *Health Care Reform and American Politics: What Everyone Needs to Know*. New York: Oxford University Press.

Jardina, Ashley. 2014. *Demise of Dominance: Group Threat and the New Relevance of White Identity for American Politics*. Ph.D. Dissertation. University of Michigan.

Jeffries, Judson Lance. 2000. *Virginia's Native Son*. Lafayette: Purdue University Press.

Jencks, Christopher. 1998. "Racial Bias in Testing." In *The Black–White Test Score Gap*. Christopher Jencks and Meredith Phillips (Eds). Washington, DC: Brookings Institution. 55–85.

Jenkins, Jay and Nasir Jones. 2008. "My President." *The Recession* [Album]. New York: Def Jam Records.

Johnson, Adam. 2012. "The New Duck Metaphor." *Stanford Daily*. September 26. Retrieved from www.stanforddaily.com/2012/09/26/the-new-duck-metaphor/, September 30, 2016.

Johnson, Lyndon B. 1965. "Commencement Address at Howard University: 'To Fulfill These Rights.' " June 4. Online by Gerhard Peters and John T. Woolley,

The American Presidency Project. Retrieved from www.presidency.ucsb.edu/ws/?pid=27021, November 2, 2017.

Jones, Maya A. 2016. "Two Lives Profoundly Changed by My Brother's Keeper." *The Undefeated*. October 11. Retrieved from https://theundefeated.com/features/two-lives-profoundly-changed-by-my-brothers-keeper/, November 10, 2017.

Kantor, Jodi. 2008. "Teaching Law, Testing Ideas, Obama Stood Slightly Apart." *New York Times*. July 30. A1.

Kantor, Jodi. 2012. *The Obamas*. New York: Little, Brown and Company.

Keeter, Scott and Nilanthi Samaranayake. 2007. "Can You Trust What Polls Say About Obama's Electoral Prospects?" *Pew Research Center*. Retrieved from www.pewresearch.org/2007/02/07/can-you-trust-what-polls-say-about-obamas-electoral-prospects/, August 1, 2014.

Kinder, Donald and Allison Dale-Riddle. 2012. *The End of Race*. New Haven: Yale University Press.

King, James D. and James W. Riddlesperger, Jr. 1996. "Presidential Management and Staffing: An Early Assessment of the Clinton Presidency." *Presidential Studies Quarterly*. 26(2): 496–510.

Klinkner, Philip with Rogers M. Smith. 1999. *The Unsteady March*. Chicago: University of Chicago Press.

Kochhar, Rakesh, Richard Fry, and Paul Taylor. 2011. "Wealth Gaps Rise to Record Highs between Whites, Blacks, Hispanics." *Pew Research Center*. July 26. Retrieved from www.pewsocialtrends.org/2011/07/26/wealth-gaps-rise-to-record-highs-between-whites-blacks-hispanics/, November 10, 2017.

LaFraniere, Sharon and Matt Apuzzo. 2017. "A Bond Over Bucking the Establishment." *New York Times*. January 9. A1.

Lane, Emily. 2016. "'Finally over': Last Danziger Defendant Pleads Guilty, Sentenced to Probation." *New Orleans Times-Picayune*. November 4. Retrieved from www.nola.com/crime/index.ssf/2016/11/danziger_katrina_gerard_dugue.html, October 18, 2017.

Leadership Conference on Civil Rights. 2010. *The Leadership Conference on Civil and Human Rights Voting Record: 111th US Congress*. Retrieved from www.protectcivilrights.org/pdf/voting-record/leadership-conference-2010-voting-record.pdf, October 25, 2017.

Levine, Bettijane. 1993. "Behind the 'Lani Guinier Mask': Politics: Months After Her Nomination Ordeal, She Says The Public Still Doesn't Know Who She Really Is." *Los Angeles Times*. December 7. Retrieved from http://articles.latimes.com/1993-12-07/news/vw-64911_1_lani-guinier, October 24, 2017.

Levine, Lawrence. 1977. *Black Culture and Black Consciousness: Afro-American Folk Thought from Slavery to Freedom*. New York: Oxford University Press.

Lewis, David E. 2012. "The Personnel Process in the Modern Presidency." *Presidential Studies Quarterly*. 42(3): 577–596.

Lillis, Mike. 2015. "Black Lawmakers Push Back on Obama over 'Thugs.'" *The Hill*. May 1. Retrieved from http://thehill.com/homenews/house/240807-black-lawmakers-push-back-on-obama-over-thugs, October 24, 2017.

Linzer, Drew. 2016. "Daily Kos Elections Final Presidential Forecast: Clinton 323 Electoral Votes, Trump 215." *Daily Kos*. November 7. Retrieved from www.dailykos.com/stories/2016/11/7/1592391/-Daily-Kos-Elections-final-presidential-forecast-Clinton-323-electoral-votes-Trump-215, October 25, 2017.

Logan, Enid. 2012. *At This Defining Moment: Barack Obama's Presidential Candidacy and the New Politics of Race*. New York: New York University Press.

Lopez, Tomas. 2014. "'Shelby County': One Year Later." *Brennan Center for Justice: Twenty Years*. June 24. Retrieved from www.brennancenter.org/analysis/shelby-county-one-year-later, August 25, 2016.

Lusane, Clarence. 2011. *The Black History of the White House*. San Francisco: City Light Books.

Mackenzie, G. Calvin. 2002. "The Real Invisible Hand: Presidential Appointees in the Administration of George W. Bush." *PS: Political Science and Politics*. 35(1): 27–30.

Maggi, Laura. 2010. "Six New Orleans Police Officers Indicted in Danziger Bridge Shootings." *New Orleans Times-Picayune*. July 14. Retrieved from www.nola.com/crime/index.ssf/2010/07/prosecutors_will_seek_detentio.html, October 18, 2017.

Malveaux, Julianne. 2016. *Are We Better Off? Race, Obama and Public Policy*. Washington, DC: Julianne Malveaux Enterprises.

Mann, E. and Zachary A. Smith. 1981. "The Selection of US Cabinet Officers and Other Political Executives." *International Political Science Review*. 2(2): 211–234.

Mansbridge, Jane. 1999. "Should Blacks Represent Blacks and Women Represent Women? A Contingent 'Yes.'" *American Political Science Review*. August. 628–657.

Martin, Janet M. 1989. "The Recruitment of Women to Cabinet and Subcabinet Posts." *The Western Political Quarterly*. 42(1): 161–172.

Martin, Janet M. 1991. "An Examination of Executive Branch Appointments in the Reagan Administration by Background and Gender." *Western Political Quarterly*. 44(1): 173–184.

McAdam, Doug. 1982. *Political Process and the Development of Black Insurgency, 1930–1970*. Chicago: University of Chicago Press.

McCarthy, Justin. 2015. "Americans Name Government as No. 1 US Problem." March 12. *Gallup.com*. Retrieved from www.gallup.com/poll/181946/americans-name-government-no-problem.aspx, July 20, 2015.

McClain, Paula D. and Joseph Stewart Jr. 1995. *Can We All Get Along? Racial and Ethnic Minorities in American Politics*. Boulder, CO: Westview Press.

McCormick, Joseph and Charles Jones. 1993. "The Conceptualization of Deracialization: Thinking Through the Dilemma." In *Dilemmas in Black Politics*. Georgia Persons (Ed.). New York: HarperCollins. 66–84.

McIlwain, Charlton. 2010. "Leadership, Legitimacy and Public Perceptions of Barack Obama." In *Whose Black Politics? Cases in Post-Racial Black Leadership*. Andra Gillespie (Ed.). New York: Routledge. 155–172.

McIlwain, Charlton and Stephen M. Caliendo. 2011. *Race Appeal: How Candidates Invoke Race in US Political Campaigns*. Philadelphia: Temple University Press.

McManus, Michael. 2016. "Minority Business Ownership: Data from the 2012 Survey of Business Owners." US Small Business Administration Office of Advocacy Issue Brief 12. September 14. Retrieved from www.sba.gov/sites/default/files/advocacy/Minority-Owned-Businesses-in-the-US.pdf, September 10, 2017.

McMillan Cottom, Tressie. 2017. *Lower Ed: The Troubling Rise of For-Profit Colleges in the New Economy*. New York: New Press.

Mendelberg, Tali. 2001. *The Race Card*. Princeton: Princeton University Press.

Milkis, Sidney M., Jesse H. Rhodes and Emily J. Charnock. 2012. "What Happened to Post-Partisanship? Barack Obama and the New American Party System." *Perspectives on* Politics. 10(1): 57–76.

Mitchell, W.J.T. 2009. "Obama as Icon." *Journal of Visual Culture*. 8(2): 125–129.

Moe, Terry M. and William G. Howell. 1999. "Unilateral Action and Presidential Power: A Theory." *Presidential Studies Quarterly*. 29(4): 850–872.

Morone, James A. and Rogan Kersh. 2013. *By the People: Debating American Government*. New York: Oxford University Press.

Muskal, Michael. 2011. "Rep. Maxine Waters Says It's Time for Obama to Fight." *Los Angeles Times*. Retrieved from http://articles.latimes.com/2011/aug/18/news/la-pn-maxine-waters-obama-20110818, July 25, 2014.

National Center for Education Statistics. n.d. "Fast Facts: Historically Black Colleges and Universities." Retrieved from https://nces.ed.gov/fastfacts/display.asp?id=667, November 10, 2017.

National Center for Education Statistics. 2015. "Table 104.10: Rates of High School Completion and Bachelor's Degree Attainment among Persons Age 25 and Over, by Race/Ethnicity and Sex: Selected Years, 1910 through 2015." *Digest of Education Statistics*. Retrieved from https://nces.ed.gov/programs/digest/d15/tables/dt15_104.10.asp?current=yes, September 10, 2017.

National Center for Education Statistics. 2016a. "Table 302.20: Percentage of Recent High School Completers Enrolled in 2- and 4-Year Colleges, by Race/Ethnicity: 1960 through 2015." *Digest of Education Statistics*. Retrieved from https://nces.ed.gov/programs/digest/d16/tables/dt16_302.20.asp, September 10, 2017.

National Center for Education Statistics. 2016b. "Fast Facts: SAT Scores." Retrieved from https://nces.ed.gov/fastfacts/display.asp?id=171, September 10, 2017.

National Center for Health Statistics. 2017. *Health, United States, 2016: With Chartbook on Long-Term Trends in Health*. Hyattsville: Centers for Disease Control. Retrieved from www.cdc.gov/nchs/data/hus/hus16.pdf#015, September 10, 2017.

Newport, Frank. 2014. "Public Opinion on the '4's' Through Recent History." *Gallup*. June 6. Retrieved from http://pollingmatters.gallup.com/2014/06/public-opinion-on-4s-through-recent.html, August 1, 2014.

Nicholls, Keith. 1991. "The Dynamics of National Executive Service: Ambition Theory and the Careers of Presidential Cabinet Members." *Western Political Quarterly*. 44(1): 149–172.

Nichols, Curt. 2012. "The Presidential Ranking Game: Critical Review and Some New Discoveries." *Presidential Studies Quarterly*. 42(2): 275–299.

Northwest Austin Municipal Utility District No. 1 v. *Holder* (557 U.S. 193 (2009)). United States Supreme Court.

Nunnally, Shayla. 2012. "African American Perspectives of the Obama Presidency." In *The Obama Presidency: Promise and Performance*. William Crotty (Ed.). Lanham: Lexington Books. 127–150.

Obama, Barack. 1982. Personal letter to Alexandra McNear. September 26. From the Barack Obama Letters to Alexandra McNear Collection, Stuart A. Rose Manuscript, Archives, and Rare Book Library, Emory University.

Obama, Barack. 1983. Personal letter to Alexandra McNear. February 10. From the Barack Obama Letters to Alexandra McNear Collection, Stuart A. Rose Manuscript, Archives, and Rare Book Library, Emory University.

Obama, Barack. 2009a. "The President's News Conference." March 24. Online by Gerhard Peters and John T. Woolley, *The American Presidency Project*. Retrieved from www.presidency.ucsb.edu/ws/?pid=85909, September 30, 2016.

Obama, Barack. 2009b. "The President's News Conference." April 29. Online by Gerhard Peters and John T. Woolley, *The American Presidency Project*. Retrieved from www.presidency.ucsb.edu/ws/?pid=86069, July 25, 2014.

Obama, Barack. 2009c. "The President's News Conference in Copenhagen." December 18. Online by Gerhard Peters and John T. Woolley, *The American Presidency Project*. Retrieved from www.presidency.ucsb.edu/ws/?pid=87009, September 30, 2009.

Obama, Barack. 2009d. "The President's News Conference." July 22. Online by Gerhard Peters and John T. Woolley, *The American Presidency Project*. Retrieved from www.presidency.ucsb.edu/ws/?pid=86456, September 30, 2016.

Obama, Barack. 2014a. "The President's News Conference." April 27. Online by Gerhard Peters and John T. Woolley, *The American Presidency Project*. Retrieved from www.presidency.ucsb.edu/ws/?pid=105142, September 30, 2016.

Obama, Barack. 2014b. "The President's News Conference." December 19. Online by Gerhard Peters and John T. Woolley, *The American Presidency Project*. Retrieved from www.presidency.ucsb.edu/ws/?pid=108089, October 24, 2017.

Obama, Barack. 2015a. "The President's News Conference with Prime Minister Shinzo Abe of Japan." April 28. Online by Gerhard Peters and John T. Woolley,

The American Presidency Project. Retrieved from www.presidency.ucsb.edu/ws/?pid=110078, October 24, 2017.

Obama, Barack. 2015b. "The President's News Conference with President Dilma Rousseff of Brazil." June 30. Online by Gerhard Peters and John T. Woolley, *The American Presidency Project.* Retrieved from www.presidency.ucsb.edu/ws/?pid=110393, October 24, 2017.

Obama, Barack. 2015c. "The President's News Conference With President François Hollande of France." November 24. Online by Gerhard Peters and John T. Woolley, *The American Presidency Project.* Retrieved from www.presidency.ucsb.edu/ws/?pid=111263, October 24, 2017.

Obama, Barack. 2015d. "The President's New Conference at the Pentagon in Arlington, Virginia." August 4. Online by Gerhard Peters and John T. Woolley, *The American Presidency Project.* Retrieved from www.presidency.ucsb.edu/ws/?pid=118787, October 24, 2017.

Obama, Barack. 2015e. "The President's News Conference With President Uhuru Kenyatta of Kenya in Nairobi, Kenya." July 25. Online by Gerhard Peters and John T. Woolley, *The American Presidency Project.* Retrieved from www.presidency.ucsb.edu/ws/?pid=110513, October 24, 2017.

Obama, Barack. 2016a. "The President's News Conference with Prime Minister Alexios Tsipras of Greece in Athens, Greece." November 15. Online by Gerhard Peters and John T. Woolley, *The American Presidency Project.* Retrieved from www.presidency.ucsb.edu/ws/?pid=119654, October 24, 2017.

Obama, Barack. 2016b. "The President's News Conference with Prime Minister Justin P.J. Trudeau of Canada and President Enrique Peña Nieto of Mexico in Ottawa, Canada." June 29. Online by Gerhard Peters and John T. Woolley, *The American Presidency Project.* Retrieved from www.presidency.ucsb.edu/ws/?pid=117879, October 24, 2017.

Obama, Barack. 2016c. "The President's News Conference With President Mauricio Macri of Argentina in Buenos Aires, Argentina." March 23. Online by Gerhard Peters and John T. Woolley, *The American Presidency Project.* Retrieved from www.presidency.ucsb.edu/ws/?pid=115068, October 24, 2015.

Oliver, Melvin and Thomas Shapiro. 2006. *Black Wealth, White Wealth.* 10th Anniversary Edition. New York: Routledge.

Ornstein, Norman and Thomas Donilon. 2000. "The Confirmation Clog." *Foreign Affairs.* 79(6): 87–99.

Parker, Christopher and Matt Barreto. 2013. *Change They Can't Believe In: The Tea Party and Reactionary Politics in America.* Princeton: Princeton University Press.

Patches, Matt. 2015. "Shepard Fairey on the Future of Political Art and Whether Obama Lived up to His 'Hope' Poster." *Esquire.* May 28. Retrieved from www.esquire.com/news-politics/interviews/a35288/shepard-fairey-street-art-obama-hope-poster/, September 30, 2016.

Peralta, Eyder. 2015. "Obama to Limit Police Acquisition of Some Military-Style Equipment." *NPR.org*. May 18. Retrieved from www.npr.org/sections/thetwo-way/2015/05/18/407631522/obama-to-limit-police-acquisition-of-some-military-style-equipment, October 18, 2017.

Perez-Rivas, Manuel. 1999. "First Lady Exhorts Graduates, Pleases Crowd." *Washington Post*. June 4. Retrieved from www.washingtonpost.com/archive/local/1999/06/04/first-lady-exhorts-graduates-pleases-crowd/24b19c44-1967-44c9-9213-9c0fca3593ba/?utm_term=.7bff13adadaa, November 1, 2017.

Peters, Gerhard and John T. Woolley. 1999–2017. *The American Presidency Project* [Online Database]. Retrieved from www.presidency.ucsb.edu/, September 30, 2016.

Philpot, Tasha S. 2007. *Race, Republicans, and the Return of the Party of Lincoln*. Ann Arbor: University of Michigan Press.

Pigford v. Glickman (206 F.3d 1212 (2000)). United States Court of Appeals for the District of Columbia Circuit.

Pigford v. Veneman (355 F.Supp.2d.148 (2005)). United States Court of Appeals for the District of Columbia Circuit.

Plouffe, David. 2010. *The Audacity to Win: How Obama Won and How We Can Beat the Party of Limbaugh, Beck and Palin*. New York: Penguin Books.

Politifact. n.d. "Obameter." *Politfact.com*. Retrieved from www.politifact.com/truth-o-meter/promises/obameter/, September 30, 2017.

President's Task Force on 21st Century Policing. 2015. *Final Report of the President's Task Force on 21st Century Policing*. Washington, DC: Office of Community Oriented Policing Services.

Preston, Michael B. 1987. "The Election of Harold Washington: An Examination of the SES Model in the 1983 Chicago Mayoral Election." In *The New Black Politics: The Search for Political Power*. Second Edition. Michael B. Preston, Lenneal Henderson Jr. and Paul L. Puryear (Eds). New York: Longman. 139–171.

Price, Melanye T. 2016. *The Race Whisperer*. New York: New York University Press.

Proctor, Bernadette D., Jessica L. Semega, and Melissa A. Kollar. 2016. *Income and Poverty in the United States: 2015*. United States Census Bureau. Retrieved from www.census.gov/content/dam/Census/library/publications/2016/demo/p60-256.pdf.

Quadagno, Jill. 1994. *The Color of Welfare*. New York: Oxford University Press.

Remnick, David. 2011. *The Bridge: The Life and Rise of Barack Obama*. New York: Vintage Books.

Report of the National Advisory Commission on Civil Disorders. 1968. New York Times Edition. New York: E.P. Dutton and Company.

Rhodan, Maya. 2017. "Has Change Come to America?" *Barack Obama: Eight Years*. [A *Time* Magazine Special Edition]. 50–53.

Rich, Wilbur C. 2012. "Making Race Go Away: President Obama and the Promise of a Post-Racial Society." In *The Obama Presidency: Change and Continuity*. Andrew J. Dowdle, Dirk C. Van Raemdonck, and Robert Maranto (Eds). New York: Routledge. 17–30.

Riddlesperger, James W. and James D. King. 1986. "Presidential Appointments to the Cabinet, Executive Office and White House Staff." *Presidential Studies Quarterly*. 16(4): 691–699.

Riffkin, Rebecca. 2015. "Racism Edges Up Again as Most Important US Problem." *Gallup.com*. July 16. Retrieved from www.gallup.com/poll/184193/racism-edges-again-important-problem.aspx?, July 20, 2015.

Rolling Stone. 2017. *The Obama Years: Inside a Historic Presidency* [*Rolling Stone* Magazine Special Collector's Edition].

Romano, Victor and Melanie Sberna Hinojosa. 2012. "Race and the Obama Presidency." In *Grading the 44th President: A Report Card on Barack Obama's First Term as a Progressive Leader*. Luigi Esposito and Laura L. Finley (Eds). Santa Barbara: Praeger. 163–182.

Ross, Sonya and Jennifer Agiesta. 2012. "AP Poll: Majority Harbor Prejudice Against Blacks." *Associated Press*. October 27. Retrieved from http://bigstory.ap.org/article/ap-poll-majority-harbor-prejudice-against-blacks, August 1, 2014.

Ryan, April. 2015. *The Presidency in Black and White*. New York: Rowman & Littlefield.

Ryan, Josiah. 2016. "'This Was a Whitelash': Van Jones' Take on the Election Results." *CNN.com*. November 9. Retrieved from www.cnn.com/2016/11/09/politics/van-jones-results-disappointment-cnntv/index.html, October 25, 2017.

Saad, Lydia. 2014. "Government Itself Still Cited as Top US Problem." *Gallup Politics*. January 15. Retrieved from www.gallup.com/poll/166844/government-itself-cited-top-problem.aspx, August 1, 2014.

Sapiro, Virginia. 1981. "When Are Interests Interesting? The Problem of Political Representation of Women." *American Political Science Review*. 75(3): 701–716.

Saturday Night Live. 2013a. "Michelle Obama Cold Open." *Saturday Night Live*. NBC, November 2. Retrieved from www.nbc.com/saturday-night-live/video/michelle-obama-at-the-white-house-cold-open/n42641#i, May 31, 2014.

Saturday Night Live. 2013b. "How's He Doing?" *Saturday Night Live*. Kenan Thompson, Jay Pharaoh, and Kerry Washington. NBC, November 2. Retrieved from www.nbc.com/saturday-night-live/video/hows-he-doing/n42645#i, May 31, 2014.

Savage, Charlie. 2017. "US Rights Unit Shifts to Study Antiwhite Bias." *New York Times*. August 2. A1.

Schlesinger, Arthur M. Jr. 2004. *The Imperial Presidency*. New York: Houghton Mifflin Harcourt.

Semega, Jessica L., Kayla R. Fontenot, and Melissa A. Kollar. 2017. *Income and Poverty in the United States: 2016*. United States Census Bureau. Retrieved from www.census.gov/content/dam/Census/library/publications/2017/demo/P60-259.pdf, September 14, 2017.

"Senator Cory Booker on NFL Anthem Protests: 'Protests is Patriotism." 2017. *CongressionalBlackCaucus.com*. September 28. Retrieved from https://congressionalblackcaucus.com/sen-cory-booker-on-nfl-anthem-protests-protest-is-patriotism/, October 20, 2017.

Shear, Michael D. and Maggie Haberman. 2017. "Trump Again Says Two Sides at Fault in Rally Violence." *New York Times*. August 16. A1.

Shelby County, Alabama v. *Holder, Attorney General* (679 F. 3d 848 (2013)). United States Supreme Court.

Singer, Natasha. 2009. "Harry and Louise Return, With a New Message." *New York Times*. July 16. B3.

SI Wire. 2016. "Sen. Booker: More Outrage Over Kaepernick than the Killing of Unarmed Black Man." *Sports Illustrated*. September 20. Retrieved from www.si.com/nfl/2016/09/20/corey-booker-disagrees-colin-kaepernick-protest, October 20, 2017.

Skowronek, Stephen. 1997. *The Politics Presidents Make: Leadership from John Adams to Bill Clinton*. Cambridge, MA: Harvard University/Belknap Press.

Skowronek, Stephen. 2008. *Presidential Leadership in Political Time*. Lawrence: University Press of Kansas.

Small Business Administration. n.d.a. Raw Data on 7(a) and ARC Loan Allocations by Race. Furnished by the Small Business Administration upon request.

Small Business Administration. n.d.b. "7(A) Loan Program: Terms, Conditions and Eligibility." *SBA.gov*. Retrieved from www.sba.gov/partners/lenders/7a-loan-program/terms-conditions-eligibility#section-header-19, November 9, 2017.

Smart, Charlie. 2017. "Obama Granted Clemency Unlike Any Other President in History." *Fivethirtyeight.com*. January 19. Retrieved from https://fivethirtyeight.com/features/obama-granted-clemency-unlike-any-other-president-in-history/, November 7, 2017.

Smith, Mark S. 2011. "Obama Congressional Black Caucus Speech: Stop Complainin' and Fight." *Huffington Post*. Retrieved from www.huffingtonpost.com/2011/09/25/obama-to-congressional-bl_n_979708.html, July 25, 2014.

Smith, Michael and Lydia Saad. 2016. "Economy Top Problem in a Crowded Field." *Gallup.com*. December 19. Retrieved from www.gallup.com/poll/200105/economy-top-problem-crowded-field.aspx, September 7, 2017.

Smith, Robert C. 1984. "Black Appointed Officials: A Neglected Area of Research in Black Political Participation." *Journal of Black Studies*. 14(3): 369–388.

Smith, Robert C. 1990. "Recent Elections and Black Politics: The Maturation or Death of Black Politics?" *PS: Political Science and Politics*. 23(2): 160–162.

Smith, Robert C. 1996. *We Have No Leaders*. Albany: SUNY Press.

Smooth, Wendy. 2006. "Intersectionality in Electoral Politics: A Mess Worth Making." *Politics and Gender*. 2: 400–414.

Social Security Administration. n.d. "Social Security History: Organizational History." Retrieved from https://www.ssa.gov/history/orghist.html, 11 July 2018.

Swain, Carol M. 1993. *Black Faces, Black Interests: The Representation of African Americans in Congress*. Cambridge, MA: Harvard University Press.

Swarns, Rachel. 2012. *American Tapestry: The Story of the Black, White and Multiracial Ancestors of Michelle Obama*. New York: Amistad Books.

Tate, Katherine. 1994. *From Protest to Politics: The New Black Voters in American Elections*. Enlarged Edition. New York and Cambridge, MA: Russell Sage Foundation/Harvard University Press.

Tate, Katherine. 2003. *Black Faces in the Mirror*. Princeton: Princeton University Press.

Tate, Katherine. 2010. *What's Going On?* Washington, DC: Georgetown University Press.

"Tavis Smiley, Cornel West on the 2012 Election & Why Calling Obama 'Progressive' Ignores His Record." 2012. *Democracy Now*. November 9. Retrieved from www.democracynow.org/2012/11/9/tavis_smiley_cornel_west_on_the, May 31, 2014.

Tell Me More. 2008. "Obama's Father's Day Speech Stirs Reaction" [Radio Interview Transcript]. *NPR.org*. June 20. Retrieved from www.npr.org/templates/story/story.php?storyId=91727635, November 13, 2017.

Terrace, Vincent. 2013. *Television Specials: 5,336 Entertainment Programs, 1936–2012*. Second Revised Edition. Jefferson: McFarland and Company.

Tesler, Michael. 2016. *Post Racial or Most Racial?* Chicago: University of Chicago Press.

Tesler, Michael and David O. Sears. 2010. *Obama's Race: The 2008 Election and the Dream of a Post-Racial America*. Chicago: University of Chicago Press.

Time. 2017. *Barack Obama: Eight Years* [A *Time* Magazine Special Edition].

Thomas, Helen. 1981. "'In Performance at the White House.'" *UPI*. September 14. Retrieved from www.upi.com/Archives/1981/09/14/In-Performance-at-the-White-House/2054369288000/, November 1, 2017.

Trump, Donald. 1987. *The Art of the Deal*. New York: Ballantine Books.

Trump, Donald. 2017. "Executive Order 13771—Reducing Regulation and Controlling Regulatory Costs." January 30. Online by Gerhard Peters and John T. Woolley, *The American Presidency Project*. Retrieved from www.presidency.ucsb.edu/ws/?pid=122556, October 25, 2017.

TV Guide. 2014. "In Performance at the … Episodes." *TVGuide.com*. Retrieved from www.tvguide.com/detail/tv-show.aspx?tvobjectid=202201&more=ucepisodelist&episodeid=620188, August 2, 2014.

US Census Bureau. n.d. "Housing Vacancies and Homeownership (CPS/HVS)." Table 16. Retrieved from www.census.gov/housing/hvs/data/histtabs.html, September 10, 2017.

US Census Bureau. 2011. "The Black Population: 2010." *2010 Census Briefs*. September 2011. Retrieved from www.census.gov/prod/cen2010/briefs/c2010br-06.pdf, November 12, 2017.

US Department of Education. n.d.a. "Title III Part B, Strengthening Historically Black Colleges and Universities Program: Funding Status." Retrieved from www2.ed.gov/programs/iduestitle3b/funding.html, October 14, 2017.

US Department of Education. n.d.b. "Press Releases." Retrieved from www.ed.gov/news/press-releases, November 9, 2017.

US Department of Education. 2016a. "New Analysis Finds Many For-Profits Skirt Federal Funding Limits." December 21. Retrieved from www.ed.gov/news/press-releases/new-analysis-finds-many-profits-skirt-federal-funding-limits, October 17, 2017.

US Department of Education. 2016b. "Fact Sheet: Obama Administration Investments in Historically Black Colleges and Universities." October 24. Retrieved from www.ed.gov/news/press-releases/fact-sheet-obama-administration-investments-historically-black-colleges-and-universities, November 11, 2017.

US Department of Health and Human Services. n.d. "News." Retrieved from http://wayback.archive-it.org/3926/20170127134614/https://www.hhs.gov/about/news/index.html, November 9, 2017.

US Department of Health and Human Services, Office of Family Assistance. n.d. "Temporary Assistance for Needy Families." Retrieved from www.acf.hhs.gov/ofa/programs/tanf, October 18, 2017.

US Department of Justice. 2017. *Federal Report on Police Killings: Ferguson, Cleveland, Baltimore and Chicago*. Brooklyn: Melville House.

US Department of Justice, Civil Rights Division. n.d. "Information and Technical Assistance on the Americans with Disabilities Act: Project Civic Access Fact Sheet." Retrieved from www.ada.gov/civicfac.htm, October 18, 2017.

US Department of Justice, Office of the Pardon Attorney. n.d. "Clemency Recipients." Retrieved from www.justice.gov/pardon/clemencyrecipients, November 9, 2017.

US Department of Justice, Office of Public Affairs. n.d. "Briefing Room: Justice News." Retrieved from www.justice.gov/news?f%5B0%5D=field_pr_date%3A2009&f%5B1%5D=field_pr_component%3A436&page=8, November 9, 2017.

US Department of Justice, Office of Public Affairs. 2010. "Felon Who Impersonated a Police Officer Pleads Guilty in Danziger Bridge Case." April 28. Retrieved from www.justice.gov/opa/pr/felon-who-impersonated-police-officer-pleads-guiltyin-danziger-bridge-case, October 18, 2017.

US Department of Labor. n.d. "New Releases and Briefs." Retrieved from www.dol.gov/newsroom/releases/filter/, November 9, 2017.

US Department of Labor. 2015. "Hiep Thai Markets Pays More Than $416K in Back Wages to Workers Following US Labor Department Investigation."

September 14. Retrieved from www.dol.gov/newsroom/releases/whd/whd 20150914, October 17, 2017.

Valentino, Nicholas, Vincent Hutchings, and Ismail White. 2002. "Cues that Matter: How Political Ads Prime Racial Attitudes During Campaigns." *American Political Science Review*. 96(1): 75–90.

Wal-Mart. 2014. Corporate Webpage. Retrieved from http://corporate.walmart.com/our-story/our-business/locations/, August 1, 2014.

Walters, Ronald. 1988. *Black Presidential Politics in America: A Strategic Approach*. Albany: SUNY Press.

Walters, Ronald. 2007. "Barack Obama and the Politics of Blackness." *Journal of Black Studies*. 38: 7–27.

Walters, Ronald and Robert C. Smith. 1999. *African American Leadership*. Albany: SUNY Press.

Wang, Sam. 2016. "Final Projections: Clinton 323 EV, 51 Democratic Senate Seats, GOP House." *Princeton Election Consortium*. November 8. Retrieved from http://election.princeton.edu/2016/11/08/final-mode-projections-clinton-323-ev-51-di-senate-seats-gop-house/, October 25, 2017.

Washington Post Staff. 2016. "The Complete Transcript of Larry Wilmore's 2016 White House Correspondents' Dinner Speech." *Washington Post*. May 1. Retrieved from www.washingtonpost.com/news/reliable-source/wp/2016/05/01/the-complete-transcript-of-larry-wilmores-2016-white-house-correspondents-dinner-speech/, September 30, 2016.

Watkins, Mel. 1994. *On the Real Side: Laughing, Lying, and Signifying—the Underground Tradition of African American Humor That Transformed American Culture, from Slavery to Richard Pryor*. New York: Simon & Shuster.

Watson, Robert P., Jack Covarrubias, Tom Lansford, and Douglas Brattebo (Eds). 2012. *The Obama Presidency: A Preliminary Assessment*. Albany: SUNY Press.

Westfall, Sandra Sobieraj. 2016. "Their Amazing Journey: The Obamas Say Goodbye." *People*. December 16. 58–73.

WETA. n.d. "In Performance at the White House." *PBS.org*. Retrieved from www.pbs.org/inperformanceatthewhitehouse/about/, November 1, 2017.

WETA. 2013. "Past Productions." *WETA Website*. Retrieved from www.weta.org/about/productions/national/past, August 2, 2014.

White House. 2016. "Progress of the African American Community During the Obama Administration." October 14. Retrieved from https://obamawhitehouse.archives.gov/the-press-office/2016/10/14/progress-african-american-community-during-obama-administration, November 11, 2017.

White House Historical Association. n.d. "New Music Styles at the White House." *WhiteHouseHistory.org*. Retrieved from www.whitehousehistory.org/new-music-styles-at-the-white-house, November 1, 2017.

"Who Will Win the Presidency?" 2016. *FiveThirtyEight.com*. November 8. Retrieved from https://projects.fivethirtyeight.com/2016-election-forecast/, October 25, 2017.

Wilder, L. Douglas. 2001. Keynote Address to the National Conference of Black Political Scientists. March 16. Richmond Marriott. Richmond, Virginia.

Williams, Joseph. 2011. "President Obama Learns Perils of Roiling Maxine Waters." *Politico*. October 20. Retrieved from www.politico.com/news/stories/1011/66418.html, July 25, 2014.

Williams, Joseph P. 2016. "Why Aren't Police Prosecuted?" *USNews.com*. July 13. Retrieved from www.usnews.com/news/articles/2016-07-13/why-arent-police-held-accountable-for-shooting-black-men, October 18, 2017.

Williams, Linda. 1987. "Black Political Progress in the 1980's: The Electoral Arena." In *The New Black Politics: The Search for Political Power*. Second Edition. Michael B. Preston, Lenneal J. Henderson Jr., and Paul Puryear (Eds). New York and London: Longman Publishers. 97–136.

Wootson, Cleve R. 2017. "Trump Implied Frederick Douglass Was Alive: The Abolitionist's Family Offered a 'History Lesson.'" *Washington Post*. February 2. Retrieved from www.washingtonpost.com/news/post-nation/wp/2017/02/02/trump-implied-frederick-douglass-was-alive-the-abolitionists-family-offered-a-history-lesson/?utm_term=.d0c989df8249, October 25, 2017.

Yates, Jeff and Andrew Whitford. 2005. "Institutional Foundations of the President's Issue Agenda." *Political Research Quarterly*. 58(4): 577–585.

Zengerle, Jason. 2017. "Who Can Beat Trump in 2020?" *New York Times*. September 30. Retrieved from www.nytimes.com/interactive/2017/09/30/opinion/who-can-beat-trump-in-2020.html?_r=0, November 13, 2017.

Index